Murderous Medicine

MURDEROUS MEDICINE

Nazi Doctors, Human Experimentation, and Typhus

Naomi Baumslag, M.D., M.P.H.

Foreword by E. D. Pellegrino, M.D.

Westport, Connecticut
London

Library of Congress Cataloging-in-Publication Data

Baumslag, Naomi.
   Murderous medicine : Nazi doctors, human experimentation, and typhus /
Naomi Baumslag.
      p. cm.
   Includes bibliographical references and index.
   ISBN 0–275–98312–9 (alk. paper)
   1. Human experimentation in medicine—German—History—20th century.
2. Typhus fever—Germany—History—20th century.   3. Prisoners of war—Medical
care—Germany—History—20th century.   4. World War, 1939–1945—Atrocities.
5. National socialism—Moral and ethical aspects. I. Title.
   R853.H8B38 2005
   174.2'8—dc22   2004028446

British Library Cataloguing in Publication Data is available.

Library of Congress Catalog Card Number: 2004028446
ISBN: 0–275–98312–9

First published in 2005

Praeger Publishers, 88 Post Road West, Westport, CT 06881
An imprint of Greenwood Publishing Group, Inc.
www.praeger.com

Printed in the United States of America

The paper used in this book complies with the
Permanent Paper Standard issued by the National
Information Standards Organization (Z39.48–1984).

10 9 8 7 6 5 4 3 2 1

Every reasonable effort has been made to trace the owners of copyright materials in this
book, but in some instances this has proven impossible. The author and publisher will be
glad to receive information leading to more complete acknowledgments in subsequent
printings of the book and in the meantime extend their apologies for any omissions.

Cover illustration: Photography Cathrine Stukhard; Sculpture:
Ewa Kaja; Title: *Gengangen/Gone*

Dedication

Medical student card of Baruch Baumslag.
Obtained through the American Red Cross Holocaust and War Victims Tracing Center.

Most of my family was murdered as a result of the hate and atrocities that were perpetrated by the Nazi regime of the Third Reich. In 1996 I was given an opportunity to present a paper at a YIVO conference on medical resistance in the Holocaust. I chose to focus on typhus because everything I had read indicated how rampant the disease was and how epidemic disease prevention practices were used to deceive victims. They were told they were going to be bathed and deloused when in fact they were being sent to the gas chambers. Cases of typhus and contacts were exterminated as a result of the radical therapy of SS doctors, and for their evil acts the doctors were rewarded with military medals. In particular, I dedicate this book to my uncle, Baruch Baumslag, who was a community doctor in Pasvalys in 1941 and whose commitment to saving lives even in that anti-Semitic village regardless of religious affiliation serves to remind us that humanitarianism must come before science. When a Lithuanian doctor did not go to help a woman delivering twins, my uncle came but by that time, the first twin had died. Under primitive conditions he performed a caesarean section to save the mother and remaining baby's life. There is a record in the Pasvalys museum in Lithuania that attests to these facts. I never got to know him, and this document is all that remains of him. So this book is dedicated to my uncle and the many doctors who saved lives or gave comfort and did not abuse their power.

The book is also dedicated to my late son Barry who was named after him and whose love of life and spirit was special.

Naomi Baumslag

Contents

Illustrations

CHAPTER 4

CHAPTER 5

Foreword

NAZI MEDICINE—THE APOTHEOSIS OF MEDICAL EVIL

Carl G. Jung in his reflections on the psychological intricacies of evil had this advice to give: "Evil needs to be pondered just as much as good . . ." (Jung 1968). We need not accept Jung's psychologized Manicheanism to appreciate the wisdom of his words. To avoid evil, we must confront it; to confront it, we must look beyond the boundaries of the good into the darkness of evil. It does not suffice simply to be scandalized by evil and piously to repudiate it. We must be reminded how subtly evil masquerades as good, and how easy it is for all of us—individuals and nations—to lose our way and cross the boundary.

Nothing illustrates this better than the moral infamy of the Nazi physicians and the silent complicity of the German medical profession. The willing, vigorous, and efficient conduct of the atrocities of the Third Reich's genocidal euthanasia and holocaust programs stands as a lurid embodiment of medical evil. Indeed, it is an apotheosis of evil—an exaltation of evil, of killing as a good for German society, and even as an act of beneficence for the victim. The Nazi physicians blatantly erased the boundaries between good and evil. Maiming, torturing, and executing became acts of healing and beneficence.

The Nazi physicians were neither the first, nor the last to put their knowledge and skill at the service of evil purpose. Physicians in Soviet Russia, Imperial Japan, and in dozens of countries ruled by petty tyrants all defected from the ethics of medicine in similar ways. Democratic societies have not been entirely immune either. What makes the German example so compelling is the degree to which it has been documented and the fact that the miscreants were some of the best educated and scientifically grounded members of their profession at the time. The details of the moral transgressions by physicians in other countries will eventually be revealed. For the moment, the Nazi physician remains the prototype of medical evil.

The enormity of the Nazi physicians' ethical misbehavior did not gain the world's attention for over two decades. Twenty-three Nazi physicians were tried at Nuremberg after the war (Trials of War Criminals Before the Nuremberg Military Tribunals 1946–1949). They were given sentences of varying severity. But the majority of Nazi physicians and their confreres in the atrocities of human experimentation, genocidal euthanasia, and the Holocaust escaped punishment.

The German medical profession distanced itself from these events. Very few raised their voices in protest during the war. After the war, most returned to their previous posts. Some achieved prominence in world medicine. One of the participants became President elect of the World Medical Association. He was forced to withdraw just in time, when his involvement was finally revealed. A report of these events, prepared in Germany, was repressed (Kater 1989).

The first widely read indictment of the behavior of the Nazi physicians appeared in 1986, in Robert J. Lifton's book, *The Nazi Doctors: Medical Killing and the Psychology of Genocide*. Lifton described eloquently and in devastating detail, just how opprobriously the Nazi physicians conducted themselves. In 1990, Hugh Gallagher gave a harrowing account of the Third Reich's "Aktion T-4" program, which systematically murdered large numbers of Germans with congenital disabilities and varying degrees of unfitness lest they contaminate the purity of the Nordic gene pool (Gallagher 1990). It was an easy step from this kind of thinking to the Holocaust where millions of Jews were sacrificed under the same bogus population genetics.

A spate of books and articles followed Lifton's. They expanded and further substantiated the details of depravity practiced in the Third Reich (Burleigh 1997; Caplan 1992, Fasching 1993; Gallagher 1990; Goldhagen 1997; Hanauske-Abel 1996; Proctor 1988 and 1992; and Wikler 1993). They provide painful proof of the pathological moral aberrancy of the Nazi physicians. Even a brief visit to the Holocaust Museums at Yad Vashem in Israel and in Washington must dispel all doubt about the complicity of physicians. At these sites, photographs, personal belongings of the victims, details of gas chambers and "processing" of victims bespeak the maniacal Nazi hatred of Jews (*Deadly Medicine* 2004–2005).

Naomi Baumslag's book deepens our perceptions of those events even further. She adds substantially to our comprehension of how science, ordinary human feelings, as well as medical ethics were drowned in a sea of hatred. Baumslag, whose family members were among the victims, presents a wealth of documents, photographic and human detail from a wide range of sources. In addition, she adds new insights into one of the most bizarre and egregious attempts at justification for the massacre of the Jews: the outrageous claim that Jews were the cause of typhus epidemics in Germany and Europe.

As a result of lurid propaganda and pseudo-scientific "evidence" about typhus, Jews were forced to live in overcrowded, dilapidated, unhygienic areas together. They were examined for lice, quarantined, and then exterminated as sources of infection. Under conditions of war and poverty, this was a sure way to spread lice among the Jewish population, generate cases of typhus and thus "prove" that the Jews were the reservoirs of the disease. This monstrous fabrication was another instrument for mass eugenic and ethnic cleansing leading to "The Final Solution." The typhus pretense was one of the many fanciful and vicious fictions elaborated to assuage whatever remnants of conscience the Nazi physicians might have retained.

Justification was, in fact, a recurrent theme. Nazi and German physicians were conscious of the gap between their former reputations as a creditable scientific and rational community and their murderous conduct. A fuller display of this urge for justification and exculpation can be extracted from the pages of testimony before the Nuremberg Military Tribunal (Pellegrino and Thomasma 2000). Each of the defendants protested his innocence and offered arguments in his own defense. How much was genuinely believed and how much was deliberate fabrication is problematic. Anyone seeking moral lessons from the Nazi conversion of ethics into vice should study these defense arguments.

The defendants claimed they were simply following orders or laws, not of their own making. They insisted repeatedly that they were obliged to comply by virtue of their roles: The state, in any case, had the right to decide on the fate and punishment of prisoners; and the physician's task was to carry out the penalties. These acts were necessitated by the fact that Germany was at war; its survival justified whatever was necessary, even if it violated medical ethics. The death of a few prisoners was redeemed by the amount of good that would benefit the whole of society. These arguments have a familiar ring for all who use them in their daily explanations of their own questionable behavior.

One of the most common of all arguments was that of non-involvement, adopted by the rest of the German profession. It is inconceivable that German physicians were not cognizant of what their colleagues were doing.

German medicine was a relatively small community whose members knew each other. Medicine is, in fact, also a moral community which recognizes a common obligation of accountability and responsibility for what its members do. Moral complicity cannot be erased by claims of ignorance, especially if one professes fidelity to the Hippocratic Oath and Ethic.

Strangely enough, the defendants of Nuremberg even argue that they had remained faithful to the Hippocratic Oath. This could not have been a claim based in ignorance since most German physicians had some education in history and the ethics of their profession. One of the defendants was the author of a textbook of medical ethics. The Nazi doctors claimed to be acting out of beneficence, the central moral precept of the Oath. By sending older and sicker prisoners to the gas chamber, the Nazi physicians claimed to spare them the hard labor they would otherwise be subjected to. Also, they claimed the prisoners died willingly, knowing that being an experimental subject would help others. Moreover, since the prisoners were already condemned to death, an earlier execution would reduce the time of their suffering. Obviously, the Nazi physicians had learned the lesson of the "big lie" very well.

Whether or not these "justifications" were *post facto* rationalizations or falsified defense mechanisms, they tell us that the Nazi physicians were not insane. They were rational, did their work efficiently, and even dared to defend it as something good. Their arguments are not unique. They are often used by most of us in far less dire circumstances. The arguments of the Nazi physicians teach us once again that erroneous premises can lead to terrifying conclusions.

Reflections on these justifications suggest some tentative answers to the question so frequently asked: "How could such civilized, educated, scientifically informed physicians act in such an inhumane way?" If we are ever to answer this question, we must study the anatomy of evil from both the emotional and the logical point of view.

Hannah Arendt demonstrated vividly in the case of Eichmann that evil is banal (Arendt 1973). Eichmann was an "ordinary" man like many of his Nazi colleagues. Serious efforts are needed to explain how banality can so easily be turned to such vicious and grossly maleficent acts. Lifton sought the answer in the psychological mechanism of "doubling," which enabled Nazi physicians to occupy two morally opposite worlds simultaneously. Goldhagan purported to find the answer in a putative deep flaw of anti-Semitism in the German soul. Burleigh located the disease in banality of anti-Semitic Germany's history. Proctor stressed the close relationship among medical interests, Nazism, and medical ethics.

None of these explanations is fully satisfying. Some other possibilities suggest themselves as well. One is the inescapable fact that evil so often masquerades as good. Doob puts it this way:

> In order to persuade a good man to do evil, it is not necessary to persuade him to become evil. It is only necessary to teach him that he is doing good (Doob 1978).

Equally pertinent is Susan Sontag's commemoration of those who refuse to do evil:

> At the center of our moral imagination are the great models of resistance; the great stories of those who have said No (Sontag 2003).

Not knowing when to say no is the relativist's congenital indisposition. Locating the No point is crucial to the viability of any defensible ethic. It is the last defense of moral integrity. The Nazi physicians clearly failed to realize the point at which medical ethics demanded a resounding, No!

On this point, the oft quoted psychological experiments of Thomas Milgrim may be useful to recall. In those experiments, Milgrim recruited ordinary people to administer what they were led to believe were real electric shocks to other people. His recruits followed orders to increase the "strength" of their bogus shocks incrementally. They were begged by the recipients to stop. Milgrim's recruits turned to the investigator who told them to continue. Despite feelings of doubt, they did so. The authority figure in a white coat was apparently too powerful an icon to resist.

The banality of evil, and the ordinariness of its perpetrators, is an important lesson to learn from the moral defection of the Nazi physicians. Democracies are not immune to specious arguments or protestations that they are so different from other humans that such evil could never afflict them. We need only recall the moral lapses in our own country of the Tuskegee Syphilis Study, the Willowbrook Hepatitis experiments, and the U.S. Radiation Exposure experiments. The participants in these events were ordinary people who voluntarily engaged in serious moral harm. They, too, believed they were doing "good." They, too, performed their duties well, failed to question authority, and did not know when to say no.

In times of war and terrorism, we are all called upon to recognize the boundaries which ought never to be crossed. We do not know how much our medical officers knew of the reputed mistreatment of prisoners in our war on Terrorism in Iraq and Afghanistan. We must remind ourselves repeatedly that physicians in the military and also in penal and other institutional settings are especially exposed to the blurring of moral boundaries. Medical ethics is readily distorted by political or military exigency. The attention today to military ethics has received reinforcement by the recent publication of the treatise on Military Ethics (Beam and Sparacind 2004).

When survival of any society is threatened, there is an understandable tendency to lay ethics aside. This is just when ethics meets its severest test. It is a mark of a morally responsible society to know when and where to set the boundaries between good and evil. If there is a lesson in Baumslag's book and the others that have so well documented the moral failures of the Nazi doctors, it is that evil can never be done that good may come of it. Good intentions are essential to virtuous acts, but virtuous acts are not totally dependent on intention.

Philosophers and theologians have debated the nature of good and evil for centuries. That debate is unlikely to be settled ontologically. Existentially it must be confronted, however, and in that confrontation, it will help to have studied the anatomy of the euthanasia and Holocaust programs so closely described by Baumslag and the others who have tried to alert the world to the dangers of blurring the boundaries between good and evil.

One mark of a morally responsive society is knowing where to set the boundary between good and evil. The Nazi moral disaster shows how blurring that boundary allows maleficence to subvert the good to its own purposes.

Philosophers and theologians have long debated the nature of good and evil. Some give them competing independent existences; some see them as intermingled with a shifting boundary between them; others define evil as the absence of good. The debate continues. However, in the realm of practical affairs, the boundary must be examined whenever we act. To ponder the Nazi physicians' conduct is to be reminded how perilously close nations, persons and organizations can come to crossing into the darkness of evil.

—E. D. Pellegrino, M.D.
Professor Emeritus of Medicine and Medical Ethics
Georgetown University

REFERENCES

Arendt, H. 1973. *The Origins of Totalitarianism*. New York: Harcourt Brace Jovanovich.

Beam, T. E. and L. R. Sparacind, eds. 2004. *Military Medical Ethics*. 2 vols., Washington, DC: Office of the Surgeon General, United States Army, Borden Institute, Walter Reed Army Medical Center.

Burleigh, M. 1997. *Ethics and Extermination: Reflections on Nazi Genocide.* New York: Cambridge University Press.

Caplan, A. L., ed. 1992. *When Medicine Went Mad: Bioethics and the Holocaust.* Totowa, NJ: Humana Press.

Deadly Medicine: Creating the Master Race, Special Exhibition. April 22, 2004– October 16, 2005. United States Holocaust Memorial Museum, Washington, DC.

Doob, L. W. 1978. *Panorama of Evil: Insights from the Behavioral Sciences.* Westport, CT: Greenwood Press.

Fasching, D. J. 1993. *The Ethical Challenge of Auschwitz and Hiroshima: Apocalypse or Utopia?* Albany: State University of New York Press.

Gallagher, H. 1990. *By Trust Betrayed: Patients, Physicians, and the License to Kill in the Third Reich.* New York: Henry Holt.

Goldhagen, D. G. 1997. *Hitler's Willing Executioners: Ordinary Germans and the Holocaust.* New York: Vantage Books.

Hanauske-Abel, H. M. 1996. "Not a Slippery Slope or Sudden Subversion: German Medicine and National Socialism in 1933." *British Medical Journal* (December) 313:1453–1463.

Jung, C. G. 1968. *Psychology and Alchemy,* Princeton, NJ: Princeton University Press. In *Collected Works of Carl G. Jung,* 2nd ed., 36, 12. Cited in Jung, C. G. *Psychological Reflections*, Jolande Jacobi and R. F. C. Hull, eds., Bollingen Series XXXi, Princeton, NJ: Princeton University Press, 1970, p. 234.

Kater, M. H. 1989. *Doctors Under Hitler.* Chapel Hill: University of North Carolina Press.

Lifton, R. J. 1986. *The Nazi Doctors: Medical Killing and the Psychology of Genocide.* New York: Basic Books.

Pellegrino, E. D. and D.C. Thomasma. 2000. "Dubious Premises-Evil Conclusions: Moral Reasoning at the Nuremberg Trials." *Cambridge Quarterly* (Spring), no. 2, 9:261–274.

Proctor, R. 1988. *Racial Hygiene: Medicine Under the Nazis.* Cambridge, MA: Harvard University Press.

———. 1992. "Nazi Doctors, Racial Medicine and Human Experimentation," in G. J. Annas and M. A. Grodin eds., *The Nazi Doctors and the Nuremberg Code: Human Rights in Human Experimentation.* New York: Oxford University Press.

Sontag, S. 2003. "Of Courage and Resistance." *The Nation* (May 5), p. 12.

Trials of War Criminals Before the Nuremberg Military Tribunals Under Control Council Law No. 10: October 1946–April 1949. Nuremberg, vol. I, Washington: U.S. Government Printing Office.

Wikler, D., and J. Barodness. 1993. "Bioethics and Anti-Bioethics in Light of Nazi Medicine: What Must We Remember?" *Kennedy Institute of Ethics Journal* 3:39–55.

Acknowledgments

First and foremost I would like to thank Rachel Goggan for contributing invaluable research and editorial assistance and for making the telling of terrible evil doable.

A paper on medical resistance with the assistance of my dear colleagues Drs. Barry Shmookler and Saul Isroff served as the beginning of this work. They have been constant advisors and critics, and have furnished a multitude of resources and insights.

I also thank Rachel Kostanian-Danzig for insights and inspiration and Rosa Bieliauskiene from the Vilna Goan State Jewish Museum who researched the Lithuanian Historical Archives for relevant materials. Drs. Myrna Goldenberg and Myra Sclarew reviewed initial documents and suggested additional resources. Dr. Claude Romney researched French articles on typhus and shared them as well as her papers with me. For translations, I thank Aggie Szvaras, Blanca Keogan, Margitt Meisner, Bert Simson, and especially Nathan Snyder (German); Paul Murphy (French); Danuta Sawika (Polish); Jelena (Latvian); and Vitalje Gircyte (Lithuanian). I also extend my appreciation to Catherine Harbour for help with the diagrams. Most particularly I am grateful to the Kaunas Jewish community survivors for sharing their experiences and recollections.

Finally, I thank my reviewers—Professors Solon Beinfeld, Paul Weindling, Dr. Pauline Aaron, Dr. Tessa Chelouche, Lisa Thaler, Dr. Saul Isroff, and Dr. Barry Shmookler; Dr. Greg Dash, Centers for Disease Control, for resources and comments; Ann Rabinowitz for encouragement; Ron Colman and Tim Baker for research USHMM; Dr. Thomas Schnelle was especially helpful; Nicholas Chevassus-au-lois, Dr. Mikoslav Bilik, Marthe Cohn, and Dr. Giovanni de Martis provided information and insight; Clifford Matheson for assistance with photo images; and Dr. Ralph Yodaiken for editing, criticism, and suffering through this book; Heather Staines, acquisition editor, Praeger, for supporting the book and author; Lindsay Claire, Greenwood Press project manager for overseeing production; and Deborah Masi, Westchester Book Services for her support and effort in making this book readable. Last but most importantly, I would like to thank Cathrine Stukhard for the cover photograph.

Introduction

He who does not learn from history is doomed to repeat it.

George Santayana

Murderous Medicine documents a policy of premeditated murder committed by doctors under the guise of public health. It is the factual story of complicity by German and Austrian doctors in human experiments and genocide through the exploitation of typhus and biological warfare. Doctors dressed in traditional white coats with stethoscopes and syringes, and traveling in Red Cross cars had the resources and training to heal but instead participated in the murder of Jews, Roma (gypsies), Slavs, the mentally disabled, homosexuals, and others who were deemed a threat to the health of German troops and civilians and unworthy of life. SS (Schutzstaffel) camp doctors and doctors who worked in the hygiene institute of the Waffen SS were cognizant of the unlawfulness of their experimental operations because in correspondence available about official experiments countless files are stamped *secret* (Marsalek 1995).

This work is not intended to be a comprehensive historical review of Nazi medicine. Much has been written on medicine in the Holocaust by survivors, historians, social scientists, and doctors, but little attention has been paid to the role of the disease typhus in the Final Solution. Instead of fighting epidemics with hygiene and proven preventative measures, Nazi doctors labeled Jews as disease carriers and a public health risk, and justified the creation of ghettos on this basis. They knew that the overcrowded and unsanitary conditions in the ghettos and camps would lead to epidemic typhus, so they were clearly carrying out a policy contrary to any rational public health policy. At the slightest sign of an epidemic and on the pretext of disinfection and quarantine, the disease became the rationale for the murder of the sick and those who may have been contacts. "Delousing baths" were a camouflage for gas chambers.

The British Foreign Office in 1942 received a report from the Czech underground that with chilling accuracy told how typhus was a pretext for killing and how Zyclon B obtained from Hamburg was used to kill 2000 persons at a time in "delousing baths." In silent complicity the International Committee of the Red Cross took no action.

Throughout World War II the disease presented a tremendous medical challenge, tackled by separation based on spurious criteria of racial purity. Jews, gypsies, Russian prisoners of war, and others were denied resources and medical treatment, while the health of German soldiers was given the highest priority. The "treatment" prescribed for Jews suspected of typhus in the concentration camps was death in the gas chamber or by intracardiac phenol or evipan administered by *Spritz* (injection).

Copy of death book (Auschwitz) kept by concentration camp resistance prisoners. The brackets indicate prisoners that were killed with phenol injected into the heart. *Auschwitz Concentration Camp Archives.*

Doctors have a special role in society. They are perceived as healers, and as humane, caring, ethical individuals dedicated to protecting patients from injury and to prolonging and restoring life. To assume that all doctors are ethical and put the health of the public ahead of their own agenda is unrealistic, however. Unfortunately, for some the pursuit of power and money supersedes the quest for science and health. The use of prisoners as subjects of pharmaceutical trials without informed consent illustrates how unscrupulous doctors can be. The euthanasia program carried out in Nazi Germany was the twisted product of psychiatrists and anthropologists. Contrary to their pledged commitment and training, doctors killed patients to serve a political cause. The practice of Nazi doctors in the ghettos and concentration camps, overtly in the name of public health but covertly in pursuit of national goals, is a blot on twentieth-century medicine.

The Hippocratic Oath is a pledge to do the best to serve patients regardless of race, color, or sex and to do no harm. Regrettably, many medical students who swear to uphold the Oath forget it after graduation. In Germany during the Third Reich, medical students did not take the Hippocratic Oath (see Appendix 1) but they knew the ethic of "nil nocere"—do no harm. In 1931 Germany had developed and circularized regulations—the Reichsrichtlinien fur Forschung an Menschen (Guidelines on New Therapy and Human Experimentation). They were the first regulations for medical research in the Western Hemisphere. In the Third Reich these regulations were ignored but never annulled.

The spread of typhus in concentration camps is an exemplar of biological warfare. At least 1.5 million prisoners died of typhus as a direct consequence of murder, malpractice, or deliberate negligence by German doctors. This was not rational public health. The military was a driving force for measures to eradicate the disease, and the pharmaceutical industry derived profits from their drugs and vaccines. They used concentration camps to test their products with little cost and no restraints. There is evidence that the Hoechst Company paid Auschwitz concentration camp pennies for human female guinea pigs to test experimental hormones. Experiments were conducted without consent and concern for the suffering and pain inflicted. The obsession with purity of the race and Germans' health did not preclude greed and financial profit. Even tissues of the dead were sold. Skeletons and skulls and death masks formed a good source of income. Tattoo skins were used for purses and lamp shades. The SS doctors also experimented with German pharmaceutical company drugs for which they were paid (Sofsky). Saving humankind was not the consideration; only the results and the opportunity for profit mattered. Science was put ahead of humanity.

German doctors were first involved in eugenics, the involuntary sterilization of the "weak," disabled, or "feeble minded." From eugenics they moved to euthanasia, testing and developing killing technologies. These public health doctors were then deployed to concentration camps where they used their technological experience to carry out extermination policies. Their preoccupation was selection, experiments, and gassing. The doctors who had attended courses, conferences, and training were aware of the potential consequences of typhus epidemics which had devastated armies and of preventive measures which had been implemented for German troops and civilians. They set up delousing centers for German troops and civilians in occupied territories such as Dunäberg, Latvia. Anti-typhus decrees and routines were spelled out clearly. Overcrowding was known to be a major factor in epidemics. Yet they isolated Jews in dilapidated crowded ghettos with poor sanitation, no electricity, restricted coal, limited water, and no soap on the pretext of epidemic control, which only fostered epidemics where previously there had been none. Ghetto hospitals suspected of housing typhus cases were burned to the ground with both patients and staff locked inside.

Ample evidence exists that infected lice are the vectors of typhus and that killing lice, not people, is what is required for eradication. In Auschwitz concentration camp, a barrack built for 52 horses housed 1000 to 1200 prisoners. Hygienic conditions were deplorable; in general, there was one spigot for 10,000 prisoners. In a room big enough for 60 persons, 1400 people in rags with no soap were expected to wash. Naked prisoners were inspected in freezing conditions for token lice checks and beaten if a louse was found. Clothing, bedding, and hygienic conditions were ignored. The notorious Dr. Josef Mengele received an award for his radical typhus therapy, which was to send prisoners with typhus and their contacts to the gas chamber.

The SS doctors ignored epidemics as long as they did not affect the SS. In Dachau in October 1944, prisoner doctor Franz Blaha, working in the Dachau pathology laboratory, reported to SS chief camp physician Dr. Fritz Hintermeyer that Hungarian corpses from a transport had brought spotted fever to the camp. Hintermeyer forbade him to mention any epidemic in the camp and threatened to shoot him if he did. No preventive measures were taken. Sick arrivals were placed in blocks with uninfected persons. Each day there were at least 300 new typhus cases and 100 deaths. Only when the epidemic spread to the SS camp was quarantine imposed. All in all there were 28,000 cases and 15,000 deaths (Nuremberg Trials Files English document No. 3249PS Affidavit by Dr. Franz Blaha). Lice were as uncontrolled as typhus was rampant in all the concentration camps.

In the early twentieth century forced disinfection and shaving hair were common practices, especially at borders when typhus epidemics erupted.

During World War I health posters delivered messages on hygiene. But during World War II the message on posters was not to practice good hygiene or wash clothes, but to avoid Jews, the carriers of typhus.

Nazi scientists were not only guilty of blatant disregard for the ethical norms of medical experiments, but were invariably involved in inflicting sadistic injury with no possible scientific purpose in view (Cornwell 2003, p. 397). They allowed unsupervised medical students to carry out experimental studies and perform serious surgical operations. They selected who would live and who would die.

Strong links existed between camp experimenters and academic science in university hospitals and scientific institutions in Germany. Concentration camp pathology laboratories sent heads, skeletons, pickled organs (fixed in formalin), and slides of victims to German universities such as Tübingen, Innsbruck, and Jena. The "great anatomist" Dr. Vos of Jena University sold skeletons and face masks obtained from concentration camps to the Vienna Natural History Museum for profit. Nearly all of the SS doctors had a pathological desire to become surgeons for which they were not trained. They were very superficial and had no human relationship with sick prisoners (Dr. J. Podlaha Nuremberg Trials).

Most of those who murdered in the name of healing and experimented on nonvolunteers sadistically and unscientifically were never prosecuted; a few were hanged but most went free. Their brutal research did not elevate German medicine or contribute to medical science. After the war, these criminals were allowed to continue to practice medicine and teach in the universities despite their criminal record.

I.G. Farben provided Zyclon B through Degesch (the German pest control company) to concentration camps for gassing. Degesch removed the irritant odor required by law in Zyclon B canisters but added a warning label "Vorsicht, ohne Warnstoff" (beware no warning odor) to protect SS executioners who handled the gas. Behring, Bayer, and Hoechst were the driving forces in the experimental drug and vaccine research. In the I.G. Farben trial, the Third Reich's policy, not I.G. Farben, was blamed for the experiments and slave labor. Only a few of their officials received short sentences and of those who did, upon their release they were given high positions with Hoechst and Bayer. Their sentences were light enough to please a chicken thief, and they showed no remorse. Meanwhile, the Red Cross failed its mission and kept silent.

The Jewish doctors in the ghettos and concentration camps continued to help people survive, provided care and compassion, and located resources, despite the draconian health measures of the Nazi doctors. They found ways to conceal typhus cases and in so doing performed acts of sabotage. They conducted nutrition research and made efforts to record the criminal activities of the Nazis and their collaborators. Nazi doctors killed in the name of healing; Jewish doctors struggled to save lives.

Disease as a weapon of war has a long history. For centuries diseased bodies were thrown over walls at the enemy, and in North America blankets infected with smallpox were given to Native Americans. During World War II epidemic typhus was deliberately fueled in the ghettos and concentration camps by SS doctors to kill inmates. Today in the twenty-first century we face biological warfare as an increasingly integral part of military weaponry. Doctors and scientists produce and monitor microorganisms while shaping public health policy. The dispersion of new genetically engineered bacteria and viruses could be devastating to our future, and the medical profession as a whole may be unprepared to ensure the containment and control of these emerging threats to public health.

Rolf Winau states that "German scientists must exorcise Nazi demons" (Winau 2004). "If we do not, then we face uncertainty, lack of information, and confusion when considering ethical questions in the future." We cannot blame the Nazi doctors alone. The German medical profession must also accept responsibility. Those who did not join the Nazi Party were not blameless. If they had objected to the killing of German children, the ideology and technology for murder would not have been developed. From the evidence available, it is necessary to conclude that far from opposing the Nazi state militantly, part of the German medical profession cooperated consciously and even willingly, while the remainder acquiesced in silence. Therefore, our regretful but inevitable judgment must be that responsibility for the inhumane perpetrations of Drs. Karl Brandt, Siegfried Handloser, and Leonardo Conti rests in large measure on the German medical profession which, without vigorous protest, permitted itself to be ruled by such men. Is it too much to say that perhaps one single courageous individual, one single representative of German medicine, could with less careful consideration for his physical comfort have saved the honor of the entire profession (Mitscherlich 1949).

German, Austrian, and Japanese doctors in World War II were involved in experimentation on a large scale, and hundreds of thousands of people were their victims. The criminal experiments were carried out without any real scientific value. Where was the German Medical Society during the Third Reich and after? Most of the perpetrators went unpunished, their work on victims was published in reputable journals, and tissues, specimens, and skeletons from victims are still in German and Austrian laboratories. The identified perpetrators were allowed to continue to practice medicine and even take high positions. Better ways of enforcing ethical codes and rules on experimentation need to be devised; it is not enough to leave it to the medical profession. A consumer oversight committee with the ability to enforce ethical laws and human rights is urgently required. And most of all ways need to be found to ensure this never happens again.

REFERENCES

Auschwitz Archives M.M. 9/4. Report by prisoner Dr. J. Podlaha.

Berlin Code of December 29, 1900.

Cornwell, J. 2003. *Hitler's Scientists: Science, War, and the Devil's Pact.* New York: Viking, p. 237.

Fox, J. P. 1992. "The Road to the Racial Millennium: German Medical Science from 1870 to 1945." *Patterns of Prejudice,* no. 1–2, 26:103–123.

Marsalek, H. 1995. *History of Mauthausen Concentration Camp.* Vienna: Linz, pp. 177–180.

Mitscherlich, A., and F. Mielke. 1949. "The Story of Nazi Medical Crimes." In *Doctors of Infamy.* New York: Henry Schuman, p. x.

Nuremberg Trials Files. 1947. English document no. 3249PS. Affidavit by Dr. Franz Blaha, Trial of Major War Criminals, Proceedings. Vol. 5, Nuremberg.

Pellegrino, E. D. 1997. *The Nazi Doctors and Nuremberg Annals of Internal Medicine.* no. 127 4:307.

Reichsrichtlinien fur Forschung am Menschen (German Guidelines of Human Experimentation). 1931. *Reich Health Circular,* no. 6, 55:174.

Sofsky, W. 1997. *The Concentration Camps in The Order of Terror.* New Jersey: Princeton University Press, pp. 214–258.

Winau, R. 2004. "German Scientists must Exorcise Nazi Demons." *The Guardian* (June 28).

CHAPTER 1

Typhus: War, Lice, and Disinfection

Graffiti on Berlin train station wall. *N. Baumslag.*

> Typhus fever was a disease which modern sanitary reform had banished from the midst of progressive communities.
>
> Dr. James Wilson, French Army Medical Corp, 1910

Typhus is a devastating disease caused by small organisms called *Rickettsia prowazekii*, which are spread from person to person by the human body louse (Figure 1.1). Scientists believe the so-called plague of the Middle Ages was typhus and not the disease we know as plague, an infection caused by the organism *Pasteurella pestis*. Endemic typhus occurs in an area when few people are infected and most have some immunity. When war, famine, and other catastrophes remove barriers against the disease, typhus spreads especially rapidly, peaking in winter. Endemic typhus becomes epidemic when there are overcrowding, infected lice, and poor hygiene.

From the fifteenth century an overwhelming fear of typhus spread throughout Europe. Mortality from the disease in untreated cases is 40 percent and even higher in starving populations.

In the mid-1920s Weigl developed a louse feces vaccine, and in 1938 Herrald Cox developed a chick embryo vaccine used by the Allies in World War II. A number of other vaccines were developed during the war, but none prevented typhus—they just reduced the severity of the disease. Much effort has been spent on searching for an effective preventive vaccine (Gross 1996). Although typhus is now treatable with antibiotics (tetracycline and chloramphenicol), it is still a feared disease. Delousing agents (vermifuges) such as DDT (now replaced by pyrethrin and other insecticides) have been important in eradicating lice.

Humankind has practiced primitive forms of biological warfare for thousands of years. A look at the history of typhus, its effects and its spread, reveals how the Nazis manipulated and used epidemic disease as a weapon of war. Medical concepts regarding the cause and prevention of the disease evolved over time. Delousing, bathing, shaving heads, quarantine, and disinfection became common measures for eradication and control of lice. From 1939 the Nazis used these measures to protect themselves from the disease and used "disinfection" to exterminate "undesirables." German doctors under the Third Reich manipulated typhus with uncanny cunning, deception, and medical deviancy to further their goal of racial purity. They forced Jews and other groups to live in conditions known to fuel epidemic typhus. Such medical negligence whether during war or peace is tantamount to murder.

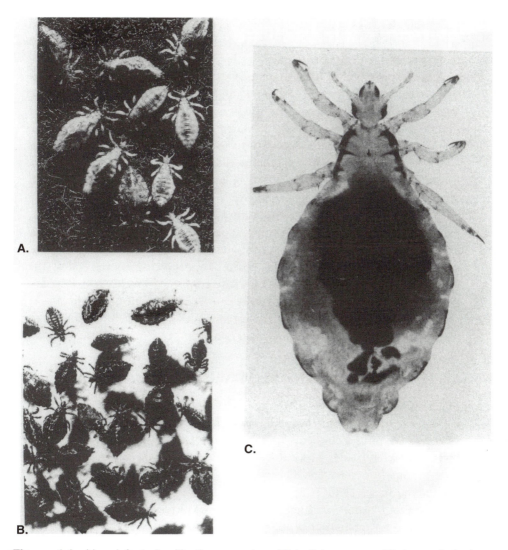

Figure 1.1: Lice infected with the organism Rickettsia prowazekii transmit typhus. **A.** Healthy lice **B.** Infected lice **C.** Louse filled with rickettsia. *Behring Archives, Emil-von-Behring-Bibliothek for Medicine, Philipps University, Marburg, Germany.*

TYPHUS: SIGNS AND SYMPTOMS

Typhus generally lasts twelve to sixteen days and is followed by a severe degree of weakness that can last several weeks.[1] It begins with muscle pain, headache, nausea, thirst, and a sudden onset of intense high fever (104–105° F). As the disease progresses over the week, the patient becomes weak and dizzy and develops temporary deafness, sleep disturbances, weakness, and exhaustion. A body rash starts in the armpit and trunk on the fifth day and then spreads but does not involve the face, palms or soles. Irregular raised pink to purple blotches (mulberry rash) that disappear on slight finger pressure characterize the rash. The second and third weeks of the disease are the most alarming and dangerous as the patient becomes delirious, may start shouting, talk incoherently, become violent, and even need to be restrained. In severe cases patients develop an infected vasculitis (inflammation of the blood vessels) resulting in gangrene of the fingers and toes, which causes a rotting odor. Cardiomyopathy (heart enlargement) is another complication of the disease, frequently misdiagnosed.

In the ghettos and concentration camps during World War II it was difficult to diagnosis typhus in the first few days because starved patients often did not develop a high fever. Some patients early on present with abdominal pain, which can mistakenly be diagnosed as appendicitis. By the end of the first week, the diagnosis of typhus is easily confirmed by the Weil-Felix agglutination test where laboratory services are available. During World War II the mere sight of the tell-tale rash (spotty fever, *Fleckfieber*) led SS doctors to order the murder of prisoners and their contacts.

TYPHUS: A DISEASE WITH MANY NAMES

The word "typhus" is derived from the Greek *typhos* meaning cloudy or confused. The disease has been known as putrid fever, spotty fever, jail fever, *Fleckfieber*, typhus exanthematicus, *cocolixtle meco*, camp fever and famine fever (Garrison 1961). Mexicans in Latin America called it *tabardillo* (red cloak). Some American Indians called typhus *cocolixtle meco*, meaning spotted fever (Zinsser 1934, p. 257). The Aztecs called it *matlazahuatl*, meaning net eruption of spots. In English prisons it was known as "gaol fever." The Polish word for typhus is *dur plamisty*.

DIFFERENTIATING TYPHUS FROM TYPHOID FEVER

The German word for typhus is *Fleckfieber* and for typhoid fever, *bauch typhus*. In 1669 the English physician Thomas Willis was first to differentiate between typhoid fever (*febris putrida*) and typhus (*febris pestilens*). Willis noted that typhus was more contagious, more extensive, and more hemorrhagic than typhoid fever. The clinical differences between the two diseases are the mode of onset, fever pattern, and rash. Typhus fever sets in rapidly and the temperature remains elevated, whereas in typhoid fever the onset is more gradual and the fever increases in a stepladder fashion. Typhus patients often suffer from severe headaches and develop transient deafness and conjunctival suffusion. In typhoid fever patients are apathetic, and the rash begins on the seventh to the tenth day and only lasts two to three days. Also, intestinal ulcers and enlarged abdominal lymph glands are found at autopsy in typhoid fever. The Widal agglutination test is the standard diagnostic laboratory test used for typhoid fever.

By the middle of the nineteenth century the differentiation of typhus from typhoid fever became clearer, but even in World War II typhus was called typhoid fever (*typhus abdominalis*) (Gerhard 1832; Kiple 1997, p. 104). In a Polish-English dictionary, both typhus and typhoid fever are translated as *tyfusowy*. Clinically, epidemics associated with diarrhea and contaminated water were those of typhoid fever, but a high fever, delirium, and a spotty rash, especially in the winter months, were more likely to indicate typhus. The confusion persists even today.[2]

DEFEAT AND RETREAT: TYPHUS BECOMES A WORLDWIDE PROBLEM

It is hard to pinpoint when typhus first appeared in the world. Evidence of lice has been found in the scalps of Peruvian and Southwestern Native American mummies (Reinard and Buikstra 2003; Watson 2004). According to Preuss (1934, in Zinsser), the foremost authority on disease in biblical times, the *Talmud*, revealed that one of the ten plagues visited on the Egyptians was lice. This information was later used in a Yiddish health poster. Many Egyptians died as a result of this infestation, but if it was due to typhus is questionable, as the absence of the disease in other parts of the world at that time makes this unlikely (Figure 1.2). Most medical scientists believe that louse-borne typhus probably arrived in Europe in the late fifteenth century.

Epidemic typhus has long played a decisive role in the defeat and retreat of armies. The disease may have first appeared in the Near East when Christian and Muslim armies clashed during the Crusades. In 1489, during an attack on Moorish Granada, typhus ravaged war-torn Southern Spain. Soon after the siege, Spanish troops began to develop an infectious disease called *tabardillo*, which was typhus. The outbreak originated with Spanish mercenaries who had been hired to fight the Moors. Spain lost 3000 soldiers in the siege of Granada and six times more to typhus (Porter 1997, p. 26).

By the 1530s epidemic typhus had spread to Italy and France. In the mid-1500s Jerome Cardan, an Italian physician, wrote about a common disease in

Italy with a rash that looked like flea bites. He described this disease in a contentious manual in which he also criticized the medical profession. Ten years later Hieronymus Fracastorius, another Italian physician, published the first clear description of typhus in which he noted that the rash resembled flea bites and was contagious in those handling the disease. Typhus was most likely introduced by the Spaniards in Latin America and in Mexico from 1570 until 1576. At about the same time, severe outbreaks of epidemic typhus occurred in Vienna, Hungary, and Poland. Outbreaks of "spotty fever" or "putrid fever" also occurred in Russia during the sixteenth and seventeenth centuries.

Battle after battle was plagued with typhus, death, and disease. By the beginning of the seventeenth century, typhus was widespread in Europe. Although people did not know lice spread typhus, they tried to get rid of lice, particularly head lice. During the Thirty Years' War (1618–1648) throughout Central Europe outbreaks of typhus occurred, which the Germans called the "Hungarian disease." Outbreaks

Yiddish health poster warning against lice.

"*Blood, Frogs, Lice - The Third Plague is the Worst ...Beware of Lice!*"

Figure 1.2: The Jews were aware that lice caused typhus. Health education posters warned people in Yiddish to beware of lice as they were one of the ten plagues. *Illustrated by Joseph Tchaikov, printed by OSE London/Berlin 1923.*

of disease during the war were often blamed on the enemy. In England, spotted fever (typhus) was reported even among the pampered aristocracy. During the siege of Reading, it ravaged parliamentary troops billeted in cramped quarters in a healthy town, and it did not take long before the troops spread the disease to the families with whom they were billeted and to their neighbors.

Typhus spread to parts of the world previously unaffected, such as the Cape of Good Hope at the southern tip of Africa, through the sea trade. In

1665 the fleet of the Dutch East India Shipping Company carried typhus to the Cape and caused the death of four-fifths of the Hottentot population. Even at that time the association between malnutrition and the virulent spread of typhus was known. Lousiness increased with water shortages, particularly during the winter, as people could not wash themselves or their clothes. Tribal customs and community rituals also aggravated the spread of the disease. When people attended a party or a funeral, they often brought lice and disease with them or took them back home (Malan 1972).

In the eighteenth century a number of typhus epidemics occurred in the Russian army, and by the end of the century Moscow physicians were familiar with the disease. Russian inns and peasant huts were heavily infested with lice and vermin. Lice were kept in check to some degree through the use of Russian baths, which were widely available. Typhus, or "camp fever," was especially prevalent during the eighteenth century in the Seven Years' War (1756–1763) and the French Revolution (1789–1799). During the devastating potato blight in Ireland, typhus was known as "famine fever" and caused much suffering and death; 700,000 contracted the disease out of a population of six million (Kiple 1997, p. 107).

As a result of the social disruption and migration of people during the Napoleonic Wars in the early nineteenth century, typhus spread rapidly among Russian soldiers and civilians as well as among the troops of the invading army and their allies. Napoleon's half million soldiers marched into battle with the Russians and typhus. During the army's retreat from Moscow, typhus and dysentery became Napoleon's main enemies. By the end of June 1813, typhus had spread from the Russian cities to the surrounding countryside. The French soldiers who escaped from Russia were infested with lice and brought typhus to France. The army was devastated by typhus, and few returned (Porter 1997, p. 27; Kiple 1997, p. 107). Napoleon's power was broken more by disease than by military opposition, as the ratio of diseased soldiers to wounded soldiers was three to one. Indeed, his soldiers were more afraid of contracting typhus than of getting shot. The social conditions were so poor that outbreaks of other contagious diseases flared up as well, but typhus more than any other factor changed the course of history.

Epidemics recurred during the Crimean War and the Russo-Turkish War in the 1850s and then spread over most of European Russia. Many cities were quarantined, and by the end of the 1860s typhus was endemic in Moscow, St. Petersburg, and other major Russian cities. Outbreaks continued into the 1870s. During an outbreak in Odessa in 1878, authorities disinfected brothels and quarantined villages, and a tenfold reduction in the incidence of typhus was attributed to these measures.

Typhus outbreaks occurred in the English courtrooms of Cambridge, Oxford, and Exeter. Fear broke out when the disease spread from lice-infected prisoners on trial to courtroom spectators, jurors and judges (Kiple 1997, p. 105). Until the late eighteenth century, typhus was prevalent in prisons. The reformer John Howard recognized that the death rate in prisons was related primarily to overcrowding, to unhygienic conditions and typhus-carrying vermin. To reduce the incidence of typhus in prisons, infected cases were isolated, inmates were required to bathe daily, and their clothes were baked in ovens. Howard, ahead of the times, was also the first person to have doctors provide medical care in prisons (Howard 1946).

Typhus resulting from and during war was greatly feared. In World War I it posed a serious threat to the troops; disease was almost as important as the strategy of generals in determining the outcomes of military campaigns. Epidemics of typhus fever in Serbia (now Serbia and Montenegro) during the war claimed the lives of thousands of people. In 1914 2500 cases of typhus were admitted to military hospitals daily in Serbia, and at the height of the epidemic mortality increased from 20 to 70 percent. In less than six months, over 150,000 people died of typhus and a quarter of the medical officers in the Serbian army died. Ironically, typhus was a blessing for the Serbs because the epidemic deterred the Austrians from attacking them (Kiple 1997, p. 108).

An International Sanitary Conference was established after World War I to contain typhus epidemics through sanitary measures. It was estimated that between 1917 and 1923, in European Russia alone there were 30 million cases of typhus and 3 million deaths (Zinsser 1934, p. 213). During the Russian Revolution epidemics of cholera, typhus and a severe famine unequaled since the Thirty Years' War added to the deplorable conditions. The typhus epidemic was so serious that by 1919 Lenin proclaimed: "Either lice will conquer socialism, or socialism will conquer lice" (Patterson 1993, p. 379). Socialism, it appears, controlled lice but did not conquer them. During the most turbulent period of the Russian Revolution, epidemic disease forced Russia into an official relationship with the rest of Europe. The international exchange and cooperation for typhus epidemic control was between the Health Commission of the League of Nations and the Soviet government; a large health education campaign was mounted that included the distribution of health posters (Figure 1.3).

During World War II there was also an international exchange between German scientists and the Allies for the production and testing of typhus vaccines (Weindling 2000). The threat of typhus was felt by all nations involved and played a key factor in Allied military plans. In 1942 President

Franklin D. Roosevelt created an extraordinary body to combat typhus wherever it might threaten U.S. military efforts (Kiple 2003, p. 1083).

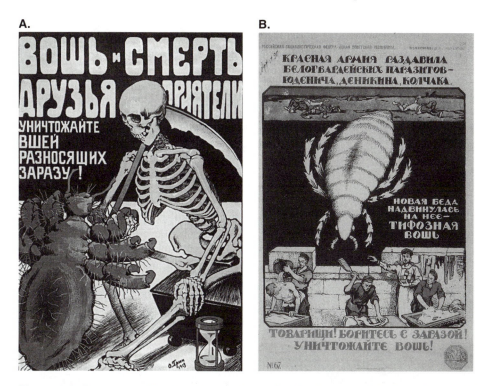

Figure 1.3: Russian health education posters.   **A.** "The louse and death are friends. Kill all lice carrying infection." The typhus louse shaking hands with death (1919, poster translated from the Russian).   **B.** After the defeat of the White Army a new peril threatens in the form of typhus louse, against which the Red soldiers fight by washing themselves and their clothes vigorously (1921, poster translated from the Russian). *Welcome Library, London.*

CAUSE AND CONTROL: EPIDEMIOLOGY OF TYPHUS

Sailors as well as soldiers contracted typhus, and ships transported the disease to people in many ports. Although the cause of typhus was unknown in the mid-eighteenth century, a remarkable British naval surgeon, Dr. James Lind, observed that whatever caused the disease could be destroyed by oven heat. Lind noted that epidemics of "ship fever" were associated with overcrowding, dirty clothing, bedding, and unwashed hair. He was the first to recommend that sailors be stripped, scrubbed, shaved, and issued with clean clothes and bedding regularly. Because of these measures British seamen did not suffer from typhus, and this gave England the upper hand in naval warfare over the French. Lind also found that sulphur, which was widely used as a vermifuge, did not destroy lice (Figure 1.4). Sulphur, however, continued to be used as a disinfectant well into the twentieth century and was employed in the concentration camps by Nazi doctors for delousing (Kiple 1997; Major 1959).

Typhus continually infested war-torn areas in the nineteenth century. The German government in 1848 sent Dr. Rudolf Virchow, a humanist and the father of cellular pathology, to assess a typhus epidemic in Upper Silesia (Poland) in 1848 (Figure 1.5). Virchow found that the disease affected the poor, uneducated, and unclean. He blamed the epidemic on the autocratic Prussian state's oppressive policies. Instead of the usual remedy of more doctors and more hospitals, he advocated revolutionary social reform, including full employment and higher wages, universal education, the establishment of agricultural cooperatives, and the disestablishment of the Catholic Church. His approach to epidemic typhus control contrasted drastically with that of the Nazi doctors a century later. As a result of his "radical" recommendations, he fell into disfavor for several years with Berlin's public health authorities. It cost him his government post, but Virchow nonetheless rose to great heights. His report on typhus in Upper Silesia is regarded as a classic of social medicine (Taylor 1985).

A.   **B.**

Figure 1.4: A. Portrait of physician James Lind (1716–1794), credited with the discovery of lime or lemon juice as a cure for scurvy. **B.** Dr. Lind had British sailors stripped, scrubbed, and shaved to prevent typhus though he did not know lice were the causative agent. *Welcome Library, London.*

Figure 1.5: Dr. Rudolf Virchow was ahead of his time. He recognized that to prevent typhus epidemics, living conditions had to be improved. *Photo Archives, Medical History Museum, Charite, Berlin. Painting by Hugo Vogel, 1891.*

A great deal of empirical knowledge about the epidemiology of typhus was known by the end of the nineteenth century. Doctors and others who cared for the sick, even laundresses, were at increased risk of contracting the disease. Customary preventive measures included prompt hospitalization of the sick and disinfection of their clothes and residences. Clothes and linens were disinfected with carbolic acid in specially constructed huts. More extraordinary lengths included hiring additional doctors, isolating the sick in hospitals, and regularly inspecting homes and institutions during epidemics. So, without any confirmation that lice were the vectors of typhus, health authorities knew to attack filth in all forms from bedding to walls (Patterson 1993). Some programs recognized the importance of providing food for patients. Epidemiological studies also indicated that the risk of typhus increased in migrant populations, prisons, trains, and moving troops.

PINPOINTING THE CULPRIT: SPREADING TYPHUS FROM LOUSE TO MAN

As early as 1606, Austrian physician Tobias Cober noticed the relationship between typhus and lice infestation in the army camps, but he did not suggest a causal relationship (Major 1959, p. 164). Little attention was paid to his observations and to the Spanish researcher Dr. Carlos M. Cortezo, who in 1903 first postulated that the louse was the carrier of the disease.

In 1909 Dr. Charles Nicolle, director of the Pasteur Institute, decided to do something about typhus, which was decimating the population in Tunis. Nicolle was determined to find out how the disease was transmitted from person to person under natural conditions. The hospital was flooded with typhus cases, and patients were even waiting in the streets to gain admission. By accident Nicolle made the critical observation that patients infected others on the streets while waiting to be admitted to the hospital. The moment these patients were admitted to the hospital, after they had a hot bath and were dressed in hospital clothing, they ceased to be infectious. "This observation," recalled Nicolle, "was so simple and uncomplicated that it could have been made not necessarily by a physician, but by an administrator without professional medical training" (Gross). He determined that there must be a transmitting vector in the clothing and underwear and that it was most likely lice. Nicolle's subsequent experiments showed that after lice were fed on infected chimpanzees they infected healthy chimpanzees. This was clear evidence that the human body louse was the vector of typhus fever (Gross 1996). He also showed that lice could be killed at high temperatures (Nicolle 1965; Kiple 2003) (see Appendix 3). The first step in the search for typhus control was thereby accomplished. The Tunisian government immediately took steps to limit the typhus epidemic by combating lice. In 1928 Nicolle was awarded the Nobel Prize for his important discovery that epidemic typhus is transmitted by lice (Figure 1.6).

The recognition that lice transmitted typhus provided the first powerful weapon for an attack against the disease. It removed the mystery of the historic association of typhus epidemics with wars, famines, and wretchedness and confirmed that camp fever, prison fever, and ship fever were all typhus in different settings. This discovery opened the door for military forces in World War I to implement preventive delousing measures, including bathing and steam-cleaning clothing to kill lice, as well as health education.

The next breakthrough occurred during the Mexican typhus epidemic of 1909 when Dr. Howard Taylor Ricketts, a young American pathologist investigating typhus in Mexico City, described a new form of organism found in the blood of typhus patients, in infected body lice, and in lice feces (Figure 1.7). He had discovered the causative organism, subsequently named rickettsia, which are smaller than bacteria and larger than viruses. He demonstrated that rickettsia could not be logically grouped with bacteria, even though they were more closely related to bacteria than to protozoa: that rick-

Figure 1.6: Dr. Charles Nicolle, at the Pasteur Institute in Tunis, was the first to clearly prove the louse was the carrier of typhus. *Pasteur Institute, Paris.*

ettsia differ from bacteria because they do not take up the same laboratory stains, do not grow on artificial media, and multiply only in the cell bodies of a living animal or in tissue culture. He thus established the need for a separate classification of the typhus organism. Unfortunately, Ricketts himself died of typhus in May 1910 before he could confirm his initial findings. He was a splendid scientist and leader, and his death at thirty-nine was a great loss. He had hoped to contribute something of permanent value to humanity in the struggle against disease, and he did.

Building on his work, in 1913 researchers at the Pasteur Institute in Tunis proved that when louse-infested persons scratched themselves they scratched microorganisms into flesh where lice had drawn blood. The actual mechanism for infection was proven through experiments on Algerian volunteers and on monkeys (Busvine 1973). In 1916, the Brazillian Dr. Henrique da Rocha Lima confirmed Ricketts's finding of the causative organism (Gross 1976). Da Rocha Lima named the organism *Rickettsia prowazekii* to commemorate the work of Howard Ricketts and the Polish protozoologist Stanislaus Prowazek, from the Hamburg Tropical Institute (which became the Bernard Nocht institute). In 1915 Prowazek also died of typhus while working on the disease in a Turkish prison with da Rocha Lima (Juenicke 2001).

A.

B. 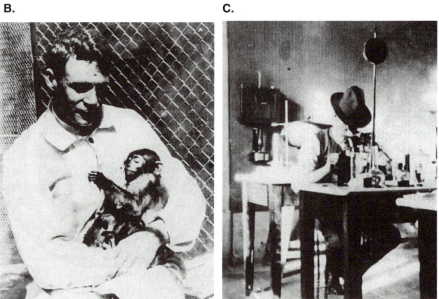 C.

Figure 1.7: A. Dr. Howard Taylor Ricketts described the organism that caused typhus, subsequently named Rickettsia prowazekii, in memory of his contribution
and that of Dr. Prowazek. Both researchers died of typhus.   **B.** Ricketts conducted
tests on monkeys.   **C.** Ricketts in the laboratory where he identified the typhus organism. *Galter Health Sciences Library Special Collections, Northwestern University, Chicago, IL.*

It was thus established that typhus is spread by the body louse, *pediculis corporis humanis*. It was recognized that louse-borne typhus is unique because it is the only rickettsial infection that is primarily a disease of humans with the human as the host which occurs in epidemic form. All other rickettsial conditions are endemic and localized. The Russians appropriately named the body louse *platyanaya vosh*, meaning clothes louse. Body lice spend their entire life cycle (twelve days) in the clothes of the human victim. They bite the host four to six times a day to consume human blood, lay eggs (nits) in the seams of the host's underwear, and cause irritating skin rashes. When the lice are infected with *Rickettsia prowazekii*, they become the source of typhus epidemics. The rickettsiae are taken in with infected blood, multiply in the louse's stomach and intestinal walls, and appear in large numbers in the feces where they look like powder. The infected lice deposit fecal material loaded with rickettsia on the skin. When the human host scratches the itchy feeding sites of the lice, the rickettsiae enter the human bloodstream. Contamination of the eye and contact with clothes and skin with infected louse feces are other modes of infection. Body lice leave a human body that is feverish or dead to search for a new host, and in this way lice spread typhus. Many typhus victims in the concentration camps knew their fellow prisoners were dead when lice left their bodies.

P. P. Orlov, a Russian scientist, recognized that typhus flared up year after year in confined areas. Rickettsiae can persist in dust through dried louse feces, in "typhus houses" in louse-infested populations, and through Brill's disease, a milder form of typhus that recurs years after recovery from an initial attack (Zinsser 1934; Kiple 2003). The recurrent disease was initially described by Dr. Nathan Brill as a new disease occurring in Jewish Hungarian immigrants in New York in 1898. In 1906 a perceptive Polish Jewish physician visiting a New York hospital recognized that the new disease was a mild form of typhus recurring in individuals who had recovered from a prior infection. The second episode was not associated with the presence of lice (Markel 1997). This recurrent form of typhus is also known as the Brill Zinsser disease.

EPIDEMICS AND ANTI-SEMITISM: SETTING THE STAGE

Typhus remained a serious endemic problem throughout Eastern Europe prior to, during, and after World War I (Figure 1.8). After World War I, 20 to 30 million people died in Eastern Europe from the disease, and an additional several million died during and after World War II (Gross 1986). The Russians had done little to eradicate the disease, but in Galicia the Austrian

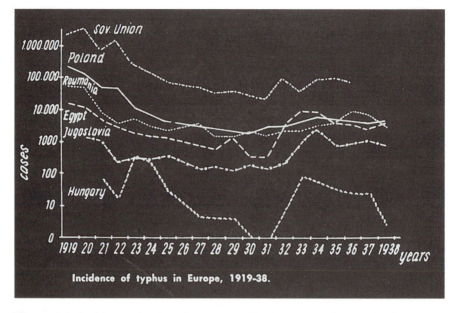

Figure 1.8: Incidents of epidemic typhus 1919–1938. Note that in 1938 the incident of typhus in Poland had decreased. *Source: Patterson.*

government enforced strict sanitary measures that controlled it. In Poland there were no regulations for reporting cases of typhus, and when food and water shortages, overcrowding, fleeing refugees, returning POWs, and chaos existed, epidemics resulted. When an epidemic occurred in Warsaw in 1917, the Polish minister of health Dr. Trenkner attributed it chiefly to Jewish food smugglers whom he claimed brought the disease into the city. Trenkner also blamed Jews living in the Jewish quarter, ignoring the fact that the German occupying forces failed to enforce consistent, sustainable sanitary measures.

Under German authority citizens were deloused by force at the point of a bayonet, but when the Germans left, hygiene deteriorated. Disruption of services and shortages of soap and water further aggravated the situation. Overcrowded trains helped increase the spread of the lice, as did the reduced availability of water during the winter. The Ministry of Health used mobile vans for delousing, but when people heard the sanitary squads were in their neighborhood, they locked their houses fearing the intimidating procedure. People infested with lice were sent to delousing centers and were denied a passport until they produced a certificate that they had been deloused.

The recurring claim that Jews were responsible for the typhus epidemics is totally unsubstantiated. The attack rate was much higher among Christians than among Jews, and the fatality of the Jews was 7 percent compared to 14 percent in the Christians. The Polish medical authorities attributed the difference to Jewish doctors treating their sick earlier. Furthermore, a report of the epidemic in Zawiercie, Poland, from November 1917 to February/March 1918, also indicated that Christians were attacked more frequently than Jews. Despite these findings, public health doctors continued to scapegoat the Jews for the epidemic. In April 1918 the Prussian minister of the interior closed the borders to Jewish workers for "medical reasons." Jews were considered the principal carriers of typhus (Maurer 1985).

The Polish health authority's typhus prevention campaign included cordoning off areas and setting up disinfection units at train stations and other central locations, but it proved too costly. In the summer of 1919 typhus was rampant in impoverished Poland, and the Polish minister of public health appealed to the international community for help. A variety of countries and organizations, including the American Red Cross and the UK's War Victims Relief Committee of the Society of Friends, provided aid. The latter sent a small unit headed by a highly respected epidemiologist, Dr. E. W. Goodall, who blamed Jews for the epidemic. Even though his beliefs were not based on statistical evidence, Jewish doctors were accused of concealing typhus cases and were stigmatized as typhus carriers (Goodall 1920).

In 1920, the health minister and the central committee were replaced by an extraordinary epidemic commissariat with an emergency staff and recovery services led by Emil Godlewski, also known as the "typhus tsar." Godlewski's measures successfully controlled the typhus epidemic in Poland. The canard that Jews were typhus carriers persisted, however, and was well ingrained and incorporated in anti-Semitic literature.

TYPHUS PREVENTION METHODS: GET RID OF THE LICE

The experience of public health doctors with typhus in Russia, Poland, China and Rumania provided practical knowledge for controlling typhus, and public health measures to prevent epidemics were well known by the onset of World War II (Mackenzie 1941). The disease could be diagnosed, and vaccines were available to decrease the severity. Most importantly, it was clear that the prevention of typhus depended on getting rid of lice.

Measures commonly instituted included delousing and disinfection in stations, trains, and mobile delousing centers, hair shaving, setting up quarantine, cordoning off healthy areas, hospitalizing typhus cases, and isolating the sick. Malnutrition was recognized as a cofactor and consequence of typhus outbreaks and was considered important because inadequate nutrition perpetuated a vicious cycle—the sick were unable to plant crops and less food resulted. The provision of supplementary food to the community improved nutrition and ended the epidemic within two years.

Many doctors and nurses contracted typhus while working with patients. During epidemics, medical personnel took special precautions to reduce their exposure and high mortality. They wore special clothing, shaved their head and body hair, and employed health workers under the age of thirty years, whose mortality was lower than that in older persons. Attention was paid to protective clothing, which was only worn for two to three hours and then changed. Special care was taken to protect the face and wrist from lice to prevent them from crawling into these areas. Snugly fitted face masks and rubber gloves were worn to cover the forearms. Ambulance drivers, sanitary inspectors, and disinfectors wore closely woven cloth gloves with gauntlets and gumboots or galoshes. For workers who had to sleep in infested peasant huts or railway trains, a special type of sleeping bag which could be boiled was provided (Mackenzie 1941, p. 154).

RADICAL APPROACHES:
RABBIS FOR HEALTH EDUCATION

The Germans feared that typhus would devastate the army and spread to Germany. During the invasion of Poland in World War II, an attempt was made to educate Warsaw Jews about typhus through posters in Yiddish and through their rabbis. Isaac Bashevis Singer, in one of his stories, "Fruitless Hopes," describes how the Germans enlisted rabbis to help prevent typhus epidemics. Two reform German rabbis who prayed and spoke in German, arrived in Warsaw and invited Polish rabbis who did not have congregations to come to a meeting and promised them official appointments and decent wages. These exclusively Yiddish-speaking Talmudic scholars were afraid of contact with *goyim* (non-Jews) and Germans. They eventually came to the meeting because they feared punishment and persecution; they came dressed in their smartest clothes, as requested by the German rabbis, so as not to appear as dirty Eastern Jews. A German military doctor came in and gave them a lecture in German about cleanliness. He told them that typhus came from the louse, and he showed a photograph of a louse enlarged a hundred times. He asked the rabbis to speak to other Jews (*Juden*) about the importance of cleanliness. After the lecture he bowed and left. The following Sabbath the rabbis spoke in the synagogue about cleanliness as they had been asked to do. "The simple Jews yawned and shook their heads. How could they keep clean in damp cellars? How could they be tidy if they had no shirts, no clothing and no piece of bread?" (Singer 1979, p. 309).

DELOUSING AND DISINFECTION: INTIMIDATION AND INCOMPETENCE

People were familiar with delousing procedures; many had seen, experienced, and feared them as they were intimidating, humiliating, and disruptive. In 1921 at one such center in Baranowice on the Polish Russian border, each day 10,000 refugees returning by trains were disinfected. They were forced to strip and leave their garments on the train, given blankets, and sent to the disinfecting station where they bathed in hot water with soft soap and paraffin. Meanwhile at the station, the train and clothes were backed up in a tunnel and disinfected with HCN gas. Then the carriages were pulled back, and the contents allowed to air. When it seemed safe, the passengers were allowed to put on their supposedly vermin-free clothes and continue their journey.

In Russia as in Serbia, each village was equipped with a "bath" housed in a log hut in which stones were heated to high temperatures and then buckets of water were thrown onto them to produce steam. The population, bedding, and clothing were deloused with heat and steam. In the entrance of some houses there was a large box half-filled with naphthalene into which all furs and outer garments were dropped and left until the following morning. Clothes were pressed with hot irons. Measures were dependent on functioning machines, cooperative people, soap and disinfectants, water, and fuel. Prevention in rural areas was particularly challenging.

In general, for disinfection to work it has to be thorough, but for the most part delousing was halfhearted and applied *pro forma* without proof that the methods were effective. The hatred, abuse, and ineffectiveness of disinfection in the bathhouse in gulag prison camps is well described by the Russian writer Varlam Shalamov, in his book, *Kolyma Tales*. Lice were so prevalent that as long as they could be brushed off, they were not considered of any consequence. Bathhouse sessions occurred before or after work, far from the living quarters. Up to 100 prisoners were packed into unheated dressing rooms constructed to hold ten to fifteen men, in various states of undress. Men had to wash with limited quantities of hot water, varying from a spoonful to a cisternful. There was not enough wood to heat iron stoves adequately, and most of the time it was cold and drafty. The process did not kill the lice because it was hopelessly inadequate. The doctors understood the process was a mere formality, but the camp could not be left without a disinfecting chamber (Shalamov 1994).

During the typhus epidemic in Poland in 1919, a number of different approaches to typhus control were tried. The American Polish Relief Expedition (APRE) of the U.S. Army attacked the lice in Poland through mobile field columns that moved from town to town. They were equipped with motorized bath plants, stoves, and bedding. When the field column arrived in a village, tents were pitched with facilities for delousing. Hair was shaved, though the Americans never insisted on shaving the religious Jews' hair and beards, out of respect for their religious traditions. After shaving, the people were sent to shower in special tents while Polish employees sterilized their clothes. Because there was a shortage of water and heat, people were only allowed a short shower and then were told to dress. They left clutching their soap, a valuable commodity in Poland, which they were allowed to keep. Five to eight hundred people were bathed each day by these field columns (Foster 1981). However, it appears that the Red Cross campaign against typhus in Poland accomplished practically nothing. According to the Rockefeller Center Archives, "the Russian crisis is so vast, . . . Private subscriptions would make almost no impression and might harm by relieving the government of a sense of responsibility" (see Appendix 8, Rockefeller Foundation 1.1/785/2/15, Letter from George Vincent to John D. Rockefeller Jr., 9 August 1921).

When the population was asked to come for delousing, they feared it was a ruse for deportation and most fled. This incomprehensible opposition frustrated the Americans; they therefore forced the Poles to participate by withholding bread from anyone without a certificate from a bathhouse unit. Years later, in 1941 in the Vilna Ghetto, evidence of bathing was again required in order to obtain a food ration card. Though an effective short-term strategy, forcing compliance subverted the long-range goals of educating the public and modernizing health practices.

Special precautions were taken when typhus cases were transported to hospitals, for typhus could be spread by a single louse. The disinfection of patient "contacts," premises, ambulances, and personnel was under the supervision of a medical officer. Saturated steam was used for disinfection, and typhus patients transported to hospital in ambulances were encased in sheets to ensure louse droppings were contained. Hospitals were required to have an admission block for typhus cases with a disinfecting unit, where all new admissions were deloused. In order to destroy the nits as well, the procedure was repeated in the second week. Although the disinfectants then available

were useless for eradicating lice, bathing with ordinary soft soap was effective if conscientiously applied after the patient was shaved.

SHAVING HAIR: RITUAL?

There are three types of lice known to infect man: head lice (*pediculis hu-manis capitis*), pubic and axillary lice (*pediculis humanis pubis*), and body lice (*pediculis humanis corporis*). Interestingly, disinfection has empirically tar-geted all three types of lice. Head, pubic, and axillary (armpit) hair have rou-tinely been shaved. Body lice are larger, more resistant to starvation, and more adaptable to captivity; therefore, they have been studied intensively. Until recently, most authorities believed that only body lice carry rickettsia, though researchers such as Dr. Gear in South Africa considered that both head lice and body lice harbor the infection (Malan 1972). Laboratory exper-iments suggest that head lice have the ability to transmit rickettsia and that they are potential vectors of typhus. Pubic lice were also found to be causally related to a typhus epidemic in China (Robinson 2003).

QUARANTINE: STIGMA AND SCAPEGOATING

Formalized practices of avoiding and isolating the ill have been a major re-sponse to contagious diseases and epidemics over time and across national boundaries. Some of the earliest recorded examples can be found in the Old Testament, which details instructions for isolating lepers and disinfecting the home. A now forgotten function of the ram's horn, or *shofar*, traditionally sounded during Rosh Hashanah (the Jewish New Year), was to warn the community that there was diphtheria or some other highly contagious disease in the community. Detention and isolation regulations started with efforts aimed at containing plague. One of the first laws to delay and isolate travelers from regions where plague was raging was enacted by Byzantine emperor Jus-tinian in A.D. 549. As early as the seventh century in China and other parts of Asia and Europe, the transmission of epidemic diseases and human migra-tion was recognized. And in the Middle Ages, in plague-ridden areas, sailors and foreign travelers were detained (Garrison 1961; Robinson 2003).

During plague epidemics ships entering the port of Venice were required to remain in isolation for forty days before their goods, crew, and passengers were allowed to disembark. This regulation was enacted in 1374, when scien-tists believed disease was spread by air and not by bacteria. This was called quarantine, a word that originated from the Italian *quarantina*. Shortly there-after the municipality of Venice established a maritime quarantine station (*lazaretto*) on the island of Santa Maria di Nazareth. Gates were closed, and sanitary cordons with armed soldiers prevented the entry of diseased fugitives. The forty-day quarantine period is believed to have been based on the fact that people with plague either died or recovered during this forty-day time period without further spread to others. Quarantine was used in France, Britain, Austria, Germany, Russia, and several other European and Asian nations from the fourteenth to the nineteenth century.

Quarantine is used not only for medical reasons but also to stigmatize social groups. Epidemics reveal deficiencies of local administrative structures and expose political, social, and moral shortcomings. The element of blame and stigma associated with quarantine is especially real for those diseases linked to the poor, alien, and disenfranchised. An epidemic hits the hardest at the lowest social classes or other fringe groups. In the United States, social scapegoating of immigrants, especially those from Eastern Europe, characterized the epidemic of typhus in New York. Historian Asa Briggs believes epidemics are a useful means of testing the "efficiency and resilience of local administrative structures" and in exposing relentlessly political, social, and moral shortcomings . . . rumors, suspicions, and at times, violent social conflicts (Markel 1997).

The Germans in World War II used quarantine and isolation to create the Warsaw Ghetto and then to justify the ghettoization of the Jews throughout German-occupied territory. According to Dr. Ludwik Hirszfeld, who studied the disease extensively in the Warsaw Ghetto: "There is little evidence that such epidemics existed to any serious degree before the ghetto was created and no evidence as expected that Jews were any more likely to suffer from or transmit typhus than any other group" (Roland 1992, p. 130). Later, a six-week quarantine was enforced for typhus cases in Auschwitz concentration camp—far in excess of the recognized two-week quarantine period—yet another measure of Nazi medical irrationality and cruelty.

DISINFECTION AND GAS: TERROR TEMPERED WITH DECEPTION

> The whole medical apparatus was nothing but a décor to disguise massacre.
>
> Elie Cohen

The Nazi policy to annihilate Jews was camouflaged from the rest of the world and to some extent from the victims themselves. The technology associated with disinfection served to mask the killing. As Jews arrived in the extermination camps of Sobibor, Belzec, and Treblinka, those selected for work were sent for head shaving and delousing. The majority were selected for extermination and packed into showers with deceptive signs "to disinfection stations" and arrows pointing "to the baths." Women were sent to one side and men to the other. They were ordered to undress, deposit their belongings, and remember where they left them. Their hair was shaved, and then they were shoved into a crowded, confined space and asked to breathe deeply as gas was pumped into the room. They were told that "inhaling is a necessary method of preventing infection" (Gerstein 1945). The elderly and invalids were ordered to proceed along a road marked with a Red Cross and the inscription "Lazarett" (military hospital). They never found the hospital but instead were shot before open pits or gassed (Hausner 1968, p. 166).

In the Chelmo camp and many others, mobile vans with "showers" were set up to look like "disinfection installations." To complete the deception, the SS handed out towels and soap to the unknowing victims. As soon as the vans were packed the doors were locked and exhaust gases were pumped into the hermetically sealed compartment. The van was then driven to a nearby forest and the dead bodies were dumped. This charade allowed the Germans to massacre millions with relative ease. The killing machines often had mechanical failures and the victims suffered slow, stifling deaths, while Nazi officials, including doctors, looked through specially created peepholes.

The Germans had a number of chemicals for delousing but used mainly Zyclon B, discovered by Carl Wilhelm Scheele in the 1780s. The generic name is prussic acid and is called blue powder (blazer) because of its color. Prussic acid, first used on the eastern front in 1917, became a popular delousing agent. It was sold in crystalline form, packed in sealed tins, and carried the name Zyclon B. Initially, the Germans ordered the gas for use as a vermifuge for delousing in the concentration camps, but after the adoption of the Final Solution to the Jewish Question at the Wannsee Conference in 1942, a need arose for a gas that could be used to murder hundreds of Jews at once. Rudolf Höss, architect and chief commander of Auschwitz, found Zyclon B suitable, and so facilities were constructed to maximize the effects of the poison. By law, Zyclon B had been combined with a small amount of irritant with a distinctive odor to warn of the presence of a dangerous substance. The SS ordered the removal of the odor. Labels on the canisters, however, as noted earlier, carried a warning "Vorsicht, ohne Warnstoff" (Beware no warning odor). The warning label was intended for protection of the SS executioners who handled the cans. Zyclon B was first tested as an

agent of mass murder on 3 September 1941, when it was used to exterminate 850 prisoners at Auschwitz-Birkenau, 600 of whom were Soviet prisoners of war (International Auschwitz Committee 1960). Zyclon B made
the notorious Hoess the most successful killer in modern history (Borkin
1997, p. 122).

The German Degesch Corporation (Deutsche Gesellschaft zur Schadlings-
bekampfung), a self-described exclusive selling agent for chemical giant I.G.
Farben, manufactured Zyclon B. Degesch netted nearly 300,000 Reich marks
from sales from 1941 to 1944. The German chemicals firm Degussa was part-
owner of Degesch and thus also profited from supplying the Nazi death camps
with the hydrogen cyanide gas pellets (Warkentin 2003) (Figure 1.9).

Interestingly, the British did not use Zyclon B for disinfection, for they
considered the chemical too toxic. They explored other substances for delousing, and even devised one notable contraption, which was a treated cloth belt
worn under the clothing and woven in folds as lice tend to congregate in
seams. This belt, tested on lousy vagrants, was determined effective and was
discussed confidentially at high levels of the Allied military command. The
British did not share this information because they feared it might fall into
the wrong hands and destroy a potential ally in the louse (see Appendix 4, secret report) (Busvine 1973).

The invention of DDT, the first truly effective delousing agent, made
British louse traps obsolete. DDT was discovered in 1874 by Othmar
Zeidler, a German chemist, and resynthesized in 1939 by Paul Mueller and
associates working for Geigy of Basle, Switzerland. Mueller had found that
DDT was a remarkable insecticide, lethal in a few minutes and effective for
two to six weeks when applied to clothing skin or blankets.[3] Geigy issued a
report in 1943 that the product was effective against the body louse. British
scientists tested it and found that it drastically reduced lice infestation in their
soldiers. It was first used on a large scale to control a typhus epidemic in
Naples, Italy, in 1943, where the U.S. military made history by bringing the
epidemic quickly under control. The powder was applied with a special
blower, and there was no need to undress. The discovery of DDT proved invaluable. It was used by the ton to coat clothes, food, and air, and the results
achieved for the control of typhus epidemics were highly effective. The adverse effects were not yet known.[4]

German soldiers, however, continued to remain heavily infested with lice
as they continued to use Zyclon B gas and assorted useless vermifuges. As
early as 1942 the Germans had two DDT derivatives available, Gerasol spray
and Neocid powder. Although in 1944 the German professor Gerhard Rose
from Robert Koch Institute proved that DDT derivatives were effective

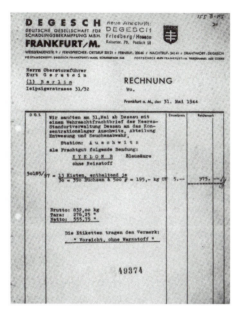

Figure 1.9: A. Invoice from DEGESCH (German Association for Pest Control) records shows shipment of 390 canisters of Zyclon B cyanide gas to be used for "disinfection and extermination" at Auschwitz concentration camp. The invoice states there is a warning label on the canisters "Vorsicht, ohne Warstoff" (beware, no warning odor). The label was for the protection of the SS executioners who handled the cans. *Invoice, DEGESCH to SS First Lt. Gerstein, May 31, 1941. RG 238, Nuremberg Document 1553 PS, Exhibit RF 350. NARA.*

B. Zyclon B canister used in Auschwitz-Berkenau for gassing. *RG 238,* United States v. Carl Krauch et al., *Exhibit DEGESCH 48. NARA.*

C. Canisters of Zyclon B poison gas pellets and a gas mask used in Majdanek concentration camp to protect the perpetrators. *USHMM.*

against the louse, still the Germans did not use them for the general public. One reason given was that large-scale production was problematic. But according to Dr. Wilhelm Hagen, a German physician who had been a medical officer in occupied Warsaw, the production of DDT derivatives was not allowed because Theo Morell, Hitler's doctor, had patented a product called *Ruslapuder* (Rusla powder) which he sold for millions of marks (Hagen 1973). It was not until March 1944 that German scientists confirmed a British finding that the Rusla powder did not work. Only then was a DDT-based derivative called Lauseto Delicia provided for troops. Civilians were given the ineffective Rusla powder, and Globol, another pesticide, was worn in a packet attached to the body. This device was abandoned once it was found to attract lice rather than destroy them.

CONTROL THE LICE, CONTROL TYPHUS: BRITISH EPIDEMIC CONTROL AT BELSEN

Typhus epidemics plagued the concentration camp victims. In Belsen concentration camp, epidemic typhus was rampant for four months prior to liberation; there were an estimated 20,000 cases. The Germans attempted to control the epidemic by isolating typhus cases, but this was a farce as the hospital was staffed by inexperienced people with inadequate facilities. Under the German hot air delousing procedure, the deloused were quickly reinfested by other prisoners who had not been adequately deloused or through clothing and bedding that had not been cleaned. They did not use delousing powder or vaccines, though the German nurses present admitted they possessed some anti-typhus vaccine. When the British army liberated Belsen concentration camp in April 1945, they found overcrowding, starvation, lack of water, and poor sanitation. Almost 100 percent of the survivors from camp one had an average of 100 lice per person.

The British controlled the ongoing typhus epidemic swiftly by attacking the lice rather than the prisoners Their approach consisted of burning infested barracks, delousing survivors, providing sanitary facilities and clean bedding, and disinfecting clothing (Figure 1.10). The British prioritized a delousing program first and foremost and complemented it with a vaccine inoculation program. Evacuees were given hot showers, clothed, and then marched through a delousing station. Most of the beds, clothing, and personal effects were dusted with DDT. During a delousing session, former prisoner Adolf Gawalewicz said to British army personnel: "It's not going to work. Even the Germans couldn't get rid of the lice!" (Jacobs 1979). But it did work. Once the British typhus control program was in place, not a single

Figure 1.10: Stretcher bearers at Bergen Belsen concentration camp clear lice-infested huts. They wore protective clothing to minimize their exposure to lice. The clothing consisted of a one-piece garment with a hood fastened down the back with a zipper, gum boots, and long fabric gloves. The Lancet, *November, 1941,* p. 688. *Photo: British Red Cross Museum and Archives.*

new case of typhus was reported within two weeks (Davies 1917). The delousing of the camp was accomplished within the incubation period of typhus, providing strong evidence that the lice were the principal cause of typhus (Figure 1.11).

Ten days after the liberation of Bergen Belsen, former prisoner Gawalewicz wrote:

> After two–three days at the hospital, we have our first encounter with the pesticide DDT. When the English soldiers enter the hospital room with sprayers filled with this product, we all look at them with contemptuous superiority. They're planning on using this puny white powder to destroy all these millions of lice! But hundreds of the most radically conducted Entläusungs hadn't helped. Yet, right in front of our eyes, something close to a miracle starts to happen! Slowly, the incessant itching, so painful on our puss infected, ulcerated skin, starts to vanish, and this great relief finally convinces us that we have really been liberated. O Great, Powerful Benefactor, Inventor of the White Powder! (Jacobs 1979).

Figure 1.11: Burning the typhus-infected barracks of camp 1, Bergen Belsen. *Yad Vashem Photo Archives.*

EXTERMINATION: SANITARY MURDER

In all areas of the world where public health and hygiene have been rigorously enforced, the incidence of typhus has decreased rapidly. By sharp contrast, the Nazis made the outbreak of epidemics inevitable among the Jews (Hausner 1968; Weindling 2000). Disinfection, lazarettos, gas, and shaving—the typhus ritual was used under the subterfuge of providing health care to marginalize and ultimately murder millions of Jews (Hausner 1968). With all their barbaric, unethical experiments and gassing, the German researchers were not able to control typhus or get rid of lice. Jews were left to starve in a diseased environment, doomed to die from "natural causes" for *eine judenvrei Europa* (Europe free of Jews). It was inexcusable murder.

NOTES

1. People of all ages are susceptible to typhus, but men of working age once exposed often have higher attack rates than females, children, or the elderly. Children usually have milder clinical courses.

2. Confusion between typhus and typhoid fever is still widespread as is evidenced by correspondence with various archives. In *Kolyma Tales*, a story from the Gulag, the "typhoid" chapter is clearly about typhus and not typhoid fever.

3. Mueller first tested it on the Colorado spring beetle which was attacking Swiss potatoes, and through the use of DDT saved the crop. It was also used as a moth-proofing agent. A small amount of this product was given to the United States where the active component was isolated and synthesized in 1942. It was also tested in the Middle East and Egypt. For a time it was thought that the formula was a closely guarded secret of Geigy until it was found in a copy of *Popular Mechanics* magazine by Major Neil Murray in Modderfontein (a South African government chemical defense factory). The essential ingredients were chlorine and benzene added to talc. After finding the recipe, South Africa was able to make 20,000 tons of DDT for delousing European populations liberated by Allied armies from German occupation.

4. It is now known that DDT is an environmental hazard, harmfully affecting certain birds, fish, and mammals, and that lice can became resistant to the toxin. DDT has since been replaced by less toxic delousing agents.

REFERENCES

American-Polish Relief Expedition. 1981. *Bulletin of the History of Medicine* 55:221–232.

Bennett, T., D.C. John, and L.B. Tyszczuk. 1990. "Deception by Immunization Revisted." *British Medical Journal*, vol. 30, no. 6766 (December).

Borkin, J. 1978. *The Crime and Punishment of I. G. Farben*. New York: Free Press, pp. 122–123.

Briggs, A. 1997. *Quarantine! East European Jewish Immigrants and New York City: Epidemics of 1892*, H. Markel, ed. Baltimore, MD: Johns Hopkins University Press, p. 2.

Busvine, J.R. 1973. "Introductory Remarks on the Control of Lice and Louseborne Diseases." Washington, DC: PAHO Symposium, pp. 149–158.

———. 1976. "Experimental Transmission of Typhus to Man." March 4, 1922. In *Insects, Hygiene and History*. London: Athlone Press, p. 186.

Buxton, P.A. 1947. *The Louse*. 2nd ed. London: Arnold.

Chronicle of the Development of Infectology in Kaunas. 1990. Trans. from Lithuanian by Dr. Panavas, Kaunas, p. 51.

Cohen, E. 1988. *Human Behaviour in the Concentration Camp*. London: Free Association Books, 1988.

Creighton, C. 1983. *History of Epidemics in Britain*. Baltimore, MD: Institute of History Medicine, Johns Hopkins University.

Cunha, B.A. 1982. "Typhoid Fever, the Typhus Like Disease, Historical Perspective." *New York State Journal of Medicine* (March), pp. 321–324.

Dadrian, V.N. 1986. *The Role of Turkish Physicians in WWI: Genocide of Ottoman Armenians. Holocaust and Genocide Studies*, no. 2, 1:169.

Dasch, G. 1998. Personal communication. Bethesda, MD: U.S. Naval Hospital, (March 18).

Davies, W. A. 1947. Typhus at Belsen. *The American Journal of Hygiene*, vol. 46, (July).

Fabre, J. 1997. Hip Hip, Hippocrates; Extracts from the Hippocratic Doctor. *British Medical Journal* (December) 315:1669–1674.

———. 1997. *The Hippocratic Doctor: Ancient Lessons for the Modern World.* New York: Royal Society of Medicine Press.

Foster, G. M. 1981. "Typhus Disaster in the Wake of War: The American Polish Relief Expedition, 1919–1920." *Bulletin of the History of Medicine.* Baltimore, MD: Johns Hopkins University Press, 55:221–232.

Francastorii. 1930. *De Contagione et Contagiosis Morbis et Eorum Curatione.* Trans. by Wilmer Cave Wright, New York: G. P. Putnam's Sons, p. 103.

Garrison, F. H. 1929. *An Introduction to the History of Medicine.* Philadelphia: W. B. Saunders.

Gawalewicz, A. 1973. *Refleksje z poczekalni do gazu.* Krakow: Wydawnictwo Literackie, pp. 146–147.

Gerhard. 1832. *Am. Jour. Med. Sc. Phial.* pp. xi, xx, 289–322, 368–408.

Gerstein, K. 1945. YVA 9/30 (6a) 460, Gerstein file, Gerstein testimony (May 6).

Goldberger, J. and J. F. Anderson. 1912. "Transmission by the Head Louse" (*Pediculus capitis*). *Public Health Report* 27:297–307.

Goodall, E. W. 1920. *Proceedings of the Royal Society of Medicine* 13:265–273.

Gross, L. 1996. "Perspective: How Charles Nicolle of the Pasteur Institute Discovered That Epidemic Typhus Was Transmitted by Lice: Reminiscences from My Years at the Pasteur Institute in Paris." *Proceedings Natl. Acad. Sci.* 93:10539–10540.

Guthrie, A. 1946. *History of Medicine.* London: Lippincott.

Haffner, D. 1946. *Aspects Pathologiques du Camp de Concentration d'Auschwitz-Birkenau.* Tours, Imprimerie Unioncoopérative (Medical Dissertation), p. 39.

Hagen, W. 1973. "Krieg Hunger und Pestilenz in Warschau 1939–43." *Gesundsheidwesen Desinfektion* 9:133–135.

Hausner, G. 1968. *Justice in Jerusalem, Chapter 10: The Death Camps.* New York: Schocken, p. 156.

Hirszfeld, L., in C. Roland. 1992. *Courage under Siege: Starvation, Disease and Death in the Warsaw Ghetto.* New York: Oxford University Press, pp. 130–131.

Howard, J., quoted in A. Guthrie. 1946. *History of Medicine.* Philadelphia: J. B. Lippincott, p. 250.

International Auschwitz Committee. 1960. *KL Auschwitz.* Kracow, Poland: Drukarnia Narodowa.

Jacobs, A. 1979. Personal interview with Adolph Gawalewicz. Kracow, Poland (June).

Juenicke, L. 2001. Stanislaus von Prowakeki: Prodigy between Working Bench and Coffee House. Institute for Biocheme Universität zu Kohn.

Kiple, K. F. 1993. *The Cambridge World History of Human Disease*. New York: Cambridge University Press, p. 1088.

————. 1997. *Plague, Pox and Pestilence*. London: Weidenfeld and Nicolson, p. 107.

Lind, J. 1965. An Essay on the Most Effectual Means of Preserving the Health of Seamen in the Royal Navy, and a Dissertation on Fevers and Infection, 1779. In Christopher Lloyd, ed., *The Health of Seamen; Selections of the Works of Dr. James Lind, Sir Gilbert Blane, and Dr. Thomas Trotter*. London Navy Records Society, p. 94.

Mackenzie, M. 1941. "Some Practical Considerations in the Control of Louse-borne Typhus Fever in Great Britain in the Light of Experience in Russia, Poland, Rumania and China." *Proceedings of the Royal Society of Medicine Section of Epidemiology and State Medicine* pp. xxxv, 141.

Major, R. H. 1959. *Classic Descriptions of Disease with Biographical Sketches of the Authors*. Springfield, MO: Charles C. Thomas, pp. 163–165.

Malan, M. 1988. "In Quest of Health." *SAIMR 1912–1972*. Johannesburg: Lowry Publishers, p. 271.

Markel, H. 1997. *Quarantine! East European Jewish Immigrants and New York City, Epidemics of 1892*. Baltimore, MD: Johns Hopkins University Press.

Maurer, T. 1985. The Medical Policing and Anti Semitism: German Policy of Closing the Borders to East European Jews in WWI. *Jahrbucher fur Geschichte Osteuropas* (West Germany), no. 2, 33:205–230.

Musto, D. F. 1986. Quarantine and the Problem of AIDS. *Milbank Q.* Suppl. 1, 64:97–117.

Nicolle, C. 1965. "Investigations on Typhus." *Nobel Lectures: Physiology or Medicine 1922–1941*. Amsterdam: Elsevier Publishing Co., p. 94.

Nicolle, C., C. Comte, and E. Conseil. 1968. "Experimental Transmission of Exanthemic Typhus Through Body Lice." In N. Hahon, *Selected Papers on the Pathogenic Rickettsia*. Cambridge, MA: Harvard University Press, pp. 37–40.

Panavas, S., Director of Infectious Disease Hospital, Kaunas, Lithuania. Personal communication. July 1996.

Patterson, K. D. 1993. "Typhus and Its Control in Russia, 1870–1940." *Medical History* 37:361–381.

Porter, R. 1997. *The Greatest Benefit to Mankind: A Medical History of Humanity from Antiquity to the Present*. London: HarperCollins, p. 29.

Preuss in Medizin Im Talmud, cited in Zinsser. 1934. *Rats, Lice and History*. Boston: Little, Brown, p. 110.

Reinhard, K. J., and J. Buikstra. 2003. Louse Infestation of the Chiribaya Culture, Southern Peru: Variation in Prevalence by Age and Sex. Mem. Inst. Oswaldo Cruz, Rio de Janeiro Suppl. I, 98:173–179.

Risse, G. B. 1985. *Bulletin of the History of Medicine* 59:176–195.

Robinson, D., N. Leo, P. Prociv, and S.C. Barker. 2003. Potential Role of Head Lice, *Pediculis humanus capitis*, as Vectors of Rickettsia Prowazekii, Parasitol. Res. no. 3, 90:209–211.

Rockefeller Foundation 1.1/785/2/15. 1921. Letter from George Vincent to John D. Rockefeller Jr. (August 9).

Roland, C. 1992. *Courage under Siege: Starvation, Disease and Death in the Warsaw Ghetto*. New York: Oxford University Press, pp. 130–131.

Rose, G. 1943. *Abhandlungen, Fortschritte in der Bekampfung der Kleiderlaus, Reichs-Gesundheitsblatt*. no. 5, 18:53–57 (February 3).

Rosenberg, C. 1992. "What Is an Epidemic? AIDS in Historical Perspective." In C. Rosenberg, *Explaining Epidemics and Other Studies in the History of Medicine*. New York: Cambridge University Press, pp. 286–287.

Service, M. W. 1996. *Medical Entomology for Students*. New York: Chapman & Hall,

Shalamov, V. 1994. "The Bathhouse." *Kolyma Tales*. London: Penguin Books, p. 336.

Singer, B. 1979. *Fruitless Hopes*. Trans. by Y. L. Joseff. Tel Aviv: Peretz Publishers, p. 309.

Taylor, R., and A. Rieger. 1985. Medicine as a Social Science: Rudolf Virchow on Typhus Epidemic in Silesia. *Intl. Journ. of Health Services* no. 4, 15:547–59.

Warkentin V. 2003. "New Blow to Much-Delayed German Holocaust Memorial." Reuters (November 6).

Watson, D. 2004. Cliff Palace—The Story of an Ancient City, I libri di na Tonga. http://www.natale.to/libri/cliff-palace.htm (accessed April 23).

Weindling, P. 2000. *Epidemics and Genocide in Eastern Europe 1890–1945*. Oxford: Oxford University Press.

Winick, M. 1979. *Hunger Disease: Studies by Jewish Physicians in the Warsaw Ghetto*. New York: John Wiley & Sons.

Wolbach, S. B., J. L. Todd, and F. W. Palfrey. 1922. "The Etiology and Pathology of Typhus." *The Main Report of the Typhus Commission of the League of Red Cross Societies of Poland*. Cambridge, MA: Harvard University Press.

Wolfe, R. 1990. *Holocaust. The Documentary Evidence*. Washington, DC: National Archives and Records Administration.

Zinsser, H. 1934. *Rats, Lice and History*. Boston: Little, Brown.

CHAPTER 2

Decline of German Medicine:
From Euthanasia to Murder

Cancer day room in Sachsenhausen concentration camp, drawn by unknown artist.
Sachsenhausen Memorial and Museum/Brandenberg Memorials Foundation.

When you take an idea or a concept and turn it into an abstraction, that opens the way to take human beings and turn them, also, into abstractions. When human beings become abstractions, what is left?

Elie Wiesel

Generally, it must be recognized that typhus was one of the most powerful extermination weapons used by the Germans in concentration camps.

Desire Haffner

CRIMES OF CALCULATED CRUELTY

Figure 2.1: Graffiti on a wall in a Berlin train station is symbolic of the evil perpetuated by the Nazi medical machine. *N. Baumslag.*

The German prewar medical association was a democratic forum with progressive concerns regarding hygiene and public health. Questions of medical ethics were handled through the German Medical Association and Reich Chamber of Physicians. During the Third Reich, German doctors ignored the traditional code of ethics—the Hippocratic Oath.[1] They ignored the Berlin Code of 1900[2] and they violated the 1931 Reichsrichtlinien directives on human experimentation and drug therapy, which explicitly requires voluntary consent, making volunteers aware of hazards, and prohibits nontherapeutic research on minors and incompetents (Michalczyk 1994, p. 177).[3]

The medical machine of destruction evolved with the full and active participation of German doctors, nurses, and scientists. They cast aside the Hippocratic Oath, the traditional medical code of ethics, and replaced it with the Nuremberg Laws.[4] Physicians in particular were responsible for cruel crimes rationalized as science. The infamous "special treatment" of the Jews was organized by public health officials, physicians, nurses, administrators, and lawyers. Physicians devised and promoted the claim that the very presence of Jews endangered German families and troops. Propaganda distributed through scientific journals and the general media fueled the denigration of Jews, who were transformed into hated, infected, polluted objects that had to be eradicated (Glass 1997).

German authorities forced Jews into ghettos where poor conditions made the outbreak of epidemics inevitable (Trunk 1972). The technologies of typhus eradication used first within the ghettos and later in the camps were murderous by design and thinly camouflaged genocidal intentions (Hirszfeld 1946). Furthermore, the Nazis used typhus as a powerful means of extermination in the camps (Haffner 1946).

No one suspected or imagined that Germany, a cultured country with a highly respected medical profession renowned for its scholarship, would provide ideas and techniques for the systematic, barbarous, unparalleled mass slaughter of human beings. These infamies occurred with the active participation of Germany's medical profession. Prior to the establishment of Auschwitz and other death camps, the Nazis had developed a policy of killing within medical channels, decided by medical means and carried out by doctors and their assistants. They called this killing "euthanasia"; Jay Lifton rightly calls it "camouflaged murder" (1986, p. 82).

KILLING THE UNDESIRABLES

The concept of race hygiene provides a necessary context for the role of German science and medicine in Nazi crimes against humanity. The race hygiene movement in Germany evolved from the theory of Social Darwinism, which had become popular throughout Europe, North America, and elsewhere by the second half of the nineteenth century. Social Darwinism holds that the weaker elements of society would naturally be selected out and that

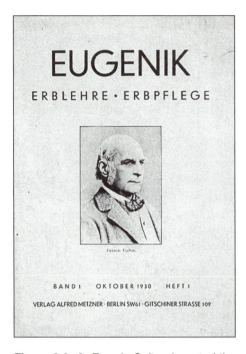

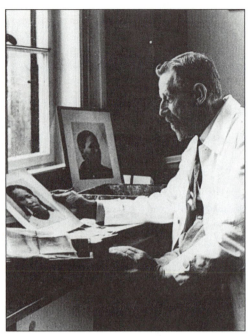

Figure 2.2: A. Francis Galton invented the term "eugenics" (good birth). He wrote the first book on the subject and would have been appalled by the extremes to which eugenics was carried out in Germany where the goal of racial purity was pushed to its horrific limit in the "Final Solution." *USHMM.*

B. Eugen Fischer, director of the Kaiser Wilhelm Institute, achieved prominence with his 1913 racist study of mixed Dutch and Hottentot children in colonial southwest Africa. *Archiv zur Geschichte der Max-Planck-Gesellschaft, Berlin-Dahlem.*

this "survival of the fittest" would ultimately lead to the improvement of the species as a whole.

Charles Darwin's cousin, Sir Francis Galton, in 1883 introduced the term *eugenics* (good birth), a science of racial improvement through controlled breeding (Nicosia and Heuner 2002) (Figure 2.2). The concept expanded on Social Darwinism to include a more proactive approach to improving the species, manipulating the natural selection process to purify a nation's bloodlines. To do so, eliminating undesirables was portrayed as healing the nation. The United States was at the forefront of the eugenics movement, and the national program included forced sterilizations, segregation laws, and marital restrictions. The Carnegie Institute established a laboratory at Cold Spring Harbor, New York, where scientists plotted the systematic removal of non-

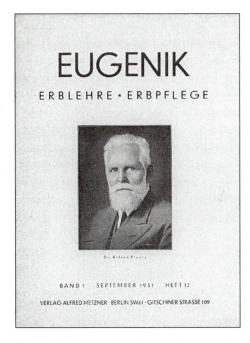

EUGENIK

ERBLEHRE · ERBPFLEGE

Dr. Alfred Ploetz

BAND 1   SEPTEMBER 1931   HEFT 12

VERLAG ALFRED METZNER · BERLIN SW61 · GITSCHINER STRASSE 109

C. Alfred Ploetz, physician and economist, founded the German racial hygiene movement. *USHMM.*

Nordic people. The American model was then transplanted to Germany where it caught Hitler's attention (Black 2003, p. 259).

The Nazi pseudoscience of "race hygiene" was well ingrained in German culture by World War II (Figure 2.3). The renowned Erwin Baur, psychiatrist and plant geneticist, Ernst Rudin, professor of psychiatry, and Dr. Eugen Fischer, professor of anthropology and Germany's most senior Nazi geneticist and rector of Berlin University, concocted an anti-Semitic "racial science."

Fischer had developed and tested his race theories in German South West Africa (now Namibia). He used concentration camp survivors of the 1904 Herero rebellion as guinea pigs for his medical experiments, from which he inferred that the genetic racial mixing of Germans and Hereros was fraught with danger. Fischer later supervised the Kaiser Wilhelm Institute for Anthropology, Eugenics, and Human Genetics in Berlin, funded by the Rockefeller Foundation (Michalczyk 1997).[5] Fischer openly advocated the extermination of Jews, mental patients, and criminals as early as 1941, a year before the Wannsee Conference and the adoption of the "Final Solution."

The race hygiene movement effectively medicalized anti-Semitism to lend legitimacy to the genocide. The term *race hygiene* (*Rassenhygiene*) was introduced by Alfred Ploetz, Ernest Haeckel advocated killing "weaklings," while the physician Fritz Lenz developed the theory of racial inequality (Proctor 1992, p. 18 in Annas and Grodin 1992). Lenz, Fischer, and Baur together wrote *The Principles of Human Heredity and Race Hygiene* (*Menschliche Erblichkeitslehre and Rassenhygiene*), part of which Hitler received in 1924 from the publisher while in prison (Watson 2003). The book strongly reinforced Hitler's notions of Germany's master Aryan race. Hitler incorporated their ideas and those of the American eugenics program in *Mein Kampf,*

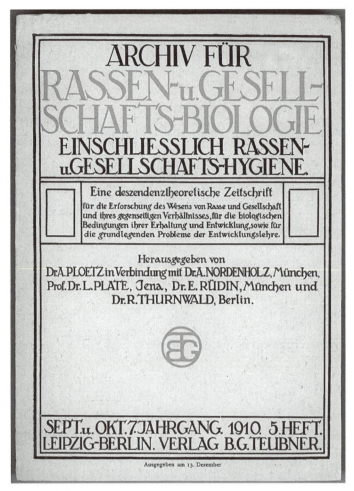

Figure 2.3: "Race hygiene" pervaded all training, activity, and research during the Third Reich. The term was introduced by Alfred Ploetz, founder of German eugenics, in *Archiv fur Rassen-und Gesellschafts,* 1910. *USHMM.*

which became the blueprint for Nazi race policies. (Throughout his book, Hitler refers to the Jewish race as one of parasites, a disease, presumably to serve as a scapegoat for Germany's defeat in World War I and for subsequent economic problems (Proctor 1992, p. 18 in Annas and Grodin 1992; Watson 2003).

When Hitler became chancellor of the Third Reich in 1933, Jewish physicians, professors, and philosophers were dismissed from their positions and

Figure 2.4: Heroic members of the White Rose, a student passive resistance organization, included Hans Scholl, Sophie Scholl, and Christopher Probst (left to right in photo, summer 1942) that called for "freedom and honor" and an end to Nazi atrocities. They were tried by the Peoples Court and executed for high treason. Other heroic members of the White Rose, Alexander Schmorell, Willi Graf, and Professor Kurt Huber, were also tried for high treason and executed. The message of the White Rose was "We are not silent. We are your bad conscience." *Dr. George Jurgen Wittenstein (White Rose survivor).*

posts. Within weeks of the Nationalist Socialist takeover, many Jewish faculty members were discharged. In 1938 medical licenses were revoked. The famed medical school of Vienna lost 80 percent of its faculty (Ernst 1995). Their replacements were known not for their clinical expertise but for their political trustworthiness. Jewish medical students were dismissed, and all remaining students were required to take courses in race hygiene. To obtain a civil or military post, a physician had to endorse race hygiene as the basis for direct medical killing, justified by the concept of "life unworthy of life" (*Lebens unwertes Leben*).

Nazi policy and programs were wholeheartedly accepted, and health care was reorganized and reoriented along Nazi lines. The German medical profession trained doctors and nurses to place the health of the nation above individual medical care. The provision of medical care and food for the impaired, aged, and sick was considered an economic drain on the nation,

Figure 2.5: Dr. Georg Groscurth, assistant professor of medicine at Charite Hospital, Berlin, followed his conscience. He was opposed to the Nazi regime and involved with the resistance. He was arrested and executed in the Brandenburg penitentiary in May 1944. *Medical History Museum, Charite Photo Archives, Berlin.*

and the doctors prescribed "mercy killing" for treatment. Because the Jewish question was presented as a medical problem, "treatment centers" were later established in places like Dachau and Auschwitz.

Although some individuals refused to participate in the killings and sterilizations, there was almost no organized group resistance. Opposition to the regime was suppressed by fear of brutal punishment, and the medical profession remained silent throughout. The few isolated attempts at resistance were dealt with quickly and drastically. One of the most tragic attempts involved the White Rose, a small organization of medical students at the University of Munich with adherents in several other cities (Figure 2.4). In 1942 and 1943, members of the White Rose denounced the regime and spread leaflets calling for "freedom and honor," stating "For Hitler and his followers there will be no punishment on earth that will expatiate their crimes." Hans Scholl, a twenty-four-year-old medical student, his twenty-one-year-old sister Sophia Scholl, and Christoph Probst were condemned to death by a Nazi people's court and beheaded publicly in February 1943 (Kater 1989, p. 168; Scholl 1983). White Rose members Alex Schmorell, Professor Kurt Huber, and Willi Graf were executed by guillotine later that year. Today, monuments to the young activists stand as memorials in Munich and in Ulm. The European Union, another anti-Nazi resistance organization founded by Dr. Groscurth (Figure 2.5), a lecturer in internal medicine at the University of Berlin, secretly aided Jews, helped soldiers fake illness to avoid being sent to the front, and was involved in sabotage. He was arrested by the Gestapo in 1943 and was executed (Kater 1989, p. 145).

FROM FORCED STERILIZATION TO MURDER

Purification of the German nation's health started with forced sterilization. In July 1933, the Nazis passed the Law for the Prevention of Offspring with Hereditary Disease. The law required the identification of all "handicapped persons" and established 200 special genetic health courts that gave doctors power to order involuntary sterilization. Each court consisted of three expert members, two of whom were doctors. As a result of this law, over 400,000 individuals including many children were sterilized. Physicians became the judges and guardians of the law, and there was no one to cross check their actions. Doctors received payment for the "expert reports" that were required for justification of involuntary sterilization. After World War II, the expert reports were analyzed, and it was found that nearly all the persons who had come before the genetic health courts had been sterilized without adequate justification (Rothmaler 1989).

Germany was not the first and only country to impose involuntary sterilization of impaired children. The United States also had a eugenics program. By 1935 over 21,000 "genetic" sterilizations had been performed in the United States, and by 1960 the number had tripled to 64,000. The program continued until 1973. Sweden started a similar program in the 1930s, which was only discontinued in 1976. The program in Sweden carried out almost the same number of sterilizations as the U.S. program in the same period, despite a significantly smaller population. Eugenics proponents in the United States were in constant contact with the Germans and admired the large number of sterilizations the Nazis performed. The German program differed, however, in that it was a national program, whereas in the United States the regulations in different states varied and were not always enforced. The Third Reich eugenics program was more extensive and systematic than any other nation's sterilization program, and nowhere except Germany did murder ultimately replace sterilization.

German psychiatrists and anthropologists based the justification of the progression from sterilization to involuntary "euthanasia" on notions of economic necessity and racial purity. Eliminating "lives unworthy of living" it was stated, would cut the financial burden of caring for the mentally and physically impaired and would enable the state to channel funds to other sectors of German society. Disabled children were the first to be killed; adults in mental hospitals and the hospitalized aged followed (Michalczyk 1997). The final extension of the rationale and technology was the gassing of the ill, aged, disabled, and otherwise unwanted in Auschwitz and other concentration camps as part of the Final Solution.

The euthanasia program in Germany was started by SS Gruppenführer Philip Bouhler under Hitler's orders after the occupation of Poland in 1939. At a secret meeting in Dr. Karl Brandt's office in June 1939, SS Colonel Dr. Viktor Brack, one of Hitler's private functionaries, presented the program to medical professionals. The program was run by approximately 50 volunteer physicians and was called Aktion T4 as it was headquartered in Berlin's Tiergarten Strasse 4. Only Dr. Gottfried Ewald, professor of psychiatry at the University of Goettingen, openly objected to the killing. Participants were sworn to secrecy, for there was fear of public reaction. Initially, in 1939 the Nazi euthanasia program operated in such strict secrecy that the doctors involved went to great lengths to falsify the death certificates of their victims. The doctors informed relatives that the victims died of natural causes such as pneumonia or appendicitis. In one case, a letter falsely informed a family that an aged relative had died of appendicitis, when in fact an appendectomy had been performed years before. Doctors proceeded to carry out thousands of murders at euthanasia facilities like Hadamar, Sonnenstein, and Bernburg (Michalczyk 1997).[6] Once identified, victims were secretly transported by the busload—often in the middle of the night—to these special centers, cursorily examined, and gassed with carbon monoxide in batches of twenty, thirty, or more, their gold teeth extracted, samples of their brains taken for research, and their bodies cremated.

By the end of 1941, more than 70,000 psychiatric patients in Germany had been murdered. Despite the secrecy, people living in areas where the killing centers were located became aware of the murders. When this special treatment in the "curative institutions" was discovered there was a public outcry, including protests from the Catholic and Protestant churches (Figure 2.6). Because of the protests, Hitler ordered the program stopped in August 1941, but this was fictitious. As the killing of individual patients in various psychiatric institutions continued, the order must have intended to end the protests, not the program. Instead of mass gassing, patients were then murdered by intracardiac phenol injections, starvation, neglect and/or an overdose of sedatives such as Luminal or sleeping pills such as Veronal, which were commonly used medicines. The effect in psychiatric institutions of this "wild euthanasia" was the same, only slower.

Creating a generation of pure Aryans now took precedence over fundamental ethics in medicine. Physicians and psychiatrists, mostly professors, hospital directors, and bureaucrats, served as medical experts, selecting victims unseen and directing the killings. The T4 program turned out to be a pilot project for the elimination of millions of concentration camp prisoners. In Bernberg euthanasia center, there were fake showers in the gas chamber

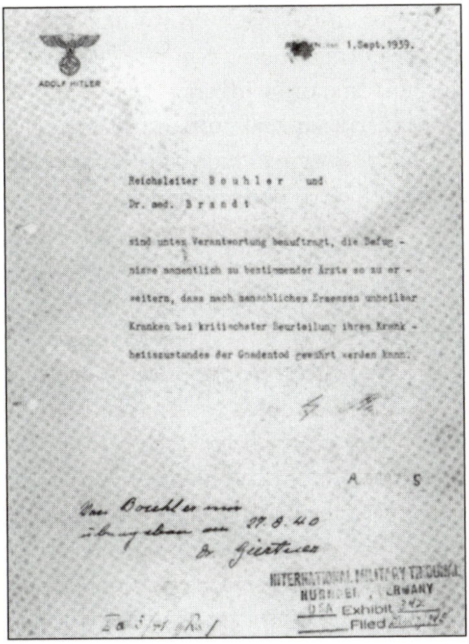

ADOLF HITLER

1.Sept.1939.

Reichsleiter Bouhler und

Dr. med. Brandt

sind unter Verantwortung beauftragt, die Befugnisse namentlich zu bestimmender Ärzte so zu erweitern, dass nach menschlichem Ermessen unheilbar Kranken bei kritischster Beurteilung ihres Krankheitszustandes der Gnadentod gewährt werden kann.

INTERNATIONAL MILITARY TRIBUNAL
NURNBERG, GERMANY
USA Exhibit 342
Filed

Figure 2.6: A. When German families complained about the killing of their "feeble-minded" relatives, the Minister of Justice requested a copy of Hitler's September 1, 1939 executive order authorizing certain doctors to kill individuals deemed unworthy of life. On August 27, 1940 he received a copy of the order signed by Adolf Hitler. *Source: Executive order signed by Adolf Hitler, September 1, 1939, Photostat, 1940. RG 238. Nuremberg Document 630 PS. Exhibit USA 342. NARA.*

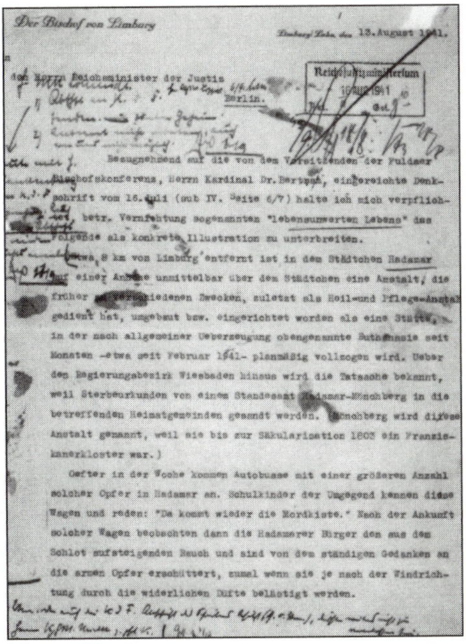

Der Bischof von Limburg

Limburg/Lahn, den 13. August 1941.

An den Herrn Reichsminister der Justiz
Berlin.

Reichsjustizministerium

Bezugnehmend auf die von dem Vorsitzenden der Fuldaer Bischofskonferenz, Herrn Kardinal Dr. Bertram, eingereichte Denkschrift vom 16. Juli (sub IV. Seite 6/7) halte ich mich verpflichtet, betr. Vernichtung sogenannten "lebensunwerten Lebens" das Folgende als konkrete Illustration zu unterbreiten.

Etwa 8 km von Limburg entfernt ist in dem Städtchen Hadamar auf einer Anhöhe unmittelbar über dem Städtchen eine Anstalt, die früher zu verschiedenen Zwecken, zuletzt als Heil- und Pflege-Anstalt gedient hat, umgebaut bzw. eingerichtet worden als eine Stätte, in der nach allgemeiner Ueberzeugung obengenannte Euthanasie seit Monaten - etwa seit Februar 1941 - planmäßig vollzogen wird. Ueber den Regierungsbezirk Wiesbaden hinaus wird die Tatsache bekannt, weil Sterbeurkunden von einem Standesamt Hadamar-Mönchberg in die betreffenden Heimatgemeinden gesandt werden. (Mönchberg wird diese Anstalt genannt, weil sie bis zur Säkularisation 1803 ein Franziskanerkloster war.)

Oefter in der Woche kommen Autobusse mit einer größeren Anzahl solcher Opfer in Hadamar an. Schulkinder der Umgegend kennen diese Wagen und reden: "Da kommt wieder die Mordkiste." Nach der Ankunft solcher Wagen beobachten dann die Hadamarer Bürger den aus dem Schlot aufsteigenden Rauch und sind von dem ständigen Gedanken an die armen Opfer erschüttert, zumal wenn sie je nach der Windrichtung durch die widerlichen Düfte belästigt werden.

B. Letter from Bishop Hilfrich of Limburg to the Minister of Justice protesting the killing of inmates, deemed "valueless lives," at Hadamar asylum. He complained that even the children in the area knew the origin of the stench from the smoky chimneys and that implausible death certificates had been received by many families. Hitler ordered a stop to the program, but it continued and the technology developed was transferred to the death camps. *Source: Letter from Dr. Anton Hilfrich, Bishop of Limburg to Franz Guertner, August 31, 1941. RG 238. Nuremberg Document 615 PS. Exhibit USA 717. NARA.*

and a peephole window, as well as a good pathology laboratory. Physicians and nurses who worked in the T4 program developed techniques and centers for mass execution and performed outrageous and cruel experiments under the pretense of scientific research. Those working in the euthanasia centers received extra pay. They were reemployed in the killing centers in the concentration camps.

ANTI-SEMITISM AND NAZI PUBLIC
HEALTH: PROPAGANDA

The hatred and suspicion of Jews in Nazi Germany was neither new nor
unique, even in academic circles. The image of the Jew as a carrier of pestilence
also appeared in anti-Semitic diatribes in France and many other European
countries. Heinrich von Treitschke, influential professor of history at the University of Berlin, was a vocal advocate of anti-Semitism. He rejected democracy,
socialism, and feminism, all of which he attributed to the Jews, and equated
Jews with vermin. In 1879 he coined the phrase "the Jews are our misfortune"
(*Die Juden sind unser Unglück*) (Weyers 1998). This saying persisted through
generations of Germans and eventually became a favored slogan of the Nazis
(Figure 2.7). Paul de Lagarde (1827–1891) was an influential and popular German anti-Semite in the nineteenth century. His father's name was Böttischer,
but in 1851 he took his mother's family name. He promoted the extermination
of the Jews, whom he referred to as "vermin." Lagarde also believed that the
death of the Slavs would benefit everyone, and his ideas were in many ways in-
distinguishable from that of Nazi ideologists (Bein 1964).

Third Reich propagandists promised to eradicate the Jewish assault on the
nation's health once and for all (Figure 2.8). The German nation was presented as a living body that needed to be "healed." Together the government

Figure 2.7: "The Jews are our misfortune" painted on a WWI plane reflects ingrained, prevalent anti-Semitism. *Stadtarchiv Nuremberg.*

Figure 2.8: "Stop the thief; the role of Jews in medicine," an anti-Semitic article appearing in a German public health journal. *Source:* Deutsche Volksgesundheit *(November 1933) p. 1.*

and the medical profession would cure the chronically ill German nation (Michalczyk 1997). Nazi doctors portrayed Jews as *carriers of sickness* and associated them with lice and typhus (Hilberg, Staron Kermisz 1979, p. 18) (Figure 2.9). The portrayal was widespread and popular among high-ranking Nazi officials. Hitler equated Jews with diseased nonhumans. He said "I feel like Robert Koch in politics. He discovered the bacillus and led medical science into new paths. I discovered the Jew as the bacillus and ferment in social decomposition" (Hillgruber 1989). Goebbels wrote in his November 1941 diary, "The Jews are like lice of civilized mankind somehow they must be

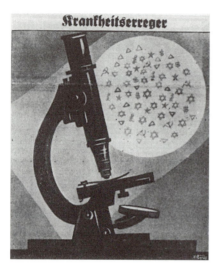

A. Looking down the microscope at infectious germs. Cartoon from the notorious Julius Streicher's anti-Semitic newspaper. Der Stürmer *(April 15, 1943)*.

B. German poster in Ukrainian reads "Beware of typhus do not come near Jews." *Museum Okregowe, Poland.*

C. German propaganda poster "The Path of Horror," depicts how a Jewish beggar woman infected forty-two people with typhus. Das Vorfeld *(1943) 3.*

Figure 2.9: Propaganda posters showing Jews as spreaders of lice and typhus.

exterminated or they will resume their tormenting and molesting role" (Hill-gruber 1989, p. 107). Heinrich Himmler, chief of the SS, also used the medical model in April 1943 when he asserted that anti-Semitism was not an ideological issue but a matter of hygiene: "We are almost deloused, we have only some 22,000 lice left and then it will be ended in Germany" (Glass 1997, p. 83; Hillgruber 1989, p. 111).

Ironically, at the same time that Jews were being dehumanized, an animal protection law was passed in 1933. The law prohibited painful or injurious operations or experiments on animals and required written authorization by the department head for special research. Dogs were not to be used to improve physicians' surgical skills. "Had this law been followed for humans this indictment [the Nuremberg judgment] would never have been filed. It is perhaps the deepest shame of the defendants that it probably never occurred to them that human beings should have been treated with at least equal humanity" (Taylor 1946).

NAZI MEDICINE: THE DOCTOR'S ROLE

> The Führer holds the cleansing of the medical profession far more important than for example the bureaucracy since in his opinion the duty of the physician is or should be one of racial leadership.
>
> Martin Bormann

According to Richard Toellner, a medical historian at the University of Muenster, "the whole range of representatives of the medical profession was involved and they all knew what they were doing. A medical profession that accepted mass murder of sick people as normal, and to a large degree explicitly approved of it as a justified act for the sake of the community, had failed and betrayed its mission" (Toellner, in Annas and Grodin 1992, p. 45).

Hitler's doctors were chosen primarily for their commitment to race hygiene, and they were also given military titles. The Nazi regime transformed German medicine by replacing the traditional doctor with the "genetic doctor" (Proctor 1992, p. 42). The doctor's role was expanded into that of medical-führer, brainchild of Kurt Blome, deputy to the Commissioner of Health, Dr. Leonardo Conti. From the second half of the nineteenth century and after German unification in 1870, the individual's health needs became subordinate to the collective health status of the state. In this way the medical profession distanced itself from its barbaric acts. This was an unprecedented change for nursing and medical care that dominated Third Reich medicine (Weindling 2000).

German physicians joined the Nazi Party in large numbers, and their medical associations actively supported Nazi policies. Of the 50 percent of doctors who joined the party, 26 percent became Storm Troopers and 6 percent joined the SS. By 1929, a number of German physicians organized the National Socialist Physicians League and rid the German medical community of "Jewish bolshevism." Nearly 300 doctors, 6 percent of the German medical profession, joined the League by 1933, and more than 38,000 doctors (45 percent of German physicians) were members of the Nazi Party by 1942—a higher percentage than for any other profession (Ernst, 1996; Lifton 1983). In Austria by 1941 60 percent of medical professionals formed the Nazi Party. The physicians' enthusiastic cooperation with the Nazis could in part be explained from an economic perspective. By 1932, Germany had suffered a severe economic depression, and 72 percent of German physicians earned less than the minimum amount necessary for survival. The Nazi Party offered a solution to high unemployment and an excess of medical students, and had tremendous appeal to German physicians as it offered power, prestige, pride, and money (Pross, in Annas and Grodin 1992, p. 33).

Third Reich nurses played a major role in public health education and in enforcing Nazi policy. By 1932 over 9 percent of German nurses had joined the nationalist nursing organization and many were later absorbed into broader Nazi nursing organizations (Hahn 1994). The Nationalist Socialist nursing organization originated from the Red Swastika nurses, and in 1934 the Red Cross nurses became part of the Nazi machine; the emblems and actions of the swastika and Red Cross became intertwined. At least forty-five nurses were involved in the killing of 5000 German children and 70,000 handicapped adults in the euthanasia program. Adoption of the Nazi ideology demanded radical changes in nursing practice. There was a political shift from government service to party-controlled duty. In 1938 nursing schools were established where entrants had to prove that they were Aryans and were politically reliable. Physicians provided training to nurses in hereditary and racial studies, eugenics, and population policy. Nurses were required to belong to the Reich's Union of German Nurses and Nursing Assistants and pledge loyalty to the state. The brutal actions of German nurses have only recently been scrutinized.

Public health became an instrument of Nazi ideology. After the Nazi takeover of the German government, the National Department of Public Health was dissolved and replaced by an "expert council" on public health. Over half of public health, social welfare, and aid programs were eliminated. By 1941 Nazi doctors, nurses, and public health officials were receptive to the Final Solution as a way out of the self-induced public health dilemma (Browning 1992, p. 145).

GERMANS FIRST AND FOREMOST: POLICIES IN THE OCCUPIED TERRITORIES

In the occupied territories, German doctors supervised local doctors because there were not enough German doctors to staff their programs. The local doctors were considered "lesser" doctors who had childish fascinations with medical instruments and gadgets they didn't know how to use. In accordance with Nazi ideology, German public health officers saw their main task as that of protecting Germans from typhus and other infectious diseases and preventing these diseases from spreading to Germany. They believed it was not Germany's task to provide the Poles with health care.

German doctors knew that typhus was endemic in Eastern Europe and was fueled by overcrowding, hunger, and filth. They were also aware of effective methods for preventing the spread of typhus, and public health officers had rules and regulations to control the spread of typhus. Examples abound. In July 1941 a "Health Palace" was established for the region centered in Riga, Latvia. The German health commissariat issued a number of health decrees "for the strict and purposive fight with epidemic diseases requiring obligatory treatment in hospital and prophylactic vaccination against typhus, diphtheria, dysentery" (Panavas 1996). Another decree for overcoming spotted fever forbade meetings in theaters and other gathering places. A law "to avoid bringing spotted fever to Germany" required forced laborers from Poland to have a doctor's certificate stating they were lice free.

TYPHUS AND GHETTOIZATION

While the Germans took public health measures to stop the spread of epidemics to Germany and Germans at the front and in the occupied territories, they isolated Jews in overcrowded ghettos and restricted their movement. It was the Nazi doctors who initiated pressure on high-ranking Nazi officials to proceed swiftly to ghettoization, a pattern that was followed by the rest of the Generalgovernement. The doctors were not acting in a strictly medical capacity, for it does not make medical sense to create conditions counterproductive to public health. These doctors were driven by typhus phobia and racial genocide. Ghettoization was "part and parcel of the Nazis' diabolical plan to hasten the physical destruction of the Jews" (Trunk 1972). Josef Goebbels, the propaganda leader of the Nazis, referred to the ghettos as "death boxes."

Ghettos had been around a long time. As early as 1280 in Morocco Jews were segregated in areas called *millahs*. The modern word "ghetto" originated in 1516 in Venice from the closed Jewish quarter called the *Geto Nuovo* (new foundry). Renowned medieval ghettos existed in Frankfurt am Main and Prague's Judenstadt. By the early nineteenth century ghettos were abolished in most of Europe. Only in Yemen did they prevail until 1948, and they finally ended due to large-scale immigration to Israel. The Nazi regime revived the notion of ghettos as preliminaries to extermination. There is no record of a general order having been issued for their establishment, although it appears that they were the result of local initiatives. The first of these ghettos was established in Poland in Piotrckow Trybunalski in the Lodz district of occupied Poland in October 1939 (Y. Gutman 2004).

Figure 2.10: Ominous signs were posted outside the ghettos warning that entry was forbidden because of epidemic typhus.   **A.** This quarantine sign was outside the entrance to the Warsaw Ghetto. *USHMM.*

In November 1939, Jews in Warsaw were ordered to relocate to a ghetto area, allegedly to avoid a typhus epidemic that coming winter. The Jewish quarter was declared a quarantine area (*Seuchensperrgebiet*), and movement in and out of the ghetto was restricted and placed off limits to German military personnel (Warsaw diary of Cherniakov ed. by Hilberg, Staron, and Kermisz 1979, p. 18) (Figure 2.10). The *Judenrat*, the Jewish council established by the Nazis, was ordered to post signs on the ghetto borders stating "Danger: Epidemics—Entry Forbidden" (*Achtung Seuchengefahr Entritt Verboten*) (Cherniakow edition by Hilberg, Staron, and Kermisz 1979, p. 90). Dr. Walbaum and Dr. Kaminski of the Warsaw district then announced that a wall was necessary because the Jews had not complied with the public health regulations. In April 1940 the Jewish Council in Warsaw was ordered to build at its own expense a quarantine wall (*Seuchenmauer*) 10 feet high and 11 miles long around the designated area. This quarantine wall cost the interned impoverished Jews $260,000 (approximately $3 million today), and the German contractor profited enormously (Hilberg, Staron, and Kermicz 1979, p. 404).[7]

A conflict developed between the SS and the health officials regarding what to do about Jews in Warsaw, but ultimately it was the racial hatred of the doctors that drove the sealing of the ghetto. At a conference on typhus control in 1940, Dr. Jost Walbaum, chief health official of the Generalgovernement, claimed that Jews posed a serious public health risk: "The Jews are

B. This sign was outside the entrance to the Lodz Ghetto forbidding entry into the Jewish area. *USHMM.*

overwhelmingly the carriers and disseminators of infection. Spotted fever endures most persistently in the regions heavily populated by Jews with their low cultural level, their uncleanliness and infestation of lice unavoidably connected with this." As if this was not enough, he went on to state: "we sentence the Jews in the ghetto to death by hunger or we shoot them even if in the end the result is the same, the latter is more intimidating, we have one and only one responsibility, that the German people are not infected and endangered by these parasites, for that any means must be right" (Walbaum 1941, p. 34).

The majority of the doctors attending the conference applauded enthusiastically. Conference participants unanimously advocated restricting the movement of Jews as a measure for typhus epidemic control. The plan was reiterated at a subsequent public health conference on epidemic disease, with special emphasis on typhus, in October 1941 at Bad Krynica on the Baltic coast. Although the doctors knew that the cause of typhus was lice, only Dr. Robert Kudicke of the Warsaw Hygiene Institute urged that "one could not successfully combat the spread of an epidemic without removing its cause." His recommendation was ignored (Browning 1992, p. 157).

SS Obersturmführer Dr. Lambrecht took over from Kaminski as chief of public health in Warsaw in August 1940. He fueled Dr. Walbaum's push for ghettoization of the Jews when he reported sixty-eight cases of typhus in the Warsaw area and warned that an epidemic was imminent if nothing was done. This was a manipulation of statistics and no cause for alarm, for there had been more cases of typhus in Warsaw in 1936, when there was no epidemic (Roland 1992). Lambrecht was new in Warsaw and had no expertise in infectious disease. In a September meeting with Governor Frank, Walbaum seized on these statistics to press his case for immediate ghettoization of Jews on the pretext of avoiding an epidemic. Using Lambrecht's statistics, Walbaum convinced Governor Frank in Cracow that typhus had spread from the Jewish quarter and that it was of the utmost importance that Jews be brought into the ghetto to prevent an epidemic of typhus, especially in Warsaw. Frank approved the order, and the Warsaw Ghetto was formally established in October 1940. The German physician in charge of public health eventually closed Warsaw Ghetto schools (Trunk 1972). The official rationale for closing the schools was also medical rather than political: that Jews are especially susceptible to typhus. The Warsaw Ghetto was sealed on November 15, 1940, Yom Kippur, the holiest of Jewish holy days.

There was nothing Jewish about typhus of course. The claim that Jews carried typhus more than any other group, as previously stated, is totally unsubstantiated. Nor is there any scientific proof of the allegation that Jews are more likely to spread the disease to others while remaining immune themselves. Nazi physicians were not scientifically ignorant; they simply made science subservient to ideology (Roland 1992, p. 123). Their allegations served to vilify Jews and justify discrimination and persecution. Nazi propaganda portrayed Jews in the Warsaw Ghetto to the world as dirty, rat-infested, rejected, starving parasites. Anti-Semitic propaganda posters and slogans linked Jews to lice and typhus (Figure 2.11). The medieval invention, the sealed ghetto, was revived as a modern medical response.

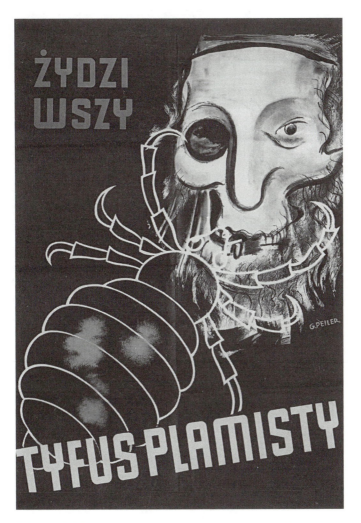

Figure 2.11: "Jews bring lice and spread typhus," 1941 German propaganda poster (in Polish). *Museum Okregowe, Poland.*

BREEDING GROUND FOR DISEASE: CAUSE AND EFFECT IN THE GHETTO

> . . . extermination of the Jews to prevent food speculation and the spread of typhus. Killing (is) a matter of sanitation.
>
> Governor Hans Frank's diary, May 3, 1942, Lublin

In the Warsaw Ghetto, over 500,000 Jews were crowded into approximately 100 acres of uninhabitable dwellings with an inadequate sewage system and a lack of water, heat, and food. As noted earlier Nazi doctors and officials well knew that these conditions were a breeding ground for disease. In his diary Governor Frank recorded that Dr. Hummel, chief of the Warsaw health district, told him:

> The danger of typhus has increased because the resistance of the population, particularly the youngsters has decreased. The ghetto inmates get insufficient food. In addition there is not enough soap and people live in overcrowded quarters. . . . The fact that the Jews have been enclosed in the ghettos is a blessing, but the ghettos have to be totally isolated (Frank's diary, September 9, 1941 in Trunk, p. 144).

Waldemar Schon, commissar of the Warsaw Ghetto, openly advocated death by starvation and cut off all food to the ghetto. Dr. Lambrecht protested energetically against an artificial famine, which he argued would bring on an epidemic. At the same time, Lambrecht urged tighter sealing of the ghetto, producing the same result. Before the ghetto was sealed, hunger and typhus did not particularly affect the Jewish population (Lenski 1975). Sealing the ghetto, however, led to a serious epidemic of typhus in the late spring of 1941.

When the results became apparent, the German public health officials announced a "fight against disease," which only served to aggravate epidemics (Trunk 1972, p. 82). In fact there were at least three epidemics in the Warsaw Ghetto. Over 100,000 persons suffered from this disease, and about 25,000 died due solely to the dreadful overcrowding and unsanitary conditions. The German prophylactic plan was repressive and it was only at great cost that the Jewish Health Council and Health Department were able to stamp out the 1940–1942 epidemic (Zablotniak 1971).

Not only did the Nazi doctors fail to fight the disease, but they also interfered with the work of the Jewish health and sanitation workers in the ghettos (see Chapter 3). German health authorities would not allow anti-typhus serum to be delivered to the Warsaw and Kutno ghettos even when epidemics were raging. After robbing the Jews of supplies in their pharmacies and hospitals, the Germans and their collaborators would not allow them to buy essential food and medicines. If they suspected typhus or other infectious diseases, they carried out bloody *Aktions* (murdering or burning the patients, doctors, and nurses) in the hospitals. The Jews concealed typhus because the Nazi methods for fighting epidemics were feared as much as the epidemics themselves (Trunk 1975) (see Chapter 3).

In 1941 after Dr Lambrecht left, Dr. Wilhelm Hagen was appointed city of Warsaw medical officer. His responsibility was, first and foremost he believed, to protect the health of the German population and then the Polish population. As a student, Hagen had been involved in revolutionary activities, and in 1933 he was fired from his public health position for political unreliability. His appointment in Warsaw was due to a doctor shortage in the occupied territories. He believed for "unclarified" reasons that spotted fever was endemic among the Jews. In 1973 Professor Hagen wrote *War Hunger and Pestilence* to justify his actions in the Warsaw Ghetto. He stated unequivocally that Jews were carriers of typhus: "this is a phenomenon of medical statistics that has nothing to do with politics," and he cited as evidence selected comparative statistics from outbreaks in Eastern Europe between 1916 and 1921. His prejudice remained despite scientific evidence to the contrary (Hagen 1973, p. 117).

Faced with the accelerating typhus death rate in the Warsaw Ghetto and the increasing danger that spotted fever would spread beyond the ghetto walls, Hagen came to the ghetto. Though not in his official domain, he came to check on the incidence of typhus and to instruct the health department to take a number of hygienic measures. This visit caused problems with the German ghetto administration and the SS who did not want him there. Hagen estimated that 8 to 10 percent of deaths in the ghettos were due to spotted fever, and he blamed the ghetto Jews for noncompliance with his orders to delouse and bathe. He accused the ghetto health authorities of reporting only one quarter of the typhus cases and stated that bribery and passive resistance had undermined enforcement. He ignored the terror his health measures created.

Hagen believed that the Jews were stubborn and in denial. With pistol in hand he threatened a group of Jewish health workers with death for not reporting a case of spotted fever. He later denied he took this action but admitted that he threatened the most severe punishment. In 1941 Hagen submitted a comprehensive report on the epidemic. He urged more food for ghetto residents and recommended that Jewish vagabonds be shot and smugglers flogged. Frank ignored his recommendations and in October 1941 proposed less food for ghetto inhabitants and death for those trying to leave the ghetto. After the war, when Hagen was accused of wartime atrocities, his defense was that he had not created the annihilation policy and that the trajectory was decided by Hitler before he took the job.

In the Kaunas (Kovno, Kauen) Ghetto, Jews were forced to work in the German Red Cross hospital to delouse soldiers returning from the front. These Jewish laborers were made to shave, wash, and delouse homebound German soldiers and their clothing before Lithuanian workers put them back on the train to Germany. Much to the surprise of the German health authorities, many of the Lithuanian hospital workers who had been vaccinated against typhus developed the disease (Tory 1990).[8] There was no doubt that the German medical authorities and their collaborators knew that they were deliberately exposing Jews to a typhus-rich environment. As a result of the typhus outbreak in the Red Cross hospital, many Jewish workers developed typhus and infected other ghetto inhabitants. The Germans looked for the cases, but the Jewish doctors treated them in hiding to avoid their drastic actions.

In the Dvinsk (Daugavpils) Ghetto in Latvia, Jews were interned in wretched unhygienic conditions. By August 1941, 16,000 Jews had been driven into the cavalry barracks with no running water or sanitation: overcrowded and filthy, it was an area unfit for human habitation. In November 1941 the ghetto was put under strict quarantine after a typhus epidemic had broken out. The quarantine was in force for four months, and while it lasted the ghetto was sealed off from its supply sources. As a result, most of the people died from starvation. By the time the quarantine was lifted in the spring of 1942, only 100 Jews had survived. In late October 1943 the Germans removed these surviving Jews to the Kaizerwald concentration camp (Gutman and Berenbaum 1998).

Normally, two weeks of quarantine was acceptable, but German doctors imposed periods of six weeks or more, with serious untoward effects. For people in the ghettos, quarantine meant starvation, theft of vacated apartments, disruption, food spoilage, and ruined clothing. Disinfection bathing known as *parówka*, or steaming, has been described as a mockery of the most elementary principles of prophylaxis. Compulsory delousing measures included standing naked in all kinds of weather; such inhumane measures did not reduce the lice infestation (Trunk 1972, p. 108). Quarantine coupled with the pernicious unsanitary conditions craftily devised by the German authority resulted in the spread of disease.

The Holocaust literature indicates that typhus was rampant in the ghettos and camps, but there are no accurate official records of the total number of typhus cases and deaths.[9] It is known that typhus in the Kutno Ghetto made up at least 42 percent of deaths from 1940 until 1941. The actual number of cases in the ghettos was much higher than available statistics suggest due to underreporting, the common practice of concealing typhus cases, and the fact that during resettlement many of the sick died before they were registered. The German policy was to deliberately kill as many Jews as possible by "natural means" (Davidowicz 1976). On July 11, 1943, Governor General Frank cunningly told a delegation of German physicians that the mass destruction of the Jews was due to "sanitary conditions" (Trunk 1972, p. 149).

TYPHUS EPIDEMICS IN THE CONCENTRATION CAMPS

> A block elder told us what it's like. THIS IS A DEATH CAMP, a Vernichtungslager. "You've been brought here to be destroyed by hunger, beating, hard labor and sickness. You will be eaten by lice, you'll rot in your own shit."
>
> Donat 1979, p. 168

Typhus was rife in the concentration camps, and the German doctors did little to protect the prisoners from disease. The inmates were overworked and starved in overcrowded, lice-infested filth without adequate hygienic facilities, clean clothes, soap, and water. A mixture of organizational sloppiness, indifference, ignoring of facts, and terror allowed epidemics to thrive. If measures were taken at all, they were half-hearted, ineffective, harassing, and/or lethal. The surest prophylactic was mass delousing, the disinfection of persons, their clothes, and their accommodations. Such a procedure, however, was expensive and time consuming and interrupted normal camp routine (Sofsky 1997). It is logical to deduce that the authorities deliberately promoted typhus in the camps because "natural death" was cheaper than gassing.

Inspections did not control the disease but instead served to terrorize the inmates and identify individuals and groups for selection and extermination. Notices posted in the concentration camps warning of the danger of typhus also served to instill fear among the prisoners. No standard public health precautions were taken, and there was nothing the prisoners could do to protect themselves. New inmates at Ravensbrück concentration camp were confronted at the gate by a printed sign in huge letters suspended over the top of the gate: "This is your death" (*Das ist dein Tod*) (Figure 2.12). Below the

A. Poster from Buchenwald. *Buchenwald Memorial Museum Archives.*

B. Poster drawn by Auschwitz concentration camp prisoner. *Auschwitz Memorial Museum.*

C. Polish poster from Dachau concentration camp. *Archives of Dachau Concentration Camp Memorial.*

Figure 2.12: "One louse, your death." These warning posters, found in many concentration camps, served only to promote fear.

words was an enormous louse painted in garish red and bright yellow with a long flat body with a small pointed head and six legs each with a hook on the end (Bernstein 1997).

Concentration camps from Buchenwald to Treblinka were rampant with typhus. When an epidemic of typhus broke out in Dachau at the end of 1942, the camp doctor placed the camp under quarantine for two months. Of the 1400 cases of typhus on record, 526 died. When an epidemic broke out in the main camp in 1944, two quarantine blocks were fenced in by barbed wire and the SS no longer entered. During the winter, as many as fifty prisoners died every day in these blocks, nicknamed "Chinatown." When an SS guard came down with the disease, the health authorities placed the SS residential area under quarantine as well.

In Majdanek concentration camp on February 1942, a typhus epidemic killed more than 1,000 people. Typhus suspects were hanged or shot. There are innumerable examples, and only a few are included in this book. In the beginning of 1943, the SS set up quarantine barracks where the sick were left to die. Only after forty SS personnel came down with the disease did camp authorities ask for disinfection and washing facilities. At the peak of the epidemic three infirmary barracks were built, and the section was declared a "no go" area, closed for a month. The barracks were disinfested only after thousands died.

When work at the Buna camp in Monowitz, a subcamp designated Auschwitz III in 1943, was interrupted by a typhus epidemic, construction was delayed. The sick prisoners and suspected contacts were gassed, and then a delousing was carried out. But it proved impossible to limit the spread of lice with the pseudo-measures used, and special death blocks were set up as elsewhere. Blocks set aside for typhus cases became waiting rooms for the gas chamber. In 1942 a wooden barrack for people suffering from typhus was added to Block 20 in Auschwitz as cases could no longer be accommodated. Near the end of the war almost everyone in the barrack was transported to the gas chamber. Birkenau was no different. During the epidemic of 1942, hundreds died every day, and doctors' selections sent more to the gas chambers (Shalit 1980, p. 6).

In Stutthof, as in the other concentration camps, high mortality was in part attributable to epidemic typhus and hunger. The Jewish camp (*Judenlager*) was the center of the epidemic because of the inmates' weakened physical condition, disastrous sanitary conditions in the barracks, and lack of medical care. There were no Jewish prisoners at Stutthof until 1944, but there were several recorded epidemics before Jews were interned (Klusak 1976). As in the other concentration camps, high mortality was attributable to epidemic typhus and hunger. From November 1944 the typhus epidemic became widespread. The commandant issued orders to try and control the spread of the disease and implemented a vaccination program for the SS and staff. The *Judenlager* was isolated from the rest of the camp by a fence. Entry was strictly forbidden for fear of spreading typhus to the nearby town. Only a special group of sanitation prisoners who transported the dead bodies to the crematorium were allowed to enter the Jewish camp from time to time.

By April 1945, sanitary conditions were terrible, especially in the Jewish barracks. In one of the isolated barracks and lying on its doorsteps were live, naked, emaciated female prisoners. In another barrack rotting corpses lay on the three-storied board beds next to prisoners who were left to die. The camp authorities did not take any action to control the epidemic, except for vaccination of a selected group of functional prisoners. Deaths caused by typhoid fever and typhus were supposed to be separately recorded in the death register. This was clearly not done, inasmuch as there were only eight typhus cases recorded in the death registry at the height of the epidemic (Orski 1995, p. 78).

Authorities were cautious when it came to reporting an epidemic to the central inspection or the local civic administration because it showed camp conditions in a bad light. Camp quarantine meant a freeze on leave for the SS, and German doctors eliminated records of epidemics by recording false diagnoses in the death certificates such as "heart disease" or general lung disease. SS doctors signed under a different name because, ironically, falsifying records was illegal. There were no death certificates for those sent to the gas chambers. When the camp authorities saw there were no more cases of typhus recorded among the prisoners they considered the problem solved (Drywa 1997).

An epidemic at Auschwitz in July 1942 claimed the lives of 4000 prisoners, and clearly the epidemic was out of control. Once the German authority felt threatened, Rudolf Höss, the camp commander-in-chief of Auschwitz concentration camp, temporarily ordered a complete blockade of the camp and restricted the movement of the SS and their families. Tons of Zyclon B were ordered to save the camp, though the requisition did not state that the Zyclon B was for delousing. It was assumed the gas was for the gas chambers. In his statement to the War Crimes Tribunal in 1945, Höss admitted that he personally arranged for the gassing of three million persons, but when asked to sign the statement to that effect he denied it. He said he only killed two million; the rest, he said, had died of other causes. When asked to state what had caused these deaths, he replied that there was a lot of typhus in the camps.

Typhus had also raged in the forced labor Messerschmidt aircraft factory in Dachau for months. Indeed, there was every indication that the SS themselves had spread the infection among the prisoners to ease the work of the crematoria. When it became evident that the war was coming to an end, the camp was locked on the pretext of quarantine. There was no longer any reason to maintain the facade. Germany was beaten (Shalit 1980).

DISINFECTION OF PRISONERS: PREVENTION?

Prisoners were subjected to frequent humiliating measures in the name of disinfection, which included degrading louse checks. When there was an attempt at disinfection, prisoners were made to shower hurriedly in the presence of SS men and certain prisoner attendants. They were forced to stand naked in the cold for hours. The incidence of pneumonia deaths increased from this exposure, and lice were left in the barrack blankets, straw mattresses, prisoners' underwear, and clothing (Czech 1990).

The disinfection of camp internees was totally ineffectual and clearly part of the extermination plan. Dr. Olga Lengyel, who was deported to Auschwitz from Cluj, Romania, in the spring of 1944, described the procedure:

> From time to time, the Germans disinfected the camp but had it been done correctly it would have improved the hygiene. But like everything else at Auschwitz the disinfection was carried out in a mocking fashion and only increased the mortality rate. Doubtless this was part of the plan. The disinfection began with the isolation of 4 and 5 barracks. We had to present ourselves by barracks at the washroom. Our clothing and shoes, items that had been acquired at the cost of great privations were taken away and placed in a fumigating oven while we passed under a shower. The operation lasted only a minute, not enough time to get clean at all. Then after being doused with a disinfectant on the head and parts of the body covered with hair, we were moved to the exit. Those who had lice had their hair clipped again. But after leaving the washroom, we had to line up outside completely naked, regardless of the season or weather. We had to wait until the line was perfectly formed, though it often took more than one hour. People were put at risk for catching pneumonia. Blankets and clothing were taken and when returned there was less clothing than disinfected—one blanket for 10 women. As a result many women had to come to roll call completely naked and were beaten and called "treacherous females, shameless." The naked were liquidated first. (Lengyel 1995)

SCENES SET FOR DECEPTION—BATHING AS A FAÇADE FOR MURDER

In order for the mass killing of Jews to run as smoothly as possible, the Nazis took great trouble to conceal their murderous activities. They had special gassing vans in Mauthausen and used medical blocks in Sachsenhausen as an execution chamber. By 1942 three extermination centers were operating—one in Belzec, which killed 15,000 per day, another in Sobibor with the capability of killing 20,000 per day, and in Treblinka which could gas 25,000 persons per day (Gerstein 1945).[10] Kurt Gerstein, a German chemical engineer in charge of the SS technical disinfection with highly toxic gasses, testified that the system was organized to cause the minimum resistance and to utilize as few staff members as possible.[11]

When prisoners arrived, they were instructed to take off all their clothes and leave valuables at the "valuables ticket office." Prisoners' hair was cut off in the barber's barrack, and they were then marched under the gun to the gas chambers (Figure 2.13). They stood stark naked and were told by an SS officer that no harm would come to them. "You just have to breathe very deeply, that strengthens the lungs, inhaling is a means of preventing contagious disease. It's a good disinfection" (Tregenza 1977, p. 8). They were packed into the gas chambers, and the doors were shut. Exhaust fumes from a diesel en-

Figure 2.13: A. Disinfection of prisoners at Mauthausen concentration camp was totally inadequate and served only to increase the spread of lice. *Fotoarchiv der KZ-Gedenkstaette Mauthausen, Stephan Matyus.*

Figure 2.13: B. Propaganda photo. Inmates await disinfection under the German gun in Mauthausen concentration camp. *Fotoarchiv der KZ-Gedenkstaette Mauthausen, Stephan Matyus.*

gine filled the room. SS doctors and professors like Wilhelm Pfannenstiel, a medical doctor and professor of hygiene at the University of Marburg/Lahn, and others watched through specially constructed peepholes on the door of the gas chamber (Figure 2.14). Metal grids covered the peepholes so that the people inside could

Figure 2.14: Nazi officials looked through this peephole in the gas chamber door while families were murdered in the Mauthausen concentration camp gas chamber. In Auschwitz the gas chamber peephole had a metal grid. *Fotoarchiv der KZ-Gedenkstaette Mauthausen, Stephan Matyus.*

not try to break it to get air. After the prisoners died, dentists were sent in to hammer out the gold teeth bridges and crowns while others inspected anuses and genitalia for hidden wealth (Gerstein 1945). Whatever valuables were found were sold.

Poison gas (HCN) was used in Treblinka and Auschwitz, and to a lesser extent in Sachsenhausen, Natzweiler, and Stutthof. Each camp had its own procedures, but all had variations on this deceptive theme—gas chambers disguised as shower rooms (Figure 2.15). The Nazis exploited expectations of routine delousing, and doctors were actively involved in all aspects of the façade. Prisoners were forced to erect the buildings and create changing rooms with hooks, towels, and soap and fake washrooms with false shower-heads and no drains. Gardens were planted to enhance the illusion of a bath-house. Prisoners were promised food and clean clothes after delousing, but they were instead robbed and murdered. In Buchenwald, the corpses were taken to the crematorium, the ashes used for fertilizer (Cohen 1988).

Figure 2.15: A. The inside of the Auschwitz gas chamber was plastered and painted white with false nozzles meant to imitate shower heads fixed to wooden blocks on the ceiling. *DÖW Documentationsarchiv des Österreichischen Widerstandes, Austria.*

Figure 2.15: B. Zyclon B was used in the Auschwitz gas chamber for mass murder. Administration of the gas was supervised by SS doctors. It took less Zyclon B to gas victims than to disinfect them. *USHMM.*

CONTAINMENT THROUGH EXTERMINATION

Nazi doctors were responsible for the murderous ecology of the concentration camps' killing programs. They were foremost in the camps selecting the weak and young, sick and suspect for death. Prisoners were paraded naked before Nazi doctors like the infamous Dr. Mengele in his immaculate white gloves. On the slightest suspicion of typhus, German doctors had prisoners murdered. "Anyone with spots or any thin muselmann was directed to the right side—the side that spelt death, the other side meant you were able to rot a little longer" (Des Pres 1976, p. 62). The incredibly brutal SS doctor Oberscharführer Jakob Fries made suspected typhus inmates run. If they were too weak to do so, they were diagnosed as having typhus and sent to the gas chambers (Vrba 1997). SS men tried to get assigned to "special actions" because they received additional rations of ⅕ liter of vodka, 5 cigarettes, 100 grams of sausage and bread (Kremer in International Auschwitz Committee 1960, p. 49).

Dr. Kurt Uhlenbrook was considered an expert on epidemic typhus control in the concentration camps. He obtained his credentials in Belsen, where he killed typhus cases and those suspected of having the disease. When a major typhus epidemic broke out in Auschwitz, the camp commander Rudolf Höss in August 1942 requested Dr. Uhlenbrook's services to solve the Auschwitz problem (Vrba 1997, p. 123). After the war, Uhlenbrook was initially brought to Frankfurt to face trial, but for some unknown reason the prosecutor dropped all charges.

Concentration camp doctor Friedrich Entress personally selected 746 typhus cases or recovering cases in the camp hospital and sent them to the gas chamber as an epidemic control measure. In November 1942 he sent 500 prisoners suffering mainly from typhus to the gas chamber and over a thousand victims the following month. Thousands more women prisoners, mostly those who suffered from typhus or were in contact with typhus cases, were also sent to their death in the gas chambers in the months that followed (5812 in October 1942, 6440 in February 1943, and 3492 in March 1943). In May 1943 over a thousand Roma (gypsy) men, women, and children suspected of having typhus were sent to the gas chambers (Wroblewski 1998).

According to the Austrian prisoner physician Lingens, in 1944 Dr. Josef Mengele personally supervised the gassing of 4000 men, women, and children with typhus. He sent 2857 Roma (gypsies) to the gas chambers in a single day in August 1944. He was awarded the War Cross Second Class with Swords for successfully combating serious epidemics (Gutman and Berenbaum 1998). However, the record also shows that his radical "therapy" did not work. Dreadful living conditions and lack of sanitary hygiene perpetuated the high incidence of disease in the camp. Again, nothing was done about the typhus epidemic until it affected the SS staff.

GERMANS PROTECTING GERMANS: EPIDEMIC CONTROL

Despite the health regulations, isolation, and quarantine measures, typhus continued to be a problem even for the military and the police. In a report from Libau concentration camp in Latvia in January 1942, the director of the camp informed the police department by telephone that several cases of typhus had been diagnosed. The camp was immediately isolated and cordoned off with police department guards. The next day a commission of military and civilian doctors determined that twenty-five persons were infected, and all sick persons were admitted to the military hospital. It became clear that the problem was larger than previously thought, as there were 1500 POWs with typhus and 300 cases in the military hospital. The Wehrmacht handled the epidemic by ensuring that the "cause" of the epidemic was destroyed. The cause of outbreak was attributed to the Russian POWs, and those with typhus were killed (Latvian Historical Archives, Report from Libau concentration camp 1942).

By sharp contrast, the Germans took precautions to protect themselves. They implemented preventive measures in occupied territories for the troops and local inhabitants. Clear directives were issued for protecting the "fatherland" from typhus. German soldiers were required to bathe at least weekly. Clothing and underwear were disinfected and changed at least twice a week. Disinfecting stations were set up for the troops, and new facilities were built in areas where they did not exist. Detailed instructions were circulated that included diagrams of disinfecting centers and called for bathing facilities to delouse up to 100 men. Vermin-free blankets and underwear were supplied for as many persons as could be bathed in two days. There were instructions for boiling clothing and ironing them on both sides, washing leather items in a 5 percent creosol solution, removing loose bedding straw, and applying a 10 percent soap solution to the furniture and floor (Latvian Historical Archives 1941).

All contact between German soldiers and civilians was discouraged. Germans in Riga, Latvia, were ordered not to have contact with civilians or prisoners, and in particular to avoid Jews. Off-duty soldiers were not permitted to use the sleeping facilities of locals, nor were they allowed to buy or wear their fur or clothing. The slightest evidence of lice was to be reported, for the danger was not just to individuals but to the whole unit, and if it was not reported it would be treated as an act of sabotage. Health workers were instructed to examine each person for scratch marks, and doctors were requested to keep records. Typhus cases were to be reported on a weekly basis to the police.

Typhus outbreaks among staff were taken seriously. When 130 cases of typhus were detected in the central Riga jail, the central prison hospital became overcrowded. Total isolation of the staff was impossible. To halt the epidemic, the entire staff that had contact with spotted fever was vaccinated, and cases of typhus were treated in a convalescent home and hospital that was commandeered as an SS military hospital (Latvian Historical Archives 1941).

In 1942, the Reich commissioner for health and treatment in the Eastern occupied territories issued a decree for the prevention of typhus epidemics. The decree stated that quarantine measures must be enforced by the local commission. Public gatherings and cultural performances were forbidden, and schools were closed; contact with POWs was prohibited; and emergency hospitals and delousing stations such as the "magnificent" Dunäberg (Da-gaupils) station, capable of disinfecting 1000 persons per day, were made available.

NAZI MEDICINE IN THE CAMPS: BRUTALITY AND OPPORTUNISM

SS doctors did not do any real medical work in the camps apart from treating German personnel. There were no proper hospitals. Prisoners in Auschwitz and other concentration camps were afraid of going to the "hospital" (*Krankenhaus*), because it was commonly known that most cases admitted were sent to the gas chambers or given phenol injections (Dawidowicz 1976). SS doctors left it to the ex-convict kapos to make selections. Although these kapos were of varying backgrounds (blacksmith, locksmith, butcher, and swimming coach) and had no medical training, they had authority over trained prisoner doctors. They amused themselves with patients, gave intracardiac injections, took blood, and performed surgery (Aroneau 1996). Generally, injections were used to murder smaller numbers, a hundred or so, because it was more economical. Larger numbers were required for gassing to be cost effective.

Treatment of ill prisoners was mostly a façade. Ill prisoners had to first pass the attendant. Then, if admitted, they reported to a prisoner physician, and then only if determined sick enough, the patient would see the block physician the next day. Having survived the obstacles, the patient would have to wait naked for hours. Those who were very ill would die, and the others were left to recover without medicine and perhaps a few strips of paper to act as bandages. The routine charting of the temperature, pulse, and course of every patient maintained the lie, and bogus medicines were prescribed even though no medicines were available (Lifton 1986, p. 82).

Doctors were also responsible for supervising their medical technicians trained in the use of Zyclon B for gassing. They brought the Zyclon to the gas chambers in Red Cross luxury cars, saw that "disinfectors" were protected with gas masks, and were responsible for declaring the "disinfected" dead. They provided technical expertise for the cost-effective burning of bodies and determined whether a prisoner was fit enough to be beaten. They falsified death certificates and conducted brutal, unethical experiments on prisoners without their consent. Many of these experiments involved testing typhus vaccines and pharmaceuticals, which yielded no real useful results owing to their flawed design and fabrications (see Chapter 4). Medical doctors also ordered that inmates be bled to death in their efforts to obtain blood for German troops. Their behavior demonstrated not only their inhumanity but also, in most cases, their mediocre science.

THE POSTMORTEM ROOM: PATHOLOGY AND PROFIT

The postmortem room present in all the concentration camps was involved not only in postmortems but also in production of specimens, tattoo skins for lamps and purses, masks, and skeletons and skulls (Figure 2.16). Prisoner doctors and kapos conducted pathological postmortems and issued official causes of death, a mere formality. In camps such as Sachsenhausen, doctors could only record one of seven causes of death prescribed by the security

Figure 2.16: The concentration camps had state-of-the-art pathology laboratories to produce specimens, skeletons, and skulls and to determine the cause of death in the victims experimented on. In the Mauthausen concentration camp postmortem room, note the skeleton and mask on the wall. Skeletons and masks were big business. *Fotoarchiv der KZ-Gedenkstaette Mauthausen, Stephan Matyus.*

office in Berlin (Figure 2.17). Typhus is suspiciously missing from this list. The absurd restriction suggests a coverup of the true purpose of the pathology laboratories. The postmortems were also conducted to determine results of experiments, identify pathological specimens, prepare histology slides and specimens (Buchenwald Archives 1963).[12]

German doctors plundered the remains of murdered individuals for university institutes of anatomy and pathology as well as prestigious research institutes (Seidelman 1998). Requests for tissues and specimens came from anatomy and pathology departments in leading German universities and scientific institutions in Heidelburg, Berlin, Berlin Charite Hospital, Tübingen, Vienna, Humboldt, Kaiser Wilhelm Institute (now Max Planck Institute), Graz, Jena, Reichsuniversität Posen, Strassburg, and the Vienna Museum of Natural History's anthropology section.[13]

Leading German scientists and professors (Hermann Vos, Eduard Pernkof) took part in this abuse. The famous Hermann Vos, professor of anatomy and dean of the Reichsuniversität Posen, is known to have sold for profit skeletons and bones, shrunken heads, and death masks to the Vienna Museum of Natural History for their display in the museum's race gallery (Seidelman 1998). Although the archives of the concentration camps appear to have no record of money exchanging hands, the Vienna Museum of Natural History has records of transactions and accounts for the specimens it received from Vos, who sold them for profit.

Skeletons and skulls were big business in Sachsenhausen concentration camp, and Berlin paid up to 3000 RM for a skull that was cooked in a bucket on an electric cooker. An immense number of the dead brought to the postmortem room were prepared as skeletons because the trade in skeletons was the best source of income (Lagerarbeitsgemeinschaft Sachsenhausen Lag V/9).

The universities of Tübingen and Vienna have removed and buried suspect remains. The University of Innsbruck and Charite Hospital of the University of Berlin have not yet honored Yad Vashem's request for an investigation of whether they have prisoner remains in their collections (Seidelman 1998). "At the end of October our pathology department (Auschwitz) received an order to send very good anatomical slides to the most important German universities and a whole collection of healthy organs, including more than 2000 slides were to be sent to Innsbruck University. These slides were very expensive as they came from healthy individuals who were then either hanged or sent to the gas ovens" (J. Tyl, Professor and Catholic priest, in Aroneau, 1996, p. 87).

Figure 2.17: A. Sachsenhausen concentration camp was a training ground for SS doctors. *N. Baumslag.*

B. The pathology laboratory was very modern and well-equipped. *N. Baumslag.*

OFFICIAL CAUSES OF DEATH

- heart weakness [*herzchwache*]
- cancer [*krebs*]
- senility [*altersschwache*]
- pneumonia [*luogenentzun dung*]
- stomach ulcers [*magengeschwure*]
- tuberculosis [*tuberculose*]
- septicaemia [*septikamie*]

C. Only one of seven causes of death could be listed in the death book at Sachsenhausen concentration camp. Note typhus was not included. *Source: Sachsenhausen Concentration Camp Archives.*

An anonymous prisoner at Sachsenhausen recalled his work in the pathology department:

> Each body has to be dissected, but when there were too many corpses, it was impossible to dissect each single one. We would then make only the prescribed incisions, and sew them up again, without doing a full autopsy. Undressing the bodies before dissection was really dangerous, especially in the case of, say, typhus fever. Because the lice carrying the disease would jump from the clothes to us, the prisoners doing this work and many people have died from the same disease. Down in the basement there would be about 200 coffins with corpses. We also had to select the best skulls, remove them and dissect these upstairs. The SS men never went down in their own cellar with the corpse, probably because they were too scared. One of us always had to come along.
>
> Written by a former unknown Sachsenhausen prisoner
> who had worked in the autopsy room

Clearly, senior officials knew about this "scientific" work and made it possible. Karl Brandt, Hitler's chief medical doctor, was an SS Obersturmbahnführer in the Wehrmacht as well as Reich commissioner for health and sanitation. He provided Colonel Dr. Wolfram Sievers, director of the Ancestral Heritage Institute and chief of the Institute for Military Scientific Research, with 115 Jewish corpses for racial research. Brandt was instructed to send the corpses with the heads detached, dipped in preservative, and placed in hermetically sealed tins. Sievers' rationale to Brandt was: "We have the opportunity of obtaining real scientific evidence by obtaining the skulls of Jewish Bolshevik commissars, who are the exemplifications of the revolting but typical sub-human type." To obtain these corpses, the living specimens had to die first of "natural causes." Care was taken to not use typhus cases because the Germans feared infecting themselves with typhus-contaminated materials. After the "specimens" were collected and dispatched, Brandt reported to Oversturmbannführer Adolf Eichmann, chief organizer of the SS police that 109 Jews (79 male, 30 female), four central Asians, and two Poles were killed to fulfill this order (Gilbert 1998).

DOCTORS OF INFAMY:
MOST PERPETRATORS GO FREE

Only a few of the many infamous criminal doctors are mentioned in this chapter. Despite the glaring evidence of gross negligence and unethical conduct, most of the guilty doctors were never held accountable for their actions. There is no complete list of doctors who were involved. Most were never found or tried, and only a few of the doctors charged with criminal acts were sentenced.

The notorious murderer Dr. Josef Mengele, "angel of death," though sentenced to death, escaped his sentence while recovering from typhus—the very disease he had taken extraordinary steps to avoid. Brandt was sentenced to death by hanging by the Nuremberg Doctors Trial for approving SS medical experiments in concentration camps. Doctors Brandt and Leonardo Conti performed unethical experiments on patients in a psychiatric institution. One study tested whether killing with gas was quicker and more "humane" than killing with intracardiac phenol injections.

The senior Reich doctor Conti, head of the SS health administration, was Swiss born and German trained. In 1923 he became the first SA physician in Berlin and went on to found the Nazi Doctors Association there. When the 1933 decree forbade Jewish physicians to treat Aryans, Conti's comment was, "It is only the elimination of the Jewish element which provides for the German doctor the living owing to him" (Cock 1997). Conti was initially in charge of the euthanasia program, but later was replaced by Bouhler and Brandt due to infighting within the Nazi hierarchy. In 1939 Hitler appointed Conti health leader and state secretary for health in the Reich and Prussia, a position he held until August 1944 (Friedlander 1995). Conti was responsible for killing a large number of Germans of "unsound mind" in the campaign to purify the Aryan race. In August 1944 he was promoted to the rank of SS Obergruppenführer, an SS equivalent of the Wehrmacht's lieutenant general. He hanged himself in his Nuremberg prison cell on October 6, 1945 (Taylor 1946; Wistrich 1992; Yahil 1987). In 1959 his estate was fined 3000 marks by the Berlin Denazification Trial Tribunal, a small price for the human damage and death he inflicted.

Phillip Bouhler was responsible for gassing Jews in occupied Poland. Rather than face trial, he and his wife committed suicide in 1945. Brandt was hanged. Christian Wirths, brother of Eduard Wirths, medical head of Auschwitz, was one of the many psychiatrists actively involved in the sterilization and euthanasia programs. For his work in the euthanasia program at Grafeneck Psychiatric Clinic, he was promoted to the position of administrative head of Brandenburg-an-der-Have euthanasia center. As a result of this experience, Wirths was made SS-Sturmbannführer and Kriminalkommissar in the Stuttgart police. He organized the death camps in occupied Poland and was responsible for the murder of Jews in Chelmno, Belzec, Sobibor, and Treblinka. In 1944 he was killed by a special Jewish unit in retaliation for his brutal mass murders.

Of the twenty-three doctors tried at the Nuremberg Doctors Trial, sixteen

were found guilty of war crimes and only seven were sentenced to death, a
mere handful. Most went free, and those who were sentenced did not serve
long (Figure 2.18). Ernst Grawitz and Enno Lolling killed themselves before
they could be arrested. Erwin Ding and Siegfried Handloser committed suicide. Professor Eugen Gildemeister, president of the Robert Koch Institute,
died in 1945 apparently from natural causes. Joachim Mrugowsky and Karl
Brandt were sentenced to death. Bernard Nocht of the Hamburg Institute
died of natural causes. Eugen Haagen, the virologist, was arrested but released by the Americans (Weindling 2000, p. 410) and rearrested and tried by
the French. Although thousands of German, Polish, Lithuanian, Ukrainian,
Estonian, French, and Dutch doctors were guilty of crimes against humanity,

Figure 2.18: There were more than 350 SS doctors in the concentration camps; only a few
were ever prosecuted. Defendants in the Doctors Trial were (front row from left to right): Karl
Genzken, Karl Gebhardt, Kurt Blome, and Joachim Mrugowsky (back row fourth from left):
Waldemar Hoven. Some members of the German defense council are seated in the front.
NARA.

only a few were tried as the money for the Nuremberg Doctors Trial ran out. Politics and German denial also played a major role. Of the many nurses who served in the Third Reich's medical services, few were tried for their crimes against humanity and fewer prosecuted. Nurses were actively involved, but little has been written about their crimes and most reports have ignored their role (Lagerwey 1998, p. 7).

There were over 1000 concentration camps in Germany and in the occupied countries. Thousands of German doctors practiced the barbaric Nazi medicine, and thousands more knew about the racial genocide and did nothing to stop it (Dvorjeszski 1974). From evidence that is available, it is necessary to conclude that far from opposing the Nazi state, a large proportion of the German medical profession cooperated consciously and even willingly, while the remainder acquiesced in silence. Had the medical profession taken a strong stand against the euthanasia program before the war, it is conceivable that the entire idea and technique of the death factories would never have materialized. But the majority of the German medical profession condoned the inhuman behavior of Nazi doctors like Brandt, Handloser, and Conti, and by not protesting vigorously, the profession allowed itself to be ruled by such men.

Medical history should record for coming generations not only the achievements of medical science but the fall of medical morality in Nazi Germany (1986). Nazi doctors, paralyzed to human feeling, were in powerful positions and used their medical knowledge to accomplish their anti-Semitic genocidal actions (Lifton 1986). The barbaric, unethical behavior of the German physicians and nurses in the Third Reich is the greatest blot on the record of medicine in the twentieth century. We are now faced with the challenge of how to educate generations of doctors, health workers, and researchers to have a conscience and a love for humankind. There is no medical science without a moral basis. Let us detest and ban science that has no conscience (Dvorjeszski 1977).

NOTES

1. In the United States in 1928 the Hippocratic Oath was only administered in 24 percent of U.S. medical schools. Today nearly 100 percent of medical students take the oath. Although it was not taken in Germany during the Third Reich, it was known, and now all medical graduates in Germany receive a copy of the oath for their offices. The oath does not address medical experiments, although the text is interpreted as doing no harm to a patient even though the words "nil nocere" are not in the oath.

2. Germany instituted the Berlin Code of 1900 following Albert Neisser's syphilis vaccine experiments on prostitute minors. Legal and legislative debate led to the 1900 instructions to the directors of clinics, outpatient clinics, and other medical facilities. This directive is the first document dealing with the ethics of human experimentation that recognizes the need to protect vulnerable populations such as minors and incompetents. The document further demands unequivocal consent and a proper description of adverse effects of the research. If research is to be carried out it can only be done by the director of the institution or with special supervision.

3. Reichsrichtlinien zur Forschungen an Menschen 1931 (Guidelines on New Therapy and Human Experimentation). In the 1920s criticism of the German medical profession for unethical conduct became widespread and included daily criticism in the press. It was unparalleled in other countries. In 1930, Dr. Julius Moses, who was a physician/legislator alerted the public to the deaths of 75 children by pediatricians in Lübeck, Germany from experiments with a contaminated tuberculosis vaccine. In view of the disaster and publicity, the Minister of the Interior in 1931 promulgated guidelines for medical experiments with humans, which were issued in a Reich Circular on February 28, 1931 as "Regulations on New Therapy and Human Experimentation." Most consider that these regulations remained binding even during the period of the Third Reich. They demanded complete responsibility of the medical profession for carrying out human experimentation.

4. Passed in September 1935, the Nuremberg Laws included the Reich Citizenship Law, which deprived Jews of their German citizenship, and the Law for the Protection of German Blood and German honor, which forbade marriage and sexual relations between "Aryans" and Jews. The laws essentially deprived Jews of their civil rights and excluded them from social and cultural life.

5. The Rockefeller Foundation continued to support eugenics research in Germany after the Nazis assumed power. According to Black (2003), the Rockefeller Foundation helped found and fund the German eugenics movement, including the project that sent Dr. Mengele to Auschwitz (Michalczyk).

6. The other three euthanasia centers were Brandenburg, Grafeneck, and Hartheim ("Euthanasia Program," Simon Wiesenthal Center).

7. Based on the United States Bureau of Labor Statistics Commodity Price Index.

8. Local health authorities asked Dr. Moses Brauns, an authority on typhus, to explain why the vaccinated Lithuanian workers contracted typhus. Brauns said that either the vaccine contained live typhus rickettsia or it was given when the workers were already incubating typhus.

9. Trunk reports that there were officially 18,579 cases of typhus in Warsaw from 1941 until 1942, making up 3.6 percent of deaths. There were 1355 cases in the Lodz, making up 1.2 percent of total inmates and 1.2 percent of total deaths. There were 3200 cases in Lublin in 1941, or 10 percent of the inmates.

10. In Majdanek the capacity for killing was in the works.

11. Gerstein testified that he joined the SS with hopes of sabotaging the Nazi extermination operations from within. He had made attempts to inform the Swedish

government and the Pope about the gas chambers but was not believed. He supplied a crucial written record of the gas chamber atrocities.

12. At Buchenwald, histology slides were produced in series, for example, 120 pieces (Buchenwald Memorial, Sign. 31/31, Der Prozeß gegen die Hauptkriegsverbrecher vor dem Internationalen Militärgerichtshof, Band VI, Nürnberg 1947, p. 281).

13. A letter of the "SS-Standortarzt" Weimar-Buchenwald dated 7 May 1942 reports that the pathology in Buchenwald was ordered to give a written report on the commissions of the SS Medical Academy Graz.

REFERENCES

Aly, G., P. Chroust, and C. Pross. 1994. *Cleansing the Fatherland: Nazi Medicine and Racial Hygiene*. Baltimore, MD: Johns Hopkins University Press, pp. 26–50.

Annas, G. J. and M. A. Grodin. 1992. *The Nazi Doctors and the Nuremberg Code: Human Rights in Human Experimentation*. New York: Oxford University Press.

Arad, Y. 1999. *Belzec, Solbibor, Treblinka: Operation Rheinhard Death Camps*. Bloomington: Indiana University Press.

Arad, Y., S. Krakowski, and S. Specter. 1989. *Einsatzgruppen Reports*. New York: Holocaust Library.

Aroneau, E. 1945. Concentration Camps: A Factual Report on Crimes. Committed Against Humanity. Document F 321 for the International War Crimes Council in Nuremberg Medical Experiments and Vivisections.

———. 1996. *Inside the Concentration Camps: Eyewitness Accounts of Life in Hitler's Death Camps*. Trans. by Thomas Whissen, Westport, CT: Praeger Press.

Auschwitz III (Monowitz) Concentration Camp and Sub-Camps: Buna, 2003. Memorial and Museum.

Auschwitz-Birkenau. 2004. http://www.auschwitz.org.pl/html/eng/historia_KL/monow ice_ok.html (accessed December 8).

Baur, E., E. Fischer, and F. Lenz. 1921. *Grundriss der Menschlichen Erblichkeitslehre und Rassenhygiene*. 1st ed. Munich: J. F. Verlag, Lehmanns.

Bein, A. 1964. "Notes on the Semantics of the Jewish Problem with Special Reference to Germany." In *The Jewish Parasite, The Leo Baeck Institute Yearbook*. Robert Weltsch, ed. London: East End Library, pp. 13, 32, 48.

Bennett, T., D. C. John, and L. B. Tyszczuk. 1990. "Deception by Immunization Revisited." *British Medical Journal*, vol. 30, no. 6766, (December).

Benno, Muller-Hill. 1994. "Human Genetics in Nazi Germany." In John J. Michalczyk, *Medicine Ethics and the Third Reich: Historical and Contemporary Issues*. Kansas City: Sheed and Ward, pp. 27–35.

Benson, E. R. 1995. A Historical Study of the Jewish Presence. *Nursing History Review*. The American Association for the History of Nursing, pp. 189–200.

Bernstein, S. T. 1997. *Seamstress*. New York: Putnam's Sons, p. 193.

Bilik, M. 2003. Personal communication (October).

Black, E. 2003. *War Against the Weak: Eugenics and America's Campaign to Create a Master Race*. New York: Four Walls Eight Windows, pp. 306, 325.

Blecker, J. and N. Jackertz. 1989. *Medizin im Dritten Reich*. Cologne, Germany: Deutcher Arteverlag.

Blome, K. 1942. *Arzt im Kampf [Physician in Struggle]*. Leipzig: J. A. Barth.

Borkin, J. 1978. *The Crime and Punishment of I. G. Farben*. New York: Free Press.

Browning, C. 1992. *The Path to Genocide*. New York: Cambridge University Press, p. 145.

Buchenwald Sign. 1963. 31/31: Collection 31: Transcripts of reports from various Buchenwald prisoners, Report No. 31: Former prisoner Heinrich Bauer (March 5).

Burleigh, M. 1994. *Death and Deliverance*. Cambridge, UK: Cambridge University Press.

Chronicle of the Development of Infectology. 1941. Lithuania: Kaunas (1990).

Cock, G. 1997. *Psychotherapy in the Third Reich*, 2nd ed. New Brunswick, NJ: Transaction Publishers.

Cohen, E. A. 1988. *Human Behavior in the Concentration Camp*. London: Free Association Books.

Czech, D. 1990. *Auschwitz Chronicle*. Foreword by W. Laqueur. New York: Henry Holt and Co.

Dawidowicz, L. S. 1975. *The War Against the Jews: 1933–1945*. New York: Holt, Rinehart and Winston.

———. 1976. *A Holocaust Reader: Library of Jewish Studies*. West Orange, NJ: Berhman House, p. 118.

Der Prozeß gegen die Hauptkriegsverbrecher vor dem Internationalen Militärgerichtshof. 1947. Nürnberg: Band VI, p. 281.

Des Pres, T. 1976. *The Survivor, An Anatomy of Life in the Death Camps*. New York: Oxford University Press, p. 62.

Distel, B. and R. Jakusch, eds. 1975. *Concentration Camp Dachau 1933–45*. Munich: Comite International de Dachau.

Dobroszycki, L. 1984. *The Chronicle of the Lodz Ghetto*. New Haven, CT: Yale University Press.

Donat, A. 1979. *The Death Camp Treblinka*. New York: Holocaust Library, p. 168.

Drywa, D. 1997. Personal communication. Museum Stutthof (April 18).

Dvorjeszski, M. 1974. Rescue Attempts During the Holocaust. Proceedings of the Second Yad Vashem Jewish International Historical Conference (April).

———. 1977. The Jewish Medical Resistance and Nazi Criminal Medicine During Disastrous Period. World Jewish Medical Congress, August 19, 1952. Tel Aviv, Jerusalem: YIVO Archives.

Dwork, D. and J. R. Van Pelt. 1996. *Auschwitz 1270 to the Present*. New York: W. W. Norton.

Encarta Plus Encyclopedia. 2004. "Galton, Sir Francis," http://encarta.msn.com/encnet/refpages/RefArticle.aspx?refid=761558485 (accessed December 5).

Ernst, E. 1995. "A Leading Medical School Seriously Damaged: Vienna, 1938." *Ann. Intern. Med.* 122:789–792.

———. 1996. "Killing in the Name of Healing Ensured the Active Role of the German Medical Profession during the Third Reich." *Excerpta Medica* p. 579.

Fejkiel, W. 1986. In Howard Fertig, *Nazi Medicine, Doctors, Victims and Medicine in Auschwitz,* Part 2. New York: International Auschwitz Committee, pp. 4–37.

Fertig, H. 1986. *Nazi Medicine: Doctors, Victims and Medicine in Auschwitz.* New York: YIVO.

———. 1996. *Nazi Medicine, Doctors, Victims and Medicine in Auschwitz,* Part 2. New York: International Auschwitz Committee, pp. 4–37.

Foster, G. M. 1981. "Typhus Disaster in the Wake of War: The American Polish Relief Expedition, 1919–1920." *Bulletin of the History of Medicine.* Baltimore, MD: Johns Hopkins University Press, 55:221–232.

Frank, H. 1996. *Governor General Diary.* September 9, 1941. Cited in Trunk, *Judenrat: The Jewish Councils In Eastern Europe under Nazi Occupation.* Lincoln: University of Nebraska Press, p. 144.

Friedlander, H. 1995. *The Origins of Nazi Genocide.* Chapel Hill: University of North Carolina Press, p. 103.

Gallager, N. 1999. *Breeding Better Vermonters: The Eugenics Project in the Green Mountain States.* Hanover, NH: University Press of New England.

Gerstein, K. 1945. Deathwatch at Belzec; Kurt Gerstein's deposition April 26, 1945. *le Monde* Juif, XIX (January–March 1964), 4–14, translated from the French by Rose Feitelson, with minor additions and recommendations by the editor in accordance with Gerstein's German text (May 4, 1945) Vierteljahrshefte fur Zeitgeschichte I (April 1953), pp. 185–193, 389.

Ghetto. 2004. Encyclopædia Britannica Premium Service. http://www.britannica.com/eb/article?eu=37405 (accessed April 28).

Gilbert, M. 1985. *The Holocaust.* New York: Henry Holt, p. 515.

Glass, J. M. 1997. *Life Unworthy of Life.* New York: Basic Books, pp. 7, 62–65, 211.

Goldhagen, D. 1996. *Hitler's Willing Executioners.* New York: Alfred H. Knopf.

Grabowska, J. 1990. KL Stutthof. Bremen, Temmen, p. 44.

———. 1997. KL Stutthof, Gdansk personal communication. Trans. from Polish by Danuta Drywa and Marsz Smierci (June 19).

Gutman, I. 1982. *Jews of Warsaw 1939–1943: Ghetto Underground Revolt.* Bloomington: Indiana University Press, p. 49.

———. 1990. *Encyclopedia of the Holocaust.* New York: Macmillan Pub. Co., 1:410.

Gutman, I. and M. Berenbaum, eds. 1998. *Anatomy of the Auschwitz Death Camp.* Bloomington: USHMM and Indiana University Press.

Gutman, Y. 2004. The Ghettos. Simon Wiesenthal Center Multimedia Learning Center Online. http://motlc.wiesenthal.com/resources/books/genocide/chap06.html#2 (accessed January 14).

Hackettt, D. 1995. *The Buchenwald Report*. Boulder, CO: Westview Press.

Haeckel, E. 1924. Naturliche Schopfungsgeschichte 1. Berlin: Teil H. Schmidt.

Haffner, D. 1946. Aspects Pathologiques du Camp de Concentration d'Auschwitz-Birkenau (thesis for the degree of doctor of medicine). Tours: Imprimerie Unioncoopérative, p. 39.

Hagen, W. 1973. "Krieg, Hunger und Pestilenz in Warshau: 1939–1943." *Gesundheitswesen und Disinfektion* 8:115–28; 9:129–43.

Hahn, S. 1994. Nursing issues during the Third Reich. In *Medicine Ethics and the Third Reich: History and Contemporary Issues*. John J. Michalczyk, ed. Kansas City, MO: Sheed and Ward, pp. 143–150.

Hilberg, R. 1985. *The Destruction of European Jewry*. New York: Holmes and Meier, p. xii, 1274.

Hilberg, R., S. Staron, and J. Kermisz. 1979. *The Warsaw Diary of Adam Czerniakov: Prelude to Doom*. New York: Stein and Day, p. 90.

Hillgruber, A. 1989. War in the East and Extermination of the Jews. In M. R. Marrus, ed. *The Nazi Holocaust, Historical Articles on the Destruction of European Jews*. Westport, CT: Meckler, 1:106–111.

Hirszfeld, L. 1946. *Historia Jednego Zycia*. Warsaw: Czytelnik.

Hitler, A. 1971. *Mein Kampf*. New York: Houghton Mifflin.

Holocaust. 2003. MSN Encarta Encyclopedia. http://encarta.msn.com/encyclopedia_761559508_/Holocaust.html#20 (accessed June 12).

International Auschwitz Committee. 1960. *KL Auschwitz: Fragment from the Diary of Dr. Johann Kremer in KL Auschwitz*. Kracow, Poland: Drukarnia Narodowa, p. 49.

Kater, M. H. 1989. *Doctors under Hitler*. Chapel Hill: University of North Carolina Press, p. 145.

Klee, E. 1997. *Auschwitz Die NS-Medizin und Ihire Opfer*. Frankfurt am Main: S Fischer Verlag Gmbh.

Klodinski, S. 1965. "Typhus in Przeglad." *Lekarski Medical Review*. Kracow: Kracow Polish Medical Society.

Klusak, M. 1976. Zachorrowalnosc Wiezniow I Lecznictwo W Stutthofie, Gdansk, (English summary) pp. 85–87.

Kogon, E. 1998. *The Theory and Practice of Hell*. New York: Berkley Books.

Kraut, A. M. 1994. *Silent Travellers: Germs, Genes and the Immigrant Menace*. New York: Basic Books, pp. 7, 145.

Lagerarbeitsgemeinschaft Sachsenhausen Lag V/9. Sachsenhausen Memorial and Museum.

Lagerwey, M. D. 1998. The Nurses Trial at Hadamar and the Ethical Implications of Health Care Values draft (October), p. 7.

Langbein, H. 1984. *Against All Hope, Resistance in Concentration Camps*. New York: Paragon House.

Latvian Historical Archives. 1941. "Control Typhus or Spotted Fever." Leiting Sanitary Office Wehmacht bef.

———. 1942. Report from Libau concentration camp. Latvian Archives (January 17).

Lengyel, O. 1995. *Five Chimneys: A Woman Survivor's True Story of Auschwitz.* Chicago: Academy Publishers, p. 132.

Lenski, M. 1975. "Problems of Diseases in the Warsaw Ghetto." *Yad Vashem Studies,* no. 3, p. 285.

Levi, S. 1980. *Beyond Dachau.* Johannesburg, South Africa: Kayor Press, p. 6.

Lifton, R. J. 1986. *The Nazi Doctors, Medical Killing and the Psychology of Genocide, Medical Experiments.* New York: Basic Books, p. 82.

Malcher, R. 1996. *Stutthof Das Konzentrationslager.* Gdansk: Marpress.

McFarland-Icke, B. R. 1999. *Nurses in Nazi Germany. Moral Choice in History.* Princeton, NJ: Princeton University Press, 1999.

Michalczyk, J. J., ed. 1994. *Medicine Ethics and the Third Reich: Historical and Contemporary Issues.* Kansas City, MO: Sheed and Ward.

———, Dir., 1997. *In the Shadow of the Reich: Nazi Medicine.* Documentary film, First Run Features.

Mitscherlich, A. and F. Mielke. 1949. *Doctors of Infamy: The Story of Nazi Medical Crimes.* New York: Henry Holt.

Nicosia, F. R. and J. Huener. 2002. *Medicine and Medical Ethics in Nazi Germany.* New York: Berghahn Books.

Orski, M. 1995. *The Last Days of Stutthof.* Gdansk: Marpress, p. 78.

Panavas, S., Director of Kaunas Clinics of Infectious Disease. 1996. Personal communication. Lithuania: Kaunas (May 2).

Perl, W. R. 1978. *The Holocaust Conspiracy: The International Policy of Genocide.* New York: Shapolsky Publishers.

Proctor, R. N. 1992. Nazi Doctors, Racial Medicine, and Human Experimentation. In *The Nazi Doctors and the Nuremberg Code,* G. J. Annas, and M. A. Grodin, eds. New York: Oxford University Press, pp. 17–31.

Pross, C. 1992. The Nazi Doctors, German Medicine, and Historical Truth. In *The Nazi Doctors and the Nuremberg Code,* G. J. Annas, and M. A. Grodin, eds. New York: Oxford University Press, p. 32.

Reitlinger, G. 1953. *The Final Solution: The Attempt to Eliminate the Jews of Europe 1938–1945.* New York: Beechhurst Press.

———. 1956. *The SS Alibi of a Nation, 1922–1945.* New York: Viking, p. 452.

Ringelblum, E. 1958. *Notes from the Warsaw Ghetto.* New York: McGraw-Hill.

Rizhov, and Bernane. 2001. Personal communication. Latvian Archives (May 25).

Roland, C. 1992. *Courage under Siege: Starvation, Disease and Death in the Warsaw Ghetto.* New York: Oxford University Press, pp. 130–131.

Romney, C. 1996. Jewish Medical Resistance in Block 10. Auschwitz paper presented at the conference on medical resistance during the Holocaust. New York: YIVO (November).

Rothmaler, C. H. 1989. Zwangesterilization nach dem Gestz vur Verhuftung des erbkranken Nachwuches. In J. Blecker, *Jackertz Neds Medizin im Dritten Reich.* Cologne, Germany: Deutscher Arteverlag.

Scholl, I. 1983. *The White Rose, Students Against Tyranny*. Middletown, CT: Wesleyan Press.

Seidelman, W. E. 1998. "Science and Murder in the Third Reich." *Dimensions, A Journal of Holocaust Studies* vol. 13, no. 1.

Shalit, L. 1980. *Beyond Dachau*. Johannesburg, South Africa: Kayor Press.

Silver, J. R. 2003. "The Decline of German Medicine 1933–45." *Coll. Physicians Ed.* pp. 54–66.

Sofsky, W. 1997. *The Concentration Camps in the Order of Terror*. Princeton, NJ: Princeton University Press, pp. 214–258, 467.

Steppe, H. 1992. "Nursing in Nazi Germany." *Western Journal of Nursing Research* no. 6, 14:744–753.

———. 1993. Nursing under Totalitarian Regimes: The Case of National Socialism, Paper presented at the Congress of Nursing, Women's History and the Politics of Welfare, Nottingham, England (July 23).

Taylor, T. 1948. Statements. *Nuremberg Medical Case* 1:57–58.

Toellner, R. 1992. Quoted in C. Pross, "Nazi Doctors, German Medicine and Historical Truths." In *The Nazi Doctors and the Nuremberg Code: Human Rights in Human Experimentation*, G. J. Annas and M. A. Grodin, eds. Oxford: Oxford University Press, p. 45.

Tory, A. 1990. *Surviving the Holocaust: The Kovo Ghetto Diary*. Cambridge, MA: Harvard University Press, pp. 43, 141–143.

Tregenza, M. 1977. "Belzec Death Camp." *Weiner Library Bulletin* 30, pp. 8–25.

Trials of War Criminals before the Nuremberg Military Tribunals. 1947. 1:496–97.

Trials of the War Criminals before the Nuremberg Military Tribunals under Control Council Law. 1950. No. 10, 1:89, Washington, D.C. Superintendent of Documents. U.S. Government Printing Office, Military Tribunal Case no. 15, *United States vs. Karl Brandt et al.*

Trunk, I. 1972. *Judenrat*. Lincoln: University of Nebraska Press.

Vrba, R. (Walter Rosenberg). 1997. *I Cannot Forgive!* Vancouver: Regent Press, p. 121.

Walbaum, J. 1941. *Kamf den Seuchen! Deutsche Arte Einsatz in Osten*. Die Aufbauarbelt im gesundheitswesen des Generalgouvernements, Cracca: Buchverlag Deutscher Osten.

Watson, J. D. 1996. President's Essay: Genes and Politics. Cold Spring Harbor Laboratory. Annual Report, p. 5. http://www.cshl.org/96AnnualReport/essay 5. html (accessed December 8, 2003).

Weale, A. 2001. *Science and the Swastika*. London: Macmillan, p. 34.

Weindling P. J. 2000. *Epidemics and Genocide in Eastern Europe, 1890–1945*. Oxford: Oxford University Press.

Weinrich, M. 1946. *Hitler's Professors: The Part of Scholarship in Germany's Crimes Against the Jewish People*. New Haven, CT: Yale University Press, pp. 6–7.

Weyers, W. 1998. *Death of Medicine in Nazi Germany*, Bernard Ackerman, ed. Madison: First Ardor Scribendi.

Wiesel, E. 1987. *The Night Trilogy*. New York: Hill and Wang.

Wistrich, R. 1982. *Who's Who in Nazi Germany*. New York: Macmillan.

Wittenstein, G. J. 1997. Memories of the White Rose. www.TheHistoryPlace.com/ Pointsof View/White Rose.htm

———. 2004. Personal communication (May 5).

Wroblewski, J. 1998. Personal communication. State Museum Auschwitz-Birkenau (March 12).

Wulf, S. 1994. Hamburg, Institute Public Health. Berlin, Hamburg: Dietrich Reimer Verlag.

Yahil, L. 1987. *The Holocaust, The Fate of European Jewry*. New York: Oxford University Press.

YVA 0-5/102/391-99 Halbjahres Bericht of Dr. Keppel. May 14, 1940.

Zablotniak, R. 1971. *Epidemic of Typhus among the Jewish Population of Warsaw during World War II*. Biuetyn Zydowskiego Instytutu Historycznego w Polsce (Poland), 80:3–21.

CHAPTER 3

Jewish Doctors Struggle to Conceal Typhus and Save Lives

Salaspils concentration camp, Latvia. *N. Baumslag.*

To you Jewish doctors, some modest words of acknowledgment
What should I tell you, dear friend and partner in suffering?
Your fate is the fate of all; slavery, famine, deportations—
those are all in the death figures of the ghetto which had not passed
    you over.
And you by your work gave the only answer to the murderers.
The answer is NON OMNIS MORIAR.

Dr. Israel Milejkovsky

Institutions in the ghetto were created to save Jews, ease their fate. Every department was a battlefield, but the hospital was the exception. It was the defense line of a true resistance movement, that fought not with arms, not with guns and grenades but with knowledge and self sacrifice to snatch as many Jewish lives from the German hands as possible.

Balberyszski, ghetto pharmacist

While the Nazi doctors worked to destroy lives, most Jewish and other oppressed doctors and nurses worked to save lives. These outstanding doctors established a resistance through mutual assistance, creativity, and courage. In so doing many risked their own lives as well as those of their family and the community. Resistance took many forms, but throughout they utilized what little they had to struggle against the genocidal plans of the Nazi regime. They upheld the noblest commandment in the *torah* and *halacha*, the saving of life and healing of the sick. It is written in the *Talmud* that "He who saves one soul saves the entire world."

Many doctors lost their lives attempting to save others, and only a few of these heroes are known. Dr. Jacob Wigodsky, "Father of Jerusalem de Litta," at the age of eighty-six became the first Jewish leader in Lithuania to revolt against Nazi authorities when he went to the Gestapo in Vilna to protest the German crimes against the Jews. The Gestapo chief Franz Murer threw him down the stairs and had him tortured to death in the Vilna jail. Dr. Janusz Korczak, a renowned Polish pediatrician and educator, became a symbol of faith and human love when he refused to abandon the children in his care. He had been offered his freedom out of the Warsaw Ghetto but chose to accompany the children to the death wagons (Zeitlin 1978).

Dr. Alina Brewda was forced to work as a camp surgeon in Majdanek. She risked her life to steal iodine, which she used as a sterilizing material, and when an epidemic occurred, she set up a special hospital for typhus patients (Minney 1966). Dr. Adélaïde Hautval, a French psychiatrist interned at Birkenau death camp, was nicknamed "the saint." Employed by the camp commander as a physician, she used her medical knowledge to treat Jewish prisoners who had typhus by secluding them in order to prevent the spread of infection. She did not report their illnesses, thereby saving them from immediate death. "Here," she said, in words engraved on the prisoners' memory, "we are all under sentence of death. Let us behave like human beings as long as we are alive" (Hautval 1991; Romney 1996).[1]

Well-known doctors died in the ghettos and concentration camps—many from typhus while treating or working with patients. The social hygienist Julius Moses and Berlin municipal doctor Manfred Bejach died in Theresienstadt; social hygienist Felix Koeningsberger was killed in Dachau by the SS because he refused to perform medical experiments on Jewish children in the concentration camp; Walter Oettinger was killed in the Riga Ghetto. Between 1933 and 1939 many Jewish doctors committed suicide, including social hygienist Leo Langstein, Theodor Plaut, Ludwik Jaffe, and Magnus Hirschfeld. Many died of typhus having contracted the disease while treating patients in the ghettos and concentration camps. Dr. Elchanan Elkes, Chairman of the Kovno Ghetto Council, died of typhus in Dachau just before liberation. These are just a few of the many who died of typhus and the few for whom there is a record of their resistance.

RESTRICTIONS: JEWISH DOCTORS AND NURSES

The traditional Jewish hospital, or *hekdesh*, developed in the seventeenth and eighteenth centuries, was a shelter for impoverished Jews.[2] Later the *hekdesh* evolved into providing medical care for the sick. Separate Jewish hospitals enabled the provision of special kosher diets for patients, observance of Jewish holidays and special handling of the dead. Because rampant anti-Semitism excluded Jews from training and specialization, which could only be obtained in hospitals, Jews set up their own secular hospitals to train their own health professionals.

For ages, restrictions have been imposed on Jews entering trades and professions. From the eighteenth century Jews were allowed to become doctors and dentists, but other areas such as law and civil and military service remained closed to them. In Russia, Jews were able to become doctors, but the number allowed was limited. Czar Nicholas I in 1835 restricted the settlement and movement of Jews to the Pale of Settlement, lands that Russia acquired under the partition of Poland; this policy held until 1917.[3] In July

1887 *numerus clausus*, the practice of setting quotas, limited Jewish student admissions to universities in the Pale to 10 percent, outside the Pale to 5 percent, and in St. Petersburg to only 3 percent. Toward the end of the century Jewish doctors were restricted from private practice and excluded from government posts. Despite the restrictions, the number of Jewish medical professionals increased greatly as many received their training in countries such as Germany, France, and England. Jewish agencies made scholarships available to them for medical training.

Anti-Semitism in Eastern Europe rose markedly in the mid-1920s, when Jews from all walks of life were again professionally restricted (Figure 3.1). In Poland, they could not become officers in the army, nor were they allowed to serve in the police force. Obtaining a good education was difficult and complicated for Jews. Those who had the means sent their children to special preuniversity schools. University medical and dentistry schools admitted no more than 10 percent of Jewish students, and these students were singled out for demeaning treatment. At a university in Lithuania a ghetto bench was placed in the back of a lecture hall labeled "here sits a Jew." Jewish students stood in protest rather than sit on those seats. Aryan medical students also harassed and physically assaulted Jewish students.

Figure 3.1: Anti-Semitic symbols. The old Jew hat was replaced by the yellow star to make Jews targets for segregation and discrimination. *Jewish Museum Prague. Photo: N. Baumslag.*

The American Jewish Committee (AJC) was established in New York in 1906 to safeguard the rights of Jews everywhere and to fight discrimination. Through the American Joint Distribution Committee (AJDC) in Poland during World War I AJC provided medical care to the desperate and needy Jews as the Polish government did not provide services for them. Jewish organizations from around the world assisted with funding the training of Jewish doctors and the establishment of Jewish hospitals, but initially AJDC was the major source of funding and helped establish the Cyste Hospital in Warsaw, Poland, in 1922. This was the largest, best-equipped hospital in Poland, and although it was a Jewish hospital, it served all sections of the community. From its inception it operated a nursing school and a nurse's aide training program, also supported by the AJDC. In 1922 AJDC's preventive medical activities were taken over by a Polish society called Tonarzystwo Ochrony Zdrowia Ludnosci Zydowskiej (TOZ). This assistance ended during World War II.

By 1925 there was a preponderance of Jews in medicine not only in Germany but also in the Union of South Africa and the USSR. By the mid-1930s, there were 21,000 Jewish doctors in the Ukraine and Belarus alone. They primarily treated Jewish patients. The number of Jewish women in medicine was smaller, partly due to the preferential treatment given to male applicants. Jewish doctors were still not allowed to obtain specialized training, attain high academic positions, or hold senior positions. Dermatology, however, was one specialty open to Jewish doctors in Germany. German doctors did not care for such work, believing much of it entailed venereal disease. Social medicine was also left to Jews (Weyers 1998).

Jews in Germany were generally more assimilated than those in the Baltic region. In 1933 Jewish physicians made up 16 percent of physicians in Germany, and in large cities approximately 50 percent of physicians were Jewish (Weyers 1998). Many were internationally famous, held high positions, and considered themselves German. German medical students carried out increasingly vicious actions against Jewish doctors and professors and took the lead in anti-Jewish student actions. Two months after Hitler became chancellor of Germany in January 1933, violent acts against Jewish physicians increased in frequency. Aryan doctors harassed and brutalized Jewish doctors openly, often calling them for a consultation and then assaulting them. In 1933 the Brownshirts, a Nazi paramilitary organization, took brutal actions against Jewish doctors from the Moabit Hospital and tortured them in a building on General-Pape-Straße. In 1999, when the building for the Robert Koch Institute's epidemiology and statistics section was being remodeled, the scientists discovered an ugly secret. They found torture rooms, instruments and records of the Brownshirts, and names of the doctor victims (Verfolgte Arzte im Nationalsocialismus 1999).

Jewish doctors in Germany were forced out of the medical profession and many emigrated. As a result, universities lost a considerable number of doctors and professors. Heidelberg University lost one quarter of its doctors, and the Berlin Charite Hospital lost over 30 percent. When Hitler came to power in 1933, there were between 8000 and 9000 Jewish physicians in Germany. By 1937 only 4000 Jewish physicians remained (Friedlander 1989). In Poland, by 1937 the Association of Polish Physicians passed a by-law that excluded Jewish doctors from membership. When Nazi occupation forces took over, all Jewish students were forced out of universities and anti-Semitic measures increased and permeated the institutions.

In 1935, the Nuremberg Laws were passed; in July 1938, Jews were officially forbidden to practice medicine; and by 1938, Jewish doctors' licenses were nullified, and they were prohibited from practicing on non-Jewish patients and Jewish patients from consulting German doctors. Jewish doctors lost their titles and positions, and physicians were downgraded to "treaters of the sick" and surgeons to "specialized treaters in surgery" (Lifton 1986, p. 3). They were also forced to give up their hard-earned membership in the fraternity of physician healers (Taylor 1946). Germany and Poland were not alone in persecuting Jewish physicians. Bulgaria, France, Italy, Norway, and Romania had all passed laws by 1939 restricting the proportion of practicing Jewish physicians (Proctor 1988).

A FORMIDABLE CHALLENGE: HEALTH AND SANITATION IN THE GHETTOS

> When we had nothing to eat
> They gave us a turnip, they gave us a beet
> Here have some grub, have some fleas
> Have some typhus, die of disease
>
> Lucy Dawidowitz

The medical profession well knew the cause and clinical picture of typhus by 1910. Doctors knew that the destruction of lice rather than quarantine was the key to epidemic control, as typhus spreads from louse to person and not person to person. Despite or because of this knowledge, German physicians played a leading role in forcing Jews to live in filthy and overcrowded conditions that ensured the presence of lice and the spread of epidemic typhus (Figure 3.2). The ghettos contained all the ingredients for the catastrophic breakdown of community health with totally inadequate and insufficient sanitary conditions. The health of tens of thousands of Jews was permanently compromised.

Typhus: A Preventable Disease
Factors Contributing to Spread of Disease

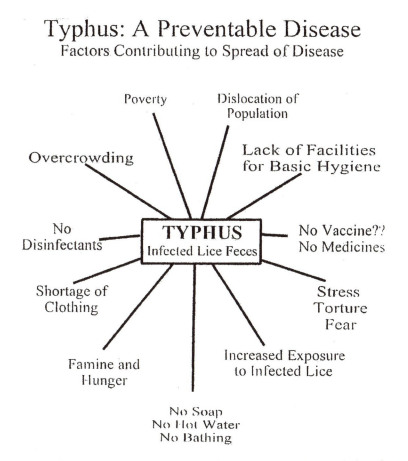

Figure 3.2: The Nazi doctors created typhus epidemics by confining Jews to dreadful unhygienic conditions, overcrowding, and starvation. *N. Baumslag.*

Dense overpopulation characterized life in all the ghettos (Figure 3.3). Ghetto inhabitants lived in dreadful condemned housing with garbage piling up and inadequate, insufficient outdoor privies. Hunger pervaded as they subsisted on 10 percent of the Minimum Daily Caloric Requirements (MDR). There was a lack of soap, water, and heating material, which became even more of a problem in winter months when pipes froze. Lack of soap was such a serious problem that in 1941 a daughter who lived in Chicago, whose father was in the ghetto, sent a special food package to him that included a pound of soap. In addition, as people had less clothing to change into and less hot water, they bathed and changed underwear less frequently. Hunger, stress, torture and lice plagued the population (Figure 3.4).

Figure 3.3: Gross overcrowding in the ghettos, food shortages, and insufficient water and soap contributed to unhygienic conditions and typhus epidemics. *USHMM.*

In addition to overcrowding, deplorable sanitary conditions, and a lack of proper nutrition, there were three other main sources of typhus in the ghettos. First, ghetto inmates were forced to work in the delousing centers for German troops. Those in forced labor had a high mortality rate because they worked in permanent hunger under flagrantly unsanitary conditions. Second, Jews were forced to work in ghetto workshops handling and repairing lice-infested clothing items that were supposedly disinfected. And third, transferees were brought in from the labor camps and given preference over Jews in ghetto hospitals. When an epidemic of typhus broke out in the so-called Kripo camp in Marysin, a camp for Polish teenagers, in December 1941 the authorities sent infected Polish children to the contagious disease hospital in the Lodz Ghetto after a commission of German physicians and officials visited and requisitioned 100 beds for Polish Aryans. Jewish patients were forced to vacate their beds, and Jewish physicians were left to handle the mass importation of typhus to the ghetto. The rule that Jewish doctors could not treat Aryans was broken for expedience, or perhaps it was another way of inducing typhus deaths among the Jews.

Health care and epidemic control in the ghettos were generally the respon-

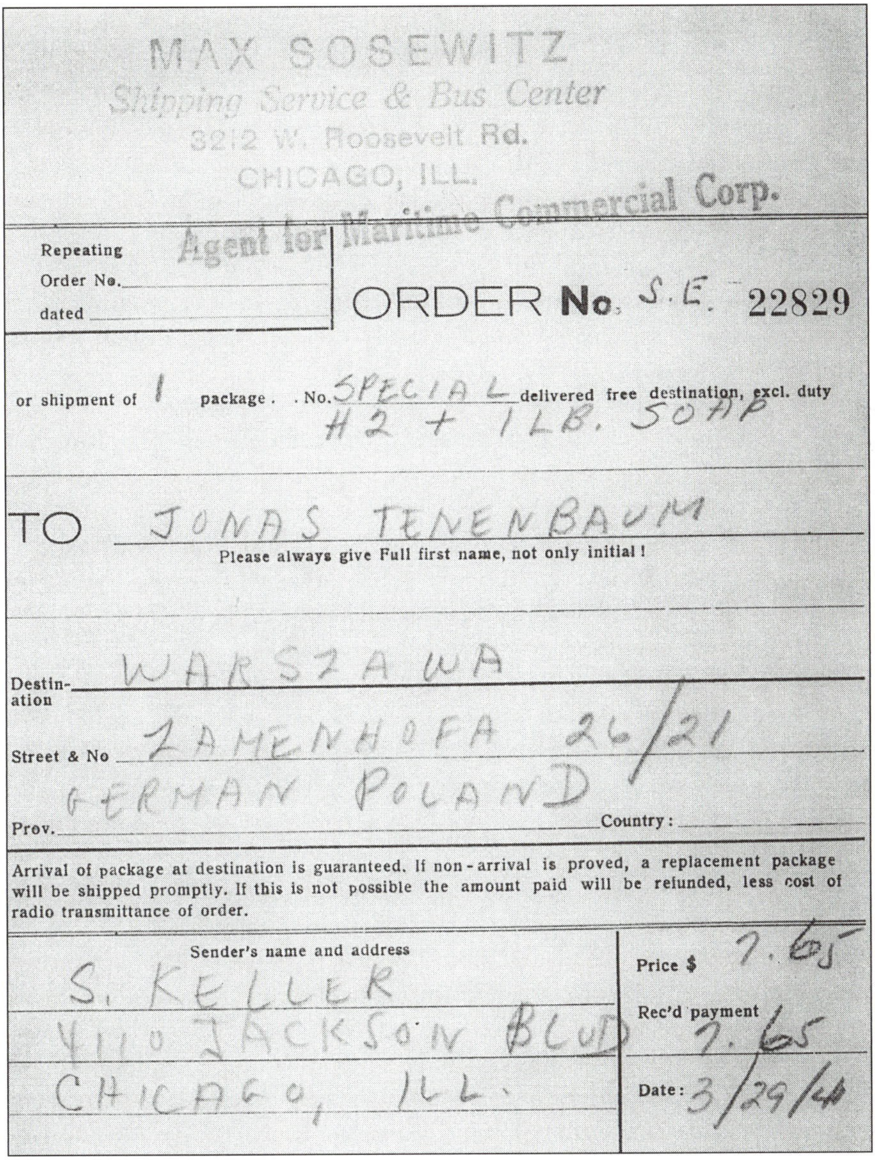

MAX SOSEWITZ
Shipping Service & Bus Center
3212 W. Roosevelt Rd.
CHICAGO, ILL.

Agent for Maritime Commercial Corp.

| Repeating Order No. | |
| dated | ORDER No. S. E. 22829 |

or shipment of *1* package. No. *SPECIAL* delivered free destination, excl. duty
#2 + 1 LB. SOAP

TO   *JONAS TENENBAUM*

Please always give Full first name, not only initial !

Destination   *WARSZAWA*

Street & No   *ZAMENHOFA 26/21*

GERMAN POLAND

Prov. _____   Country: _____

Arrival of package at destination is guaranteed. If non-arrival is proved, a replacement package will be shipped promptly. If this is not possible the amount paid will be refunded, less cost of radio transmittance of order.

Sender's name and address	Price $ *7.65*
S. KELLER	
4110 JACKSON BLVD	Rec'd payment *7.65*
CHICAGO, ILL.	Date: *3/29/44*

Figure 3.4: This receipt for a food package from a daughter, in Chicago, to her father in the Warsaw Ghetto, indicates that a one pound bar of soap was included in the package. *USHMM.*

sibility of the Jews under German supervision. Each ghetto was required to have a Jewish Council (*Judenrat*) to communicate with the Nazi rulers and carry out their orders. The German authority ordered the Jewish Council to organize a health administration to deal with treating illness, fighting lice, and preventing epidemics by maintaining strict hygienic measures. The Jews in the ghettos had to provide and pay for their own health care. In most of the ghettos, well-trained health professionals were employed by the ghetto administration. The German authority demanded weekly or biweekly statistical reports in German to keep track of their work and disease.

When the German authorities suspected a typhus outbreak they ordered the Jewish health departments to establish hospitals for infectious diseases. The authorities demanded detailed statistics of admissions, deaths and diagnoses of infectious diseases in German. They inspected the hospitals whenever it suited them, arriving unannounced to add to the prevailing atmosphere of suspicion and fear. At the slightest indication of typhus in a ghetto hospital, the Germans took radical action. In some cases, as noted earlier, hospitals were set on fire with the staff and patients trapped inside.

The ghetto health department's underground organization waged an epidemiological war against typhus and other infectious diseases primarily through disinfection and immunization and concealment when possible. They organized bathhouses and laundry rooms and set up "tea-rooms" to provide hot water. They treated typhus cases in organized hospitals, which were often robbed. In addition to a hospital, there were usually ambulatory clinics and, of prime importance, an epidemiological sanitary division. As preventive vaccines, medicines, sanitation, warmth, and food were generally unavailable, the ghetto health administration had to tackle enormous public health problems (Figure 3.5).

The ghetto health departments fought the war against the disease with only a few archaic weapons and made good use of well-known measures for typhus prevention and containment. In Vilna (Vilnius) and Kovno (Kaunas) ghettos they were able to prevent epidemics through education, training, organized health services, and sanitary brigades, as well as through the provision of hot water, wood for heat, soap, and extra food rations. Sanitary conditions might have deteriorated even more were it not for the Jews themselves who tried to improve the situation. Although more than a quarter of the ghetto administration budget was spent on providing hospital and health care, neither health nor sanitary conditions were improved owing to the hostile attitude of the authorities.

Conditions worsened when the authorities interfered with the ghetto health departments, as happened in the Warsaw and Lodz ghettos. Although

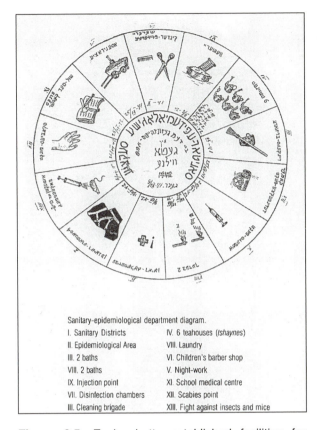

Sanitary-epidemiological department diagram.

I. Sanitary Districts	IV. 6 teahouses (*tshaynes*)
II. Epidemiological Area	VIII. Laundry
III. 2 baths	VI. Children's barber shop
VIII. 2 baths	V. Night-work
IX. Injection point	XI. School medical centre
VII. Disinfection chambers	XII. Scabies point
III. Cleaning brigade	XIII. Fight against insects and mice

Figure 3.5: Each ghetto established facilities for bathing, disinfection, and improving hygienic conditions. *Kostanian R. Vilnius Goan,* Spiritual Resistance in the Vilna Ghetto, *Jewish State Museum, p. 52, LCVA, f.R-1421 ap. 1, b. 198, p. 2.*

typhus was present in Warsaw in 1939, there was no epidemic. Within the first few months of the German occupation there was an epidemic.[4] The Jews were forced to work with the Polish sanitary supervisors in disinfection units. In September 1941 the Poles were dismissed because they extracted bribes, broke furniture, stained clothing, stole property and physically abused women. Because their brutal behavior and the measures they took did not prevent the spread of typhus, the Poles were finally replaced by Jewish sanitarians. In Warsaw a select number of Jews were sent to the Polish State Hygiene School for twelve days of disinfection training; previously, Jews had been barred from the faculty (Trunk 1953).

The German doctors and their Lithuanian, Latvian, and Polish counterparts interfered with treatment by Jewish doctors. German public health doctors from the Hamburg Tropical Institute forced doctors in the Cyste Hospital in Warsaw to treat spotted fever (typhus) patients with Uliron, an experimental sulphonamide, and other pharmaceuticals. The Jewish hospital staff was threatened with penalties if the prescribed protocol was not followed. The drug was toxic and the treatment interfered with circulation, causing blueness and coldness. Many patients died as a result of this treatment. German doctors ordered each patient photographed after treatment and conducted postmortems on those who died to determine the cause of death. The results are not available, but in all probability the deaths were caused by this experimental drug (see Chapter 4).

The genocidal plan of the Nazi regime was undoubtedly aided by epidemic typhus in the ghettos, although the actual number of deaths is extremely difficult to estimate. Existing statistics are incomplete and patchy. Ghetto mortality figures dropped because the old, sick, and feeble were selected for execution (Trunk 1953, p. 159). Cases were hidden out of fear of quarantine or deportation and only the hospital cases were recorded. In Warsaw in 1941, using Emmanuel Ringelblum's estimation (1958), only 15,449 of 38,150 cases were reported (Trunk 1953, p. 97). Typhus mortality was high as is documented in all the reports and writing on the subject. Still, doctors in the ghettos tried to prevent epidemics and developed resources.[5]

SAVING LIVES: CASE STUDY OF VILNA GHETTO

> The medical personnel in the Vilna Ghetto developed an activity of real military resistance, which fought not with guns and grenades, but with knowledge and dedication.
>
> Mendel Balberyszski

In Vilna Ghetto, health workers coped with the catastrophic health and sanitation challenges in courageous and innovative ways. As in all ghettos, Vilna Ghetto was overcrowded, and unsanitary conditions prevailed. The congestion in the ghetto was indescribable, and the challenge facing health professional staggering. There were no sewers; the water supply, toilets, and showers were totally inadequate for the population; drains were clogged; pipes burst in many houses, and garbage piled up in the courtyards. There were shortages of food, clothing, and firewood, ideal conditions for disease and epidemics. Once the Jews were forced into the ghetto, mortality increased fivefold, according to Dr. Lazar Epstein, head of the sanitary epidemiological section of the ghetto health department (Beinfeld 1998).

Vilna Ghetto had less typhus than other ghettos, and undoubtedly numerous factors played a role. The people interned in Vilna Ghetto were not as poor and undernourished as those in other ghettos (Roland 1992). This ghetto also had a large number of highly trained doctors with overseas training and many well-trained nurses and pharmacists—130 Jewish doctors remained in the ghetto throughout its existence. The nursing and medical school continued to operate in secret through a number of ruses. The German medical officer of Vilna, Dr. Zulch, had studied with Dr. Lyuba Cholem, who was a ghetto inmate. Dr. Zulch made it possible for Jewish doctors to have special passes that enabled them to walk the streets and meet at the Jewish hospital in safety, and he arranged for their personal property to be protected from confiscation (Beinfeld 1998).

In the Vilna Ghetto vaccines for typhus and cholera were given to older people when available. On one notable occasion the German authorities sent a batch of vaccine to the Vilna Ghetto Health Department. The Jews were afraid and tested it on dogs first because they thought it might be poisoned.

One of the five members of the Vilna Jewish Council, a lawyer, was given sole responsibility for health administration. He was advised by a supervising doctor and five medical colleagues. The health department activities were diversified and intensive, and the Jewish Council employed 380 health workers. Initially, there were two ghettos; ghetto 1 had a clinic and a hospital; ghetto 2 had clinics for specialists. Both ghettos operated sanitation epidemiological units to supervise cleanliness and prevent the spread of contagious diseases. The infectious disease unit functioned surreptitiously under the guise of the Department of Laboratory Medicine.

The Vilna Ghetto health department was fortunate to have the 150-year-old Jewish Hekdesh Charity Hospital within the ghetto confines. The Lithuanians originally planned to confiscate the hospital for their own use because it was well equipped, but for unknown reasons the German authorities let the ghetto Jews keep it. The reason they did so is not clear. According to Rosa Bieliaunskiene, the Germans planned to use it themselves but never did (Bieliaunskiene 1996). Dr. Zulch visited the Hekdesh Hospital from time to time and maintained a benevolent interest.

As a precaution to reduce the incidence of typhus and infected lice, by providing bathing in the Vilna Ghetto an engineer constructed a bath and disinfection chamber. From early morning to late at night, groups of twenty-two people came to wash and disinfect clothes, which they did without soap. Each person was allowed to wash 5 kilos of clothing, and the procedure took one hour. Conditions during the winter months promoted lice as pipes froze and water for washing became scarce. The preventive medicine as well as the epidemiology section eventually had two hygiene stations for bathing people and disinfecting their clothes, and six "tea-houses" which provided boiled water for drinking or washing.

Other public health measures contributed to the successful containment of infectious disease in the Vilna Ghetto. Large public assemblies were prohibited, and the library was closed when there was danger of spreading disease. An isolation chamber was set up near the ghetto gates to screen and disinfect people who returned to the ghetto from labor camps outside Vilna. Hairdressers and barbers shaved the hair of the poor as needed. Just before liquidation of the ghetto, the children's heads were not shaved so that those children secretly sent to Lithuanian families outside the ghetto could be better hidden. Closely cropped heads would have identified them as ghetto children.

Ghetto sanitation workers in Vilna had an opportunity to show initiative and act without much interference from the Germans. The sanitation office, with fourteen employees, collected garbage and disinfected refuse dumps through cleaning brigades. Brigade workers washed floors and cleaned halls, and there was a special brigade to fight vermin. To enforce general sanitary supervision in the ghetto, a special sanitary and epidemiological police force was established to supervise the cleanliness of the buildings, windows, and the like. For sanitary inspection, the ghetto was divided into four districts, each headed by a district doctor and seven nurses who assisted the doctors as needed (Figure 3.6). The housing department was divided into eleven and later twelve residential districts, each headed by a house administrator and one assistant. In each district there were six buildings, and each had between four and ten house guards or watchmen. Women were usually responsible for cleaning courtyards, streets, gutters, and toilets. A parallel organization was set up for supervising sanitary conditions in apartments, headed by a block commander. Every apartment had a commander who was personally responsible for sanitary conditions and was required to report dirt and other violations to the regional director. The block commander reported to sanitary police if an apartment was dirty or was not inspected at least weekly and properly reported. Block commanders allocated space, food rations, and ration cards. Cleaning women were given special passes called *scheine*, which ensured rations when they performed their job properly. Most of the women in the cleaning unit were the wives of intellectuals. They were assisted by homeless seven- and eight-year-old boys who served as sanitary youth auxiliaries and wore special armbands to enable them to check the cleanliness of apartments.[6] The number of people who visited the baths and the number of apartments checked for cleanliness were charted. About 61,000 persons bathed and were disinfected in the first half of 1942.

In April 1943, both the sanitary police and the epidemiology section of the health department were transferred to the ghetto police. Violators of the strict hygiene measures were fined or imprisoned in the ghetto jail. The council imposed a penalty of three days' imprisonment or a 10 mark fine on ghetto inmates who ignored the sanitation department's louse disinfection instructions.

The struggle against typhus in Vilna Ghetto included innovative public health education programs. A notable example was a public mock court case against lice which was held when a few new typhus cases were diagnosed in the ghetto in 1942. Dr. Lazar Epstein acted as the prosecutor and accused the lice of tormenting (*matering*) the inhabitants of the ghetto, eating their blood, and murdering them. One doctor defended the lice while other doctors acted as expert witnesses for the prosecution, telling the audience that the lice brought typhus and were very dangerous. The lice were found guilty and sentenced to death by burning in the disinfection chamber. The ghetto health department also continued to publish the prewar edition of *Folksgesund,* a public education magazine, as a newsletter on a biweekly basis. Popular lectures on hygiene and preventive medicine taught the people how

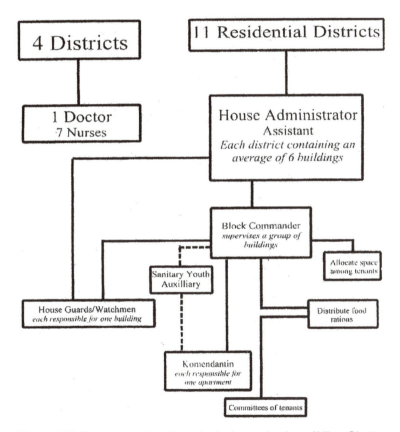

Figure 3.6: Sanitary and epidemiological organization of Vilna Ghetto. *N. Baumslag.*

to protect themselves from contagious disease. There was also a mailbox for suggestions (Kostanian-Danzig 2002).

Typhus cases existed in the Vilna Ghetto but not in epidemic proportions. The large number of devoted nurses, doctors, and pharmacists made survival in the Vilna Ghetto possible. The ghetto health workers had professional expertise, high standards, and a devotion to the public interest that protected the ghetto from severe epidemics like the ones that decimated the Warsaw and Lodz Ghettos. The greater poverty and malnutrition among the Polish Jews made them more vulnerable to disease, as mentioned previously, and contributed to the mortality rate. The administration was well organized and systematic. Typhus outbreaks, like the one that occurred after the influx of Jews into the Vilna Ghetto from outlying villages in 1943, were swiftly and effectively contained by the Jewish health authority.

RESISTING THE FARCE OF EPIDEMIC CONTROL: QUARANTINE, DISINFECTION, AND DELOUSING

The German authority favored brutal quarantine, inadequate disinfection, and nasty delousing for controlling typhus in the ghettos. Not surprisingly, many Jews resisted these procedures. Lice were a constant problem, and people sought out all sorts of alternative delousing measures. Some even bought Austrian World War I lice protection belts impregnated with mercury (Roland 1992). They appear to have been effective but may have been toxic.

Typhus quarantine imposed isolation, hunger, and freezing, and was thus feared (see Chapter 2). When a case of typhus was reported in the Warsaw Ghetto, the homes of typhus victims were isolated by the German and Polish authorities for an excessive period of six weeks and all the members of the household and their bed clothes were forcibly disinfected (Figure 3.7). In many cases, property from the homes was stolen. Sometimes the authorities, upon police orders, quarantined entire buildings where typhus cases had been reported. At times half the ghetto was in quarantine, isolated and condemned to death from hunger. Ghetto inhabitants actively resisted the dangerous, unpopular quarantine, and some bribed doctors to suppress reporting typhus cases (Lenski 1975, p. 141).[7] Others went to more extraordinary lengths. In the Warsaw Ghetto in one building, when one of the inhabitants contracted the disease, the other residents took away his identification, put him in a rickshaw, bribed a Polish policeman, and sent the unconscious patient to the ghetto hospital. He died there as an unknown, but they escaped quarantine and disinfection (Ringelblum 1958).

A. Quarantine of the individual household made starvation a real problem in the ghettos. This photo was taken in the Warsaw Ghetto. *Bundesarchiv Koblenz (1011-134-0791-31A).*

B. When a typhus case was discovered, the whole building was quarantined for six weeks and a sanitary policeman stood guard allowing no one in or out of the building. This created hardships for the inhabitants. *Bundesarchiv Koblenz (1011-134-0782-35).*

Figure 3.7: Typhus quarantine.

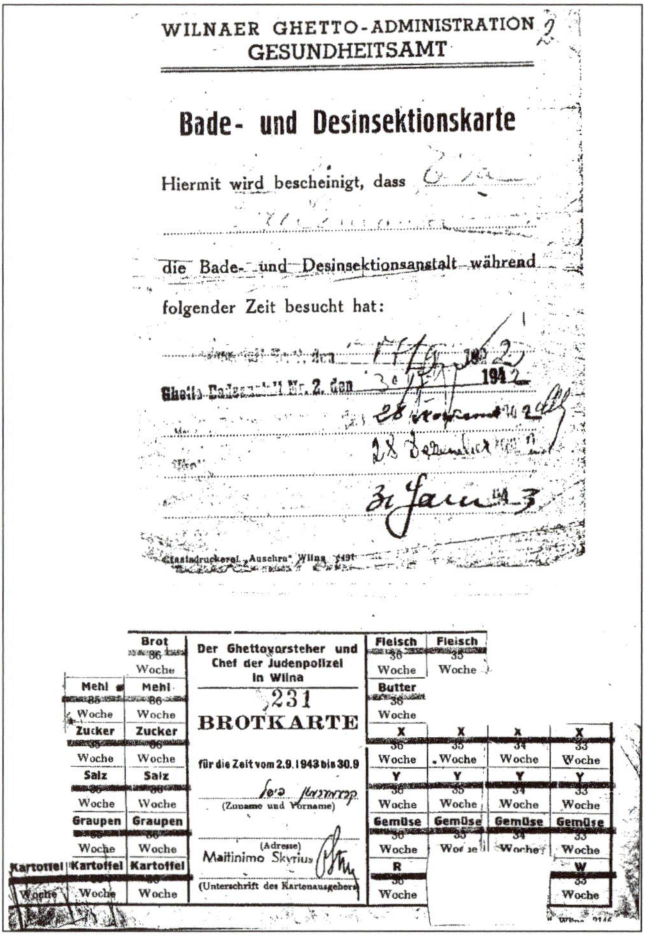

Figure 3.8: Mandatory delousing certificate from Vilna Ghetto, without which there was no ration card. *Source: Lithuanian Archives.*

The disinfecting process, supposedly intended to reduce the incidence of typhus, was ineffectual, inconvenient, and degrading. Sometimes the power in the ghettos was shut off, and often there was no coal, so clothes could not be sterilized. Facilities were inadequate and there were long lines, excessive waits, and frequent breakdowns of the equipment. At best, only one quarter of the people in the Warsaw Ghetto could bathe per day (Roland 1992, p. 142).[8] People often had to stand naked in the cold as they waited in long lines and many ghetto inhabitants avoided the procedure because it was unnecessarily degrading (Lenski 1975, p. 141). In Vilna in August 1942, the Jewish Council made certificates of delousing (*Entlausungssheine*) mandatory before bread cards would be issued (Trunk 1953, p. 163) (Figure 3.8). To avoid degradation, lice exposure, and long waits at the disinfection bath, people who still had some money resorted to bribery to avoid standing naked in the cold. Some paid 7000 Polish zloty to obtain a certificate without going to the bathhouse or paid other women to stand in for them[9] (Figure 3.9).

Figure 3.9: Women in the Warsaw Ghetto were forced to use the public baths for disinfection. *Bundesarchiv Koblenz.*

Dr. Ludwik Hirszfeld, a well-known bacteriologist who was interned in the Warsaw Ghetto despite being a Catholic convert, scathingly denounced the entire Nazi disease control procedure. With the cooperation of a German colleague, he conducted an experiment on the effectiveness of disinfection of rooms and their contents sprayed with sulphur and then sealed until it was judged that the lice were destroyed. To test the effectiveness of this regimen, Dr. Hirszfeld placed matchboxes full of lice in clothes bundles in the room being disinfected. As expected, the lice in the bundles survived the

Figure 3.10: Professor Ludwik Hirszfeld, a world-renowned infectious disease scientist with much knowledge and experience with ty-phus, blamed the German doctors for the ty-phus in the ghettos. *Oxford University Press.*

treatment and demonstrated that the process was useless. Hirszfeld's experience with ty-phus in Serbia in World War I had made him aware of the most basic public health mea-sures necessary for preventing typhus epidemics. He knew that for prevention one needed a modest supply of clothing—two day shirts and two nightshirts, regularly changed and washed. Rather than covering these basic needs, the German physicians preferred to fight lice with complex equipment, police regulations and circulars, and gassing (Figure 3.10).

JEWISH HEALTH CARE IN THE GHETTOS: HEROES AND INNOVATORS

Jewish health workers faced conditions ripe for typhus epidemics with tire-less dedication. Each ghetto had its own unique set of circumstances, but all were plagued with disease, pitiful resources, and dreadful conditions. Dislo-cated from their home base, Jewish doctors were forced to function in con-fined, inadequate, and overcrowded conditions. Drugs, medical supplies, and other resources were practically nonexistent, and Jews were not allowed to purchase essential drugs. Terror and fear, with exceedingly sparse resources, made the doctors' work difficult.

Despite the odds, Jewish doctors and nurses were able to contain some epi-demics through commitment and ingenuity. They created public health mea-sures in the ghettos, whereas previously state and local authorities had this responsibility. They created hospitals even when the Germans confiscated their buildings, drugs, bandages, instruments, linen, and equipment. To pro-tect the population, charts and statistical reports were falsified and diagnoses altered. Cases were labeled as "influenza" or "fever of unknown origin." Vac-cines and medicines were smuggled in or stolen. A few doctors in the Lodz

Ghetto, concerned with the general state of hunger, refused their special food allocation for physicians (Dobroszycki 1984).

Jewish health professionals created an underground medical and nursing school in the Warsaw Ghetto, though the training of doctors and nurses was forbidden by German edicts. Hundreds of young people received extensive medical training similar to that required by medical schools. The doctors used health education lectures for grand rounds and clinical training and quarantine notices to cover up resistance meetings. The German authorities were told that the sanitary courses were for epidemic control. At the beginning and end of every lesson, disinfectant powder was sprayed in every room to keep up the deception (Roland 1992). Luba Bielicka Blum, the director of the nursing school, continued to operate the school in the relocated Cyste Hospital until the ghetto was destroyed (Roland 1992, p. 73). Blum survived and received the Florence Nightingale award after the war for her courageous efforts in maintaining clandestine nurse training.

Numerous individual doctors distinguished themselves in the ghettos. Dr. Daniel Weiskopf was active in the formation of an underground group in the Lodz Ghetto. He was severely beaten when discovered hiding from the transport during the liquidation of the ghetto. He was later shot through the heart (Dobroszycki 1984). Another example of individual heroism is Dr. Anna Braude-Heller (Figure 3.11). During the siege of Warsaw, under her guidance the Bauman-Berson Children's Hospital became a center for first aid and care of the wounded. With the establishment of the ghetto, despite the depletion of the staff from hunger, typhus, and resettlement, the hospital became increasingly important. After each setback, Dr. Braude-Heller started over again to make the hospital a functioning place for the healing of sick children. She refused repeated offers of help to escape from the ghetto, and even the total destruction of the hospital did not stop her work as a doctor for the resistance fighters. She was killed in a bunker under the courtyard of the hospital in May 1943 (Tushnet 1966, p. 75).

The resourcefulness of Jewish health care workers was widespread and is well documented in the diaries and case histories of the survivors. Two engineers in the Lodz Ghetto, Dawidowicz and Wertheim, manufactured an X-ray machine (Dobroszycki 1984, p. 33). A facility was established to produce glucose for medical purposes from potato peels (Dobroszycki 1984, p. 198), and four different species of herbs for cardiac, gastric and other ailments were grown in the ghetto and distributed to ghetto pharmacies. In the Vilna Ghetto, a vitamin laboratory was established to produce a vitamin B cream made from beer yeast, legally and illegally acquired from the beer brewery in the "Aryan" part of the city. Vitamin D was manufactured from pulverized burnt horse bone, or "ghetto phosphate," and a special iodine was made for

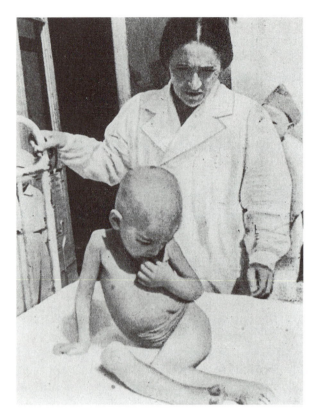

Figure 3.11: Anna Braude-Heller was the director of the Berson and Bauman Jewish Children's Hospital in the Warsaw Ghetto until mid-1942 when the hospital closed. She was a splendid human being and died in the ghetto after a lifetime of service. *USHMM.*

children with endemic goiter (Trunk 1953, p. 159). Improving health lowered the overall risk of disease.

Prior to World War II, it was possible to immunize susceptible populations against typhus. The vaccine did not prevent the disease, but it did reduce its severity. Doctors in the ghettos managed to secure small amounts of typhus vaccine and other medications, even though it was illegal for Jews to buy them. In Poland the Germans obtained vaccines from the Nazi-controlled laboratories of the Institute of Hygiene in Lwow (also known as Lvov or Lemberg) under Professor Rudolf Stefan Weigl. Weigl's vaccine was costly and time consuming to produce. In Warsaw two rich Polish merchants, aware of the value of this vaccine, traveled to Lwow and cornered the market. They bought as much of the *weiglowski* vaccine as they could, and through agents in Warsaw they sold it at high prices on the black market (Roland 1992, p. 147; Shoskes 1945). Several of the vaccines for sale were fake or of doubtless value. Some were available at enormous cost—800 to 1000 Polish zloty per vial (Shoskes 1945). Only a few could afford this luxury. Still, when it was possible it was purchased.

At one stage Dr. Israel Milejkowski in the Warsaw Ghetto bought vaccines from the Nazi profiteer Dr. Deuhler, who sold the vaccine fully aware that the Germans had forbidden Jews to purchase or use them (Shoskes 1945).

Early on, some vaccine was obtained from Switzerland for use in the ghetto and there is evidence that Dr. Rudolf Weigl sent some vaccine from the typhus institute in Lwow for Dr. Hirszfeld to use in the Warsaw Ghetto (Hirszfeldowna n.d.). But there was not enough for the whole ghetto population. Jewish forced labor working in the German Red Cross and military hospitals also smuggled in medicines into the ghetto at great personal risk (Dvorzhetsky 1958, pp. 204).

Jewish health professionals exposed themselves to danger, and, as noted earlier many died from the very disease they tried to contain. According to Fenigstein, 20 percent of the admitting staff at Cyste Hospital and 8 percent of the physicians and orderlies died of typhus. In the Lodz Ghetto, only isolated typhus cases occurred, whereas epidemics erupted in neighboring camps among Roma (gypsies) and Polish juvenile delinquents (Dawidowicz 1975, p. 215). One of the Jewish doctors attending the Roma camp, Dr. Dubski, contracted typhus and died. His replacement was chosen by the department of health through a lottery of all doctors under the age of forty-five, and precautions were taken every evening to disinfect the replacement doctor on his return from the camp (Dobroszycki 1984, p. 96). For others typhus provided a means of survival, as it did for Leon and Mina Deutsch, who survived in German-occupied Ukraine because they assisted villagers by fighting typhus (Deutsch 1994).

CONCEALMENT AND CONTAINMENT IN THE GHETTOS

The concealment of typhus became widespread of necessity, as authorities used every case of typhus to justify the isolation and murder of ghetto Jews (Roland 1992, p. 141). The German methods of fighting infectious diseases were well known and feared more than epidemics. In August 1941, on the pretext of typhus eradication, authorities burned the Kovno Ghetto Hospital together with its doctors, nurses, and patients. The fear of draconian measures against suspected typhus cases increased when it became known that Russian POWs suspected of typhus were shot. The ghettos were subject to constant inspections by the local health authority, and more so when typhus broke out among the Aryan population. At all costs the presence of typhus had to be hidden.

The concealment and containment of typhus cases was of paramount importance to the survival of ghetto inhabitants, and Jewish doctors took great risks to do so. Jewish self-organization such as in the Vilna Ghetto prevented the spread of typhus despite overcrowding and deprivation. In the Warsaw Ghetto, typhus cases were mainly treated at home in a massive clandestine operation to cover up the presence of disease from German inspection teams who periodically threatened to seal off the entire affected area (Dawidowicz 1975, p. 215). Doctors also fudged the bimonthly health reports they had to submit to the local authorities.[10]

Dr. Moses Brauns, a respected physician epidemiologist and head of the Kovno Ghetto's sanitation and contagious disease department of the Jewish Council, recognized that the greatest danger for the ghetto did not come from lice but from the attitude of the Germans toward the disease. On October 4, 1941 a reinforced squad of the German police (fifty men) and Lithuanian partisans (about one hundred) boarded up the doors of the small Kovno Ghetto infectious disease hospital and set it alight with sixty-seven patients, doctors, and staff inside (Figure 3.12). Bearing this in mind, Dr. Brauns successfully fought typhus while hiding its existence from the Germans and Lithuanians, who might have otherwise obliterated the ghetto (Tory 1990, pp. 43, 90). Rumors of typhus in the ghetto made it imperative to hide cases, delouse them and their families, and isolate and nurse them together with a family caretaker at home. Patients were given extra food rations, soap, and firewood for heat and nursed at home. Dr. Brauns would visit the typhus cases twice a day (Tory 1990).

Figure 3.12: Drawing of the burnt Kovno Ghetto hospital by Ester Lurie where sixty-seven people including patients, doctors, and nurses were burned alive on the pretext that they were infected with typhus. *The Ghetto Fighters Museum, Israel.*

In October 1942, a commission of Lithuanian doctors, suspecting a typhus epidemic, came to inspect the ghetto hospital, for a number of Lithuanian

Workers had contracted the disease. Jews were made to wash and delouse German soldiers; once cleaned-up, Lithuanian workers took over their care. At the time of their visit there were already twenty-nine cases of typhus in the ghetto, but they were not discovered because they were being nursed at home. The commission continued to search for typhus cases in the ghetto but did not find any. The home nursing of cases had been handled so secretly that even the ghetto inhabitants were unaware that there was typhus in the ghetto (personal interviews with survivors in Kovno).[11] Of the seventy cases of typhus that were diagnosed, only three died—a mortality of 4.3 percent. These cases were not recorded and the causes of death were falsified in the official biweekly report of the ghetto health administration to the local health authorities. The visiting Lithuanian doctors asked Dr. Brauns to explain why there was a high case fatality among the vaccinated Lithuanian workers at the delousing station and no trace of the disease in the unvaccinated Jews working there. Dr. Brauns, an authority on typhus, explained that the Lithuanian workers contracted typhus because they were vaccinated with a live lice preparation while incubating the disease. By hiding the ghetto typhus cases Dr. Brauns risked his life, his family's lives, and his reputation as well as the lives of everyone in the ghetto.

CONCEALMENT FOR SURVIVAL IN THE CONCENTRATION CAMPS

Prisoners of concentration camps were starved, overworked, terrorized, brutalized, and forced to live under the most unsanitary conditions. New people were brought into the camps daily on transports and infected lice spread the disease rapidly. Typhus, if suspected, let alone diagnosed, meant death.

But many people survived the epidemics through the ingenuity and dedication of inmates and doctors, nurses and scientists. At all levels there were people who, despite horrendous circumstances, were determined to resist the brutality and oppression. The literature and survivor testimony show how rampant the disease was and how the people tried to cope. Some smuggled vaccines, and others hid and sheltered friends and relatives. The struggle to survive was ever present, and in the concentration camps, hiding typhus patients and concealing diagnoses were simple steps taken to save lives:

"In Treblinka it was winter and the thermometer never rose above freezing. News of the epidemic spread quickly. In one week half of the prisoners had been stricken. Typhus, a fatal disease in their condition, was the ally of the Germans." The prisoners barely eating, sleeping little, ill clad, and beaten, constantly tried to resist it with determination. The sick went to work with fevers of 105°F and they managed to elude the Germans, who now more than ever, tracked down the weak. The fever lasted from 2–3 weeks and left men panting with weakness, anemic, exhausted, and with only the fierce will to survive. Ninety percent of the prisoners had typhus but only 50% were judged unfit and were executed by the Germans. There were no vaccines or medicines. The doctors advised the prisoners to eat more. The necessity of procuring food became vital, and with gold, food could be bought through the Ukrainian guards but because of the demand the prices soared. . . . When the Germans got wind of the epidemic an infirmary was opened and the sick who got there were in fear of the angel of death. To cope with the situation resting places were needed. In the sorting square there had been a small shed that served as a latrine. The prisoners transformed it into a "house of rest." It had served as a "social center." People came to smoke, chat, eat a stolen crust. The latrines designed for five were made to contain twenty people and became an underground infirmary. The stink offered protection (adapted and modified from Steiner 1967, p. 172).[12]

In Auschwitz help was forbidden, of course, but there was safety in numbers. Among the many thousands of prisoners packed together, the SS could only view any one group briefly (Figure 3.13). But despite the danger, the need to help persisted and often in elaborate ways. Many men and women were nursed back to health by friends who organized extra food, shuffled the sick back and forth from barrack to barrack, propped them up at roll call, and when they were delirious kept them out of sight during selections. One man who had typhus was smuggled every day into "Canada," a warehouse in Auschwitz where possessions and clothes taken from inmates on their arrival were sorted and cleaned. He was hidden in the great piles of clothing where he could rest. This particular rescue involved getting the man through a gate guarded by a kapo, whose job was to spot the sick and feeble and club them to death. Each day two prisoners supported the sick man almost to the gate and then left him to march through on his own. Once past the guard they propped him up once again (Des Pres 1976).

Prisoners exhibited a lot of resistance and solidarity. Some survived typhus attacks without staying in bed. In one reported case, two friends took a sick friend when she had a temperature of 103°F and saw everything as a blur, and dragged her along with their labor gang. Out in the fields they laid her down under a shrub, and in the evening they marched her back to camp—all in order to avoid having her being sent to a hospital hut and exposed to selection.

Prisoners also took great risks to support those subjected to the Nazi doctors' brutal experiments. These subjects were called "rabbits" (*Kaninchen*)

Figure 3.13: Two prisoners support a sick comrade in a concentration camp during roll call to avoid his extermination. From a Nazi photograph. *USHMM.*

because they hobbled when they walked as they were severely disabled by the sulphonamide and bone transplant experiments conducted by German doctors in Ravensbrück concentration camp. *Kaninchen*—guinea pig of sorts—is a common word for an experimental victim. The victims came up with the term to express their indignation at their mistreatment, but it also gave them a sense of solidarity. Wladyslawa Karolewska, one of these experimental victims, protested when it came to the third operation. In February/March 1943 the Rabbits protested in writing to the camp commandant Fritz Suhren, stating that "international law does not even permit experimental operations on criminals/political prisoners without their consent." This was an audacious stance, separating their status as internees from their ordeals as experimental victims. While inspired by the Red Cross agreements on the rights of detainees, the International Committee of the Red Cross (ICRC) did nothing to halt the medical abuses, and the camp authorities conceded that the experiments went beyond an appropriate punitive regime. The victims marched in protest to the camp commandant and demanded that he inform them as to whether the operations were part of their sentence. It was an epic protest, which the judges cited when delivering judgment on Karl Gebhardt, Fritz Fischer, and Herta Oberheuser at the Nuremberg Medical Trial (Weindling 1996).

Everyone tried to help these victims. Those who worked in the agricultural fields smuggled in fresh vegetables and fruit, and prisoners working in the kitchen sent marmalade, slivers of bread, and margarine when available. If they could not manage to smuggle food, they sent notes, drawings, and poems. When the doors were unlocked, they sneaked in and delivered painkillers, terrified that the SS would find out and take revenge (Laska 1983, p. 227; Michalczyk 1994, p. 140). In early 1945 when it was rumored that they were to be killed, fellow inmates hid them (Morrison 2000). Assisted by solidarity among the victims and their fellow prisoners, fifty-five survived despite severe and crippling wounds.

PRISONER DOCTORS: SICKNESS IS A DEATH SENTENCE

> Those who seek to protect the body at all cost must die many times over. Those who risk the body to survive as men have a good chance to live on.
>
> Bruno Bettelheim, University of Chicago, May 1960

According to the French journalist Bernadec, almost half of all concentration camp survivors owed their lives to prisoner doctors. Faced with the atrocities of Nazi medicine, prisoner doctors attempted to save lives by whatever means they had, be it sanitary, epidemiology, sabotage, resistance, or concealment. Those who were able to work in camp hospitals and laboratories did their utmost to save their fellow inmates or at least reduce their suffering. In Auschwitz as in other concentration camps, the Nazis used prisoner doctors in their hospitals and laboratories. Initially, Polish doctors were used in the prisoner hospitals and Jewish doctors were demoted to nurses and orderlies, but in Auschwitz when Eduard Wirths became camp physician, the Nazis used them in the hospitals. Many were highly qualified and were made to help the inexperienced Nazi doctors learn to operate, do research, and conduct laboratory work. They also provided the patients' only comfort.

The existence of hospitals or infirmaries for inmates in Nazi concentration camps is a paradox, for the camps themselves were geared toward mass murder (Romney 1996) (Figure 3.14). There were no real hospitals or medical care for Jews in the camps. The so-called hospitals were often filthy and lacked drugs, bandages, and any basic equipment. For bandages, paper was

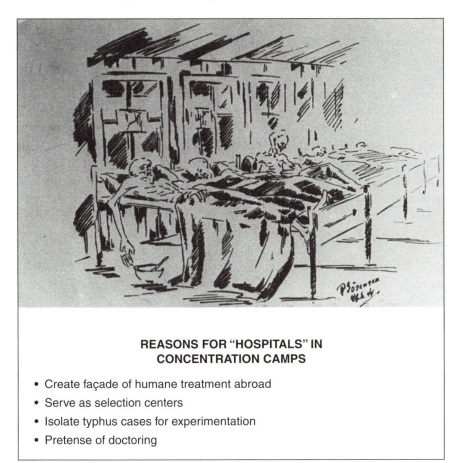

**REASONS FOR "HOSPITALS" IN
CONCENTRATION CAMPS**

- Create façade of humane treatment abroad
- Serve as selection centers
- Isolate typhus cases for experimentation
- Pretense of doctoring

Figure 3.14: Drawing of the "hospital block" by a Sachsenhausen prisoner, Thornwald Davidson. *Sachsenhausen Memorial and Museum/Brandenburg Memorials Foundation.*

used. The conditions were deplorable, and patients lay dying, infected, starving, ready for the ovens. Why then were there hospitals for concentration inmates? Several reasons have been suggested, including creating the façade for world news that sick prisoners received medical care. Hospitals really served as selection centers where ill patients were given intracardiac phenol or sent to the gas chambers. They were also used to isolate infectious diseases cases (e.g., typhus) for human experimentation and research.

Medical care for camp prisoners was largely in the hands of prisoner doctors and attendants. As in the ghettos, medicines had to be obtained through smuggling or bribery. There was such a shortage of medical supplies that prisoner doctors stole from the SS when they could. In the housing blocks prisoner doctors tried to control disease through meager makeshift measures. The only remedies available were hiding the sick and applying cold compresses. Scarce bread was bartered for soap or clean underwear, and underwear was cleaned with warm herbal infusions. Manual removal of lice and nits at night was all they could do to reduce their risk of contracting typhus.

Prisoners were not always aware of the danger of getting admitted to the hospital barracks. Attendants and prisoner doctors sent the sick back to their blocks instead of to the infirmary to save them from the clutches of the executioners. If they suspected there was to be a selection, prisoner doctors often refused to admit sick people and ordered those already hospitalized who were able to walk to leave. When there were very ill patients whom they thought they could save, prisoner doctors changed their charts and moved them into areas where they were safer. At the very least, they uttered words of encouragement and support to the suffering patients. Auschwitz survivor Rudolf Vrba recalls, "Even among the degradations of Auschwitz most of the doctors managed to retain their humanity and their professional integrity." A prisoner doctor smuggled drugs into the hospital to successfully treat Vrba after a severe beating from the authorities (Vrba 1997, p. 141). Vrba miraculously escaped in 1942 to report the atrocities in Auschwitz.

As in the ghettos, Jewish doctors concealed cases of typhus to prevent a pretext for further killings in the camps. A noted example from Auschwitz illustrates how even the most traitorous prisoner doctor falsified laboratory results to save lives. Dr. Nyiszli, a Hungarian Jewish doctor who is known to have collaborated with Mengele's barbaric procedures even more than some members of the SS, took at least one risk. Nyiszli was the personal research pathologist to the notorious Dr. Mengele. He didn't have to wear the usual uniform, had plenty of food, and generally followed orders. When Dr. Mengele sent him the bodies of two women from B camp hospital for autopsy, Dr. Nyiszli noticed the diagnosis in the files was typhoid fever and heart failure followed by question marks. Knowing what this diagnosis would do to the other inmates, and although it was classic typhoid, he wrote it up as nonspecific ulceration. Mengele was deceived, reprimanded the doctors for alarming him, and there was a stay of execution for the people in these barracks (Nyiszli 1993, p. 97).

Those researchers who were forced to work in the concentration camp laboratories helped to increase morale, stole vaccines for resistance workers and sabotaged vaccines by making them ineffective or infective for German soldiers and staff. In 1943 the typhus incidence was extreme in Auschwitz, and prisoner doctors smuggled letters out requesting medicines and anti-typhus vaccine. As a result, beginning in October 1943 a Lublin-based charity organization through the Polish Red Cross supplied Polish prisoners in particular areas with medicines and anti-typhus vaccine. Despite the high mortality in the Auschwitz camp from the disease in 1943, the prisoners were not inoculated. Through letters smuggled out there was a call for anti-typhus vaccine. Some vaccine reached the camp through Dr. Maria Mostowska and her husband who transferred the vaccine from Cracow through an organization named Pomoc Wiezniom Obozow Koncentracyjnch (PWOK) or aid for concentration camp prisoners (Wroblewski 1998).

Exercising their profession at the risk of their lives, prisoner doctors created supreme examples of the ethical practice of medicine even in dreadful places like Auschwitz. Some did not accept their fate but found a way to fight it. They wanted to survive and tell the world about the Germans' murderous activities. Braving the storm, doctors saved their patients' lives and gave comfort when there was nothing else to give (Pawelczynska 1979, p. 73).

RESISTANCE TOOK MANY FORMS

Since vaccines against typhus and pharmaceuticals were not available, doctors tried to find treatments from local resources. Under German occupation in Lvov Ghetto in 1942, typhus was the leading cause of death and no vaccine was available. Given this dire situation, Professor Dr. Ludwik Fleck developed a preventative vaccine utilizing the urine of typhus patients as a source of specific antigens. Thirty-two volunteers and later 500 people in the ghetto at Lvov were vaccinated. The results were lost, but Fleck, his family and two others contracted typhus and recovered after a mild abortive disease. A large number of those in the ghetto who were given the vaccine did not get typhus; by contrast, the nonvaccinated who contracted typhus had a 30 percent fatality. Fleck's practical vaccine was responsible for his and other prisoners' survival in the camps (Figure 3.15).

The German occupiers knew of Fleck's work and recognized that he was a leading European authority on typhus. When one of the Germans asked Fleck whether the vaccine could be used for Germans, he replied, "that was doubtful, since Germans were after all another race, and the vaccine was made from the urine of sick Jews" (Israel: Memorial Museum Archives Document Nr 0-3/650 cited in cited in Cohen and Schnelle 1986). Fleck and his family were arrested in December 1942 and deported to the Laokoon pharmaceutical factory where he was forced to produce his serum. In February 1943 the family was sent to Auschwitz, and in August 1943 he was commanded to move to

Figure 3.15: Professor Ludwik Fleck, humanist, philosopher, and extraordinary physician researcher, created a typhus vaccine from typhus patients' urine to save lives when other resources were denied the Jews in Lvov Ghetto, Ukraine. *Yad Vashem Photo Archives.*

Buchenwald to produce vaccine for the troops (see Chapter 4). After he was liberated he worked in Poland and in 1957 became head of the experimental pathology section at the Israeli Institute for Biological Research (Fleck 1947).

Typhus exposed medical doctors to danger but could also facilitate survival. The Polish director of Zamość County Hospital, Dr. Zygmunt Klukowski, extolled the value of the louse as typhus cases kept the Gestapo out of his hospital. Until August 1942 he admitted Jewish cases with typhus to save them from deportation. He used the white coat to ward off arrest and medical consultation to conceal a meeting with a member of the resistance (Diary of Klukowski, cited in Weindling 1996).

Resistance also took the form of documenting conditions in the ghettos. Physicians in Warsaw conducted starvation studies. Artist Esther Lurie documented conditions in the Kovno Ghetto and photographer George Kadish took incredible pictures secretly through a buttonhole. Historians like Ringelblum (1958) and Tory (1990) collected and buried documentation. Other ghetto inmates like Adam Cherniakow kept a diary. Their surviving documentation continues to inform researchers today.

DECEPTION: DEMONIZING LICE

In many instances the Germans' fear of typhus was used against them, often to the Jews' advantage. Notices with a red cross stating *"Achtung Seuchengefahr"* (warning danger of epidemic) were often used to keep the Germans and SS out of certain areas in the camps. The Auschwitz resistance used one of the signs ingeniously to keep the SS away from their meetings in block 20, the hospital ward, by posting a notice *"Fleckfieberverdacht"* (typhus suspected) on the door. The resistance knew that because the Germans were terrified of the disease they would not enter the barrack (Bennett 1990). In Novogrodek, Belarus, the dirty conditions inside the work camp afforded some protection against the brutality of the Germans and their henchmen. Commandant Reuter, who put on white gloves before hitting a Jew, believed that if he stepped inside the camp living quarters he would catch a disease (Kogon 1998, p. 175). Germans confiscated fur coats, and when a Jewish man was ordered to give up his coat he said they could have it, but they should know he had just been discharged from the typhus ward at Cyste Hospital. Needless to say they did not request this coat.

In January 1941 the Jews in Warsaw were moved out of the Cyste Hospital, which was built for and funded by Jews. The hospital had an excellent reputation and had treated non-Jews as well as Jews. The Jews were ordered to leave the hospital equipment, and had Nazi orders been followed they would have lost everything. Fortunately, the Jewish staff smuggled out much needed operating room instruments and equipment. One nurse recalled putting the instruments under a patient's pillow while he was being transferred (Roland 1992, p. 81). When German soldiers entered the ambulances looking for contraband, they left quickly when told the patients had typhus.

FAKE EPIDEMIC SAVES VILLAGERS FROM NAZIS

In Rozwadow and surrounding villages Eugene Lazowski, a Polish soldier and doctor in the Polish Underground Army and Red Cross during World War II, created a false typhus epidemic to save lives. During the German occupation of Poland one out of five Poles were sent to forced labor camps. The Germans required a Weil-Felix blood agglutination test to confirm a clinical diagnosis of typhus, so that drafted Poles could not avoid deportation.[13] Lazowski's friend, Dr. Stanislav Matulewicz, found that an artificial Weil-Felix reaction could be induced under the guise of giving patients protein stimulation therapy. They immunized selected patients who had symptoms suggestive of typhus, controlling the numbers in accordance with seasonal incidence and injected these healthy patients with a suspension of Proteus OX19-Proteus, which caused false positive Weil-Felix tests. For each case of typhus "confirmed" by the test, the Germans would send a red telegram, and eventually enough fake cases were produced in twelve villages that Rozwadow and the surrounding area were quarantined and declared an "epidemic area." As a result, Polish laborers were not conscripted from this area, and there was relative freedom from Nazi oppression.

The Germans were successfully fooled by a combination of factors: undue reliance on laboratory tests, lack of thoroughness in clinical examination, and fear of contagion. But by late 1943, the Germans became suspicious because there were no deaths from the disease. A Nazi deputation consisting of an elderly doctor and two assistants was sent to investigate the high number of positive laboratory results. The Polish doctors plied the investigators with food and vodka, and the lead investigator sent two junior doctors to investigate while he enjoyed the refreshments. As they feared the risk of infection, they made only a cursory investigation of the village and were easily dissuaded from closer inspection. The Germans left satisfied that it was indeed an epidemic area.

Dr. Lazowski risked his life on many occasions throughout the war to save lives. His back fence bordered the Jewish ghetto, and he told his Jewish neighbors to hang a white cloth on his back fence when they required medical help. When he saw this signal, he would wait until the safety of nightfall before sneaking under his fence to help. In a time when one could be shot for even giving a Jew a glass of water, he risked his own life and his family's welfare. He faked his medical inventory to conceal his nightly medical treatment of Jewish people. He did not dare send positive blood tests from Jewish patients, for that would have meant their death. After the Rozwadow Jews were rounded up and sent to labor and death camps, Lazowski continued to help those who were hiding in the countryside (Sun Times Company 2004).

MORAL DILEMMAS FACED BY PRISONER DOCTORS DURING THE HOLOCAUST

As the Nazis used highly skilled prisoner doctors to do their dirty work, research, and training, there were doctors who sold their souls performing unethical acts in the hope of prolonging their own lives. Some doctors collaborated willingly and performed the most evil acts, for example, the pathologist Dr. Nyiszli who volunteered to collaborate with the SS with medical experiments and dissections under Dr. Mengele's supervision. In his memoirs he attempts to justify his horrific actions by pointing to his professional skill, regardless of the moral implications, a morality that Bettelheim suggests made the Germans' job easier as well. Dr. Lucie Adelsburger worked for two years as a prisoner doctor in Birkenau's women's hospital under the supervision of Dr. Mengele. Her memoirs (1995), by sharp contrast, indicate that despite inadequate supplies and the prevailing threat of death, she persevered and did whatever she could to help others (Nevins).

Some doctors hid their professional identities rather than assist the criminals

in their experiments. Jewish doctors who refused to perform unethical murderous work for Nazi doctors and the SS were threatened and tortured when
they resisted. Dr. Adelaide Hautval, an imprisoned French Protestant,
worked in the women's hospital in Auschwitz where Nazi doctors conducted
inhumane experiments. With regard to the moral dilemmas the prisoner doctors faced she wrote: "Nobody could live during the nightmare years who in
some instance was not forced to break the rules of traditional behaviour. The
impossibilty to live without dirty hands belonged to that phenomenon."
Many compromised their ethics because they were in positions that required
them either to follow instructions or to be killed for refusing. Dr. Victor E.
Frankl chose not to assist with SS experiments and did not pervert his calling
(Bettelheim 1991). Some chose suicide rather than become henchmen for
German doctors' atrocities, and others committed suicide because they could
not continue inhuman, unethical practices (e.g., Dr. Fingerhut from Warsaw
and Dr. Sophia Camber from Kovno) (Yodaiken 1996).

Jewish doctors in the ghettos and later the camps faced obvious moral
dilemmas during the Holocaust, for they were often burdened with choosing
between their own safety and that of others. Concealing typhus cases was
problematic because without isolating those infected, there was the danger of
spreading the disease to many more. Jewish doctors often chose to take that
risk in order to save those already infected or to safeguard the community
from another horrifying action. The Jewish doctors' efforts at concealment
risked the lives of the entire community, but at the same time, these efforts
were a marked act of resistance.

Rabbi Shimon Efrata, rabbi of the surviving community in Warsaw after
the war, concluded that *halacha* does not require one to die in an attempt to
spare the life of another. Rather, if one opts to die, that person shall be
called holy. The previously mentioned pediatrician, Janusz Korczak, is an example of an unparalleled act of defiance and courage. He chose to die with
the 200 orphans in his care rather than escape the Warsaw Ghetto. They
were transported together to their deaths at Treblinka concentration camp
(Nevins 2004) (Figure 3.16). Other doctors such as the pediatrician Dr. Ad-
ina Blady Szwajger, made more morally ambiguous decisions. When her patients were ordered for deportation from the Warsaw Ghetto in 1942, Dr.
Szwajger acted to spare her patients the painful death awaiting them and eu-
thanized fifteen children and several of her elderly patients with morphine
(Nevins 2004). She had to live with the uncertainty of her decision for the
rest of her life.

Generally, Jewish doctors in the ghettos and concentration camps tried to
save lives even when it meant risking their own. Many risked their lives to steal

Figure 3.16: Janusz Korczak was a physician in the Warsaw Ghetto totally committed to the care of orphaned children. He went to the gas chamber with them. *USHMM courtesy of Yad Vashem Photo Archives.*

a vaccine or a drug from the SS medicinal workers to save the life of an ill prisoner. They sabotaged experiments and prepared drugs from herbs and vegetables to reduce suffering and illness in the concentration camps. Many became models of righteousness by risking, and in some cases sacrificing, their own lives to save others. Their efforts at prevention, containment, and concealment of typhus in the ghettos and the concentration camps were forms of resistance.

NOTES

1. Yad Vashem named Hautval one of the "Righteous Among the Nations" in 1965.

2. *Hekdesh* is Yiddish meaning "communal poorhouse."

3. The Pale was designated as an area for Jews. Special documents were needed if they moved out or were traded out of the area.

4. Disinfection units were formed in the winter of 1940, and by September 1941 there were eight operational units.

5. Ringelblum was a historian in the Warsaw Ghetto who wrote and collected documents, stories, and papers to ensure there were records of the horrors of Ghetto life. The papers were buried in milk cans and found after the war.

6. The sanitary epidemiology section had four distinct doctors; each doctor had seven nurses and supervised 1216 apartments, 71 courtyards, and 154 private enterprises; 620 apartments were disinfected. By August 1942 there had been 84,000 inspections since inception.

7. The going rate was 800 Polish zloty per day, which today equals more than U.S. $200. It was a much more substantial amount at the time.

8. There was a need in the Warsaw Ghetto for 8000 to bathe per day, but existing baths could only accommodate 2000.

9. 7000 Polish zloty today is almost U.S. $1800.

10. In October 1941 there were an estimated 9000 cases of typhus in ghetto hospitals and 7000 cases treated at home. The official number in the ghetto was 1805 (Ringelblum 1958).

11. Kovno is Yiddish for Kaunas.

12. Although this is fiction it is borne out by survivor testimony.

13. This easy and specific test depends on a high titre of O agglutinin developed in the blood to a strain of Proteus X19. A titre of 50 is diagnostic of typhus.

REFERENCES

Adelsberger, L. 1995. *A Doctor's Story*. Trans. by Susan Ray. Boston, MA: Northeastern University Press, p. 101.

Arad, Y. 1990. *The Pictorial History of the Holocaust*. New York: Macmillan Pub. Co.

———. 1992. *Ghetto in Flames: The Struggle and Destruction of the Jews in Vilna*. New York: Holocaust Library, pp. 315–318.

Balberyszski, M. 1967. *Shtarker fun Ayzon [Stronger Than Iron]*. Tel Aviv.

Baumslag, N. and B. Shmookler. 1996. Presented at the Medical Resistance During the Holocaust conference. YIVO, New York.

Beinfeld, S. 1998. Health Care in the Vilna Ghetto. *Holocaust and Genocide Studies*. New York: Oxford University Press, no.1, 12:80.

Bennett, T., D.C. John, and L.B. Tyszczuk. 1990. "Deception by Immunization Revisted." *British Medical Journal* no. 6766 (December), p. 22–29.

Berger, N., ed. 1997. The Jews and Medicine: Religion, Culture, Science Based on the Exhibit at Beth Hatefutsoth. Philadelphia: The Jewish Publication Society, pp. 205–215.

Bernadec, C. 1981. *Les Medecins de l'impossible*. Quebec: Le Nordais, Mont–royal.

Bettelheim, B. 1991. Janucz Korczak: A Tale for Our Time. In *Freud's Vienna and Other Essays*. New York: Vintage Books.

Bieliaunskiene, R., Chief Curator, Jewish State Museum, Vilnius. 1996. Personal communication.

Browning, C. 1988. "Genocide and Public Health: German Doctors and Polish Jews 1939–41." *Holocaust and Genocidal Studies* 3:21–36.

Cohen, M. 1997. *Norway's Physicians and the Nazis*. Detroit: Wayne State University Press.

Cohen, R. S. and Schnelle, T. 1986. *Cognition and Fact: Materials on Ludwik Fleck.* Dordrecht: Reidl D. Publishing Co., pp. 19–29.

Dawidowicz, L. S. 1975. *The War Against the Jews 1933–1945.* New York: Holt, Rinehart and Winston, pp. 214–215.

Des Pres, T. 1976. *The Survivor: An Anatomy of Life in the Death Camps.* New York: Oxford University Press, pp. 122, 152, 135.

Deutsch, M. 1994. *Mina's Story: A Doctor's Memoir of the Holocaust.* Toronto: ECW Press.

Dobroszycki, L. 1984. *Chronicle of the Lodz Ghetto 1941–1944.* New Haven, CT: Yale University Press, pp. 217, 267, 280, 357, 424.

Dvorzhetsky, M. 1958. Jewish Medical Resistance During the Catastrophe. In *Extermination and Resistance: Historical Records and Source Materials.* Israel: Hagettaot, 1: 118–119.

Engelking, B. 2001. *Holocaust and Memory.* London: Leicester University Press.

Fejkiel, W. 1986. Health Services in Auschwitz I Concentration Camp/Main Camp. International Auschwitz Committee. *Nazi Medicine, Doctors Victims and Medicine in Auschwitz,* Part 2. New York: Howard Fertig, pp. 4–37.

Fenigstein, H. 1992. The Holocaust and I, pp. ix–x. Cited in C. G. Roland, *Courage Under Siege, Starvation, Disease, and Death in the Warsaw Ghetto.* New York: Oxford University Press, p. 152.

Fleck, L. 1947. Specific Antigenic Substances in the Urine of Typhus Patients. *Texas Reports on Biology and Medicine* 6:169–172.

Fleck's report. 1998. Cited in E. Kogon, *The Theory and Practice of Hell.* New York: Berkley Books, p. 182.

Frank, Governor General. 1996. Warsaw Diary, August 24, 1942. Cited in I. Trunk, *Judenrat: The Jewish Councils in Eastern Europe under Nazi Occupation.* Lincoln: University of Nebraska Press, p. 144.

Friedlander, S. 1989. *Nazi Germany and the Jews—The Years of Persecution 1933–39.* Tel Aviv: pp. 258–259, 293.

Gutman, I. 1994. *Resistance.* New York: Houghton Miflin, pp. 88–89.

Hagen, W. 1973. Krieg, Hunger and Pestilence in Warshau 1939–1943. *Gesundheitswesen und Disinfektion,* 8:115–128; 9:129–143.

Hautval, A. 1991. Medecine et crimes contre l'humanite. Temoignage manuscrit ecrit en 1946, revu par l'auteur en 1987, Actes Sud, Arles, p. 36.

Hilberg, R., S. A. Staron, and J. Kermisz. 1968. *The Warsaw Diary of Adam Czerniakoz.* New York: Stein and Day.

Hirszfeldowna, H., ed. *The Story of One Life from Historia Jednego Zycïa by Ludwig Hirszfeld.* Trans. by F. R. Camp and F. R. Ellis. Fort Knox, KY: Blood Transfusion Division, United States Army Medical Research Library, p. 368.

Kogon, E. 1998. *The Theory and Practice of Hell.* Trans from the German by Heinz Norden. New York: Berkley Books, p. 182.

Kostanian-Danzig, R. 2002. *Spiritual Resistance in the Vilna Ghetto.* Vilnius: Vilna Goan Jewish State Museum, pp. 41–52.

Laska, V. 1983. *Women in the Resistance and in the Holocaust: The Voices of Witnesses.* Foreword by Simon Wiesenthal. Westport: Greenwood Press.

Lazowski, E. S. and Matulewicz, S. 1977. "Deception by Immunization." *ASM News* (Monthly Bulletin), American Society of Microbiology (June) pp. 43, 300.

Lenski, M. 1975. "Problems of Disease in the Warsaw Ghetto." *Yad Vashem Studies* 3:283–293.

Lifton, R. J. 1986. *The Nazi Doctors: Medical Killing and the Psychology of Genocide.* New York: Basic Books.

Lingens, E. 1966. *Eine Frau im Konzentrationslager.* Vienna: Europa Verlag, p. 23.

Ludwik Fleck: Founder of the Philosophy of Modern Medicine. 1992. *The Canc. J.* no. 6, 5:304–305.

Michalcyzyk, J., ed. 1994. *Medicine Ethics and the Third Reich: Historical and Contemporary Issues.* Kansas City: Sheed and Ward, p. 84.

Minney, R. J. 1966. *I Shall Fear No Evil: The Story of Dr. Alina Brewda.* London: Kimber.

Mishell, W. W. 1988. *Kadish for Kovno: Life and Death in a Lithuanian Ghetto 1941–1945.* Chicago: Chicago Review Press, pp. 320–322.

Morrison, J. G. 2000. *Ravensbruck.* Princeton, NJ: Marcus Weiner Publishers, p. 298.

Nahon, M. 1989. *Birkenau: The Camp of Death.* Tuscaloosa: University of Alabama Press.

Nevins, M. 2004. Moral Dilemmas Faced by Jewish Doctors During the Holocaust. Chevra/Sig. http://www.apfmed.org/chevra/holocaust.htm (accessed May 17).

Nyiszli, M. 1993. *Auschwitz: A Doctor's Eyewitness Account.* New York: Arcade Publishing, p. 95.

Pawelczynska, A. 1979. *Values and Violence in Auschwitz.* Berkeley: University of California Press.

Perl, G. 1979. *I Was a Doctor in Auschwitz.* New York: Arno Press.

Proctor, R. 1988. *Racial Hygiene: Medicine under the Nazis.* Cambridge, MA: Harvard University Press, p. 167.

Ringelblum, E. 1958. *Notes from the Warsaw Ghetto.* New York: McGraw-Hill.

Roland, C. 1992. Hirszfeldowna: The Story of One Life. In C. G. Roland, *Courage Under Siege.* New York: Oxford University Press, pp. 214, 266.

Romney, C. 1996. Ethical Problems Encountered by Auschwitz Prisoner Doctors. Paper presented at YIVO, New York.

Shoskes, H. 1945. *No Traveler Returns.* Garden City, NY. Doubleday, Doran and Co., pp. xiii, 56, 267.

Sloan, J., ed. 1974. *Notes from the Warsaw Ghetto: The Journal of Emmanuel Ringelblum.* New York: Schocken Books, p. 219.

Steiner, J.-F. 1947. *Treblinka.* Preface by Simone de Beauvoir, trans. from the French by Helen Weaver. New York: Signet Books, New American Library, pp. 172–173.

Sun Times Company. 2004. He Duped Nazis, Saved Thousands. http://www.stjoenj.net/lazowski/lazowski.html (accessed March 30).

Taylor, T. 1946. Statements: Nuremberg Medical Case. 1:57–58.

Tory, A. 1990. *Surviving the Holocaust: The Kovo Ghetto Diary*. Cambridge, MA: Harvard University Press, pp. 43, 141–143.

Trunk, I. 1953. Epidemics and Mortality in the Warsaw Ghetto 1939–1942. In YIVO annual of *Jewish Social Science*, vol. vii.

———. 1996. *Judenrat: The Jewish Councils in Eastern Europe*. Lincoln: University of Nebraska Press, pp. 115–143.

Tushnet, L. 1966. *The Uses of Adversity. Studies of Starvation in the Warsaw Ghetto*. New York: Thomas Yoseloff.

Yodaiken, R. 1996. Moral Dilemmas Faced by Jewish Doctors During the Holocaust. Paper presented at the Medical Resistance During the Holocaust conference. YIVO, New York.

Verfolgte Arzte im Nationalsozialismus. 1999. Dokumentation zur Ausstellung uber das SA-Gefangnis General–Pape–Strasse, Berlin: RKI.

Vrba, R. (Walter Rosenberg). 1997. *I Cannot Forgive!* Vancouver: Regent Press.

Weindling, P. 1996. Delousing and Resistance During the Holocaust. Paper presented at the YIVO Medical Resistance During the Holocaust Conference, New York.

Weyers, W. 1998. *Death of Medicine in Nazi Germany: Dermatology and Dermatopathology under the Swastika*, B. Ackerman, ed. Philadelphia: Madison Books, p. 2.

Wroblewski, J., Director State Museum Auschwitz-Birkenau. 1998. Personal communication (December 3).

Wulf, S. 1994. *Das Hamburger Tropeninstitut 1919–1945*. Hamburg: Dietrich Reimer Verlag, p. 117.

Zeitlin, A. 1978. *Janusz Korczak Ghetto Diary: The Last Walk of Janusz Korczak*. New York: Holocaust Library.

CHAPTER 4

Pharmaceutical Companies, Typhus Vaccines, Drugs, Doctors, and Inhuman Experiments

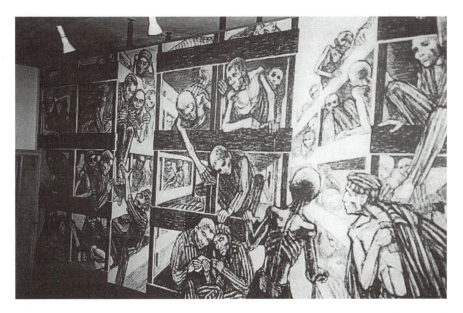

Drawing of prisoners in barracks. *Sachsenhausen Memorial and Museum/ Brandenberg Memorials Foundation. Photo: N. Baumslag.*

Sure, there are people who have hated each other for centuries, but that one kills people so systematically, with the help of physicians, only because they belong to another race. That is new in the world.

Brother of Chief SS Auschwitz doctor

The results of the experiments were of minimal value and were carried out by insufficiently competent individuals without much scientific rigor and in complete contempt for and total negation of human beings.

Waitz, Buchenwald prisoner doctor

Health care professionals enjoy an elevated position in society. For this reason it is all the more reprehensible when some doctors commit atrocities and conduct horrific unethical experiments. Never in the history of humankind has a medical profession as a whole perpetrated and tolerated without protest such widespread atrocities as were performed by German health professionals and researchers during World War II. Furthermore, never has such a grand scale of human experimentation occurred. After World War I, Germany attempted to win back colonies and regain international prestige and pharmaceutical markets (Wess 1993; Wulf 1994). In the absence of colonies, they used the occupied territories, ghettos and concentration camps to continue their unethical research and pharmaceutical and vaccine development.

A lack of adequate documentation and contradictory evidence makes it difficult to determine the exact scale of the experiments, although we may draw conclusions from what is available from concentration camp archives and transcripts from the medical trials and survivor testimony. Because the SS destroyed most records when they left the camps, it is not known exactly how many SS doctors, medical students, and foreigners were involved. At least 350 qualified doctors (including university professors and lecturers) were involved in concentration camp experiments and this represents one out of every 300 members of the medical community (Cornwell 2003, p. 357; Mitscherlich and Mielke 1949, p. 17). This figure is likely a gross underestimate. Evidence of the participation of medical schools suggests a much higher figure.

The same medical officers who supervised disinfection and delousing in the East and supplied Zyclon B gas to the extermination camps were also responsible for coordinating typhus research. They worked with or within public health institutions and concentration camp research stations that were integrated into the network of Nazi SS typhus research. There was international cooperation in typhus research, and the vaccines tested in the camps came from many centers such as Copenhagen, Zurich, Bucharest, Paris, and research institutes throughout Germany and the occupied territories.[1] Supplies were also obtained from different countries. Sweden, for example, provided the Nazis with ultraviolet technology for their rickettsial research (Weindling 2000).

The perpetrators of the large-scale experimentation were neither psychotic nor disturbed. They were doctors and scientists, many of them extremely well trained and experienced. Nevertheless, they pursued their own vicious, unconscionable research. Professor Kurt Gutzeit, a gastroenterologist at Breslau University, carried out hepatitis experiments on Jewish children. Professor Heinrich Berning of Hamburg University conducted famine experiments on Russian POWs, watching them starve to death as he recorded the results. Professor Robert Neuman carried out liver biopsies and other dissections on healthy subjects while they were alive, and other professors like Rose, Gildemeister, and Haagen directed and supervised concentration camp research. For the most part, however, the SS doctors were incompetent and poorly trained, including the cruel Drs. Ding, Hoven, Vetter, and Entress. Younger Nazi medical officers passed through medical school shortened by two years, with a distorted militarized curriculum focused on race hygiene. The doctors trained from 1933 to 1945 during the Nazi regime lacked medical expertise and emerged as a professional liability. Medical students practiced surgery on prisoners without supervision, adequate training, or regard for the victims.

Why were these doctors so unscrupulous in their professional conduct? It seems that many doctors in the camps were outright opportunists. Some German doctors took assignments in the concentration camps to give the impression they were conducting important and prolonged research so that they could avoid going to the front. Others, like Entress and Vetter, who carried out research on behalf of chemical and pharmaceutical companies had a financial motive for their experiments. The concentration camps provided opportunities for promotion, status, improving skills, living well, and even prospering. Doctors were able to conduct unsupervised research, and many researchers considered the ghettos and concentration camps a vast reservoir of experimental material. They hoped they would gain a reputation from the experiments, and the grandeur of the science and its practitioners completely eclipsed the suffering of the subjects involved (Kogon 1980, p. 95). No doctor–patient relationship existed, and doctors distanced themselves by classifying Jews, Slavs, Roma (gypsies), the disabled, and impaired as *untermenschen*—lesser beings of no consequence—or more aptly as *nonmenschen*.

A. Block 46 was a dreaded forbidden area where typhus cases were isolated and experiments on prisoners conducted.

B. In block 50 typhus vaccines were produced by prisoner doctors and researchers for the German army.

C. Special accommodation was provided for prisoner doctors and researchers in block 50.

Figure 4.1: Buchenwald concentration camp conducted typhus experiments and produced vaccines. *Museum of the Resistance and Deportation, Besancon, France.*

Many experiments bordered on lunacy. Widespread and varied research in the camps included outright cruelty, whims of fancy, experiments to determine the effects of sterilization, gas, gangrene, freezing, and altitude. Doctors also were involved in researching a variety of infectious diseases, including typhus, yellow fever, smallpox, paratyphoid, cholera, diphtheria, malaria, and tuberculosis, and investigated associated toxic chemicals. This chapter focuses primarily on the conduct of physicians with typhus epidemics and their experiments with vaccines and pharmaceuticals.

From December 1941 until near the end of World War II a large program of medical experimentation was carried out on concentration camp inmates at Buchenwald and Natzweiler, and to a lesser extent at Auschwitz, Mauthausen, Gusen, Dachau, Sachsenhausen and Ravensbrück, to investigate the value of typhus vaccines and drugs (Figure 4.1). Nazi doctors saw their vaccine research as revitalized but were only applying vaccines already developed in the United States, Poland, and France. The stated aim of their research was to give German soldiers better medical aid, but the typhus (*Fleckfieber*) experiments had little or no scientific value and thousands died as a result (Cohen 1988). Nazi doctors like Erwin Ding and Eugen Haagen deliberately infected hundreds of prisoners with typhus at Buchenwald and Natzweiler concentration camps for vaccine experiments. Dr. Karl Gross infected prisoners with typhus for vaccine experiments at Gusen. The mortality from these experiments was enormous and in some series as high as 98 percent (Kogon 1980).

The chemical giant I.G. Farben, with close ties to the drug companies Bayer and Hoechst, was heavily invested in the experiments in an attempt to dominate vaccine and pharmaceutical production and sell incalculable amounts to the army. Moreover, the conglomerate was a driving force behind drug experiments that caused horrific side effects and death. The exact number of victims and substances tested are not known, for the majority of I.G. Farben's files marked "Auschwitz" were empty. Officials declared materials had been sent to the paper mills because of an acute paper shortage in the Third Reich (Mikulski 1976, p. 224).

UNETHICAL EXPERIMENTS: SCIENTIFIC BUTCHERY

The Nazi medical professionals violated standard ethical practice by conducting experiments on concentration camp prisoners. Their oath of allegiance to Hitler took precedence over any ethical code. In the pursuit of scientific knowledge, these scientists put their own convenient moral standard forward: killing or maiming a few was justified in order to save the masses—especially if those few were considered enemies of the state or expendable.

There is a long history of experimentation on prisoners and people of so-called inferior races. With improved technology in the 1880s bacteriologists approached research with renewed vigor and saw themselves as waging war on disease. Their rationale was that as long as they advanced medical science through their research, scientific progress took precedence over the rights of an individual. Rudolf Virchow, the renowned pathologist and humanist, condemned bacteriologist researchers as "poisoners and murderers" for their excessive experiments. For some doctors there were no limits. In 1895, Professor Albert Neisser, in his search for a syphilis vaccine, injected young prostitutes with a cell-free syphilis serum. The subjects were not volunteers, and one prostitute was only ten years old. Some of the women developed syphilis and there was a public outcry when his unethical research was exposed. Neisser received a warning and an insignificant fine (Ley and Ruisinger 2001, pp. 23–25). Public clamor continued to increase against human experimentation, and the Berlin City Council, of which Virchow was a member, issued an official response to the Neisser controversy. As a result, the Berlin Code of 1900 declared that human experiments could only be conducted on fully informed, consenting volunteers. Research on children and the incompetent was also banned (Deutsch 2003). Many researchers ignored the code, however.

In the early twentieth century, German doctors experimented on colonials in South West Africa (Namibia). The German anthropologist Eugen Fischer conducted racial tests on German settlers who had interbred with Hottentots. He later conducted tests on Hereros in German concentration camps in South West Africa (Namibia) designed to confirm their racial inferiority (Weale 2001). Robert Koch experimented on Africans to study sleeping sickness. In 1916 Turkish physicians conducted typhus experiments on Ottoman Armenians at a hospital in Central Turkey. The subjects were given the blood of typhus patients and told the injections were meant to cure them. As a result, a great number of Armenians contracted typhus but the experiments yielded no useful results. Drs. Nazim and Benhaeddin Sakir, leading physicians in the experiments, later fled the country and took refuge in Berlin (Dadrian 1986).

In the 1920s Dr. Julius Moses, a social democrat, mounted a campaign against human experimentation. In the early 1930s, a scandal in Lubeck resulted in a major resurgence in public outrage. Dr. Ernst Deycke injected hundreds of newborns against TB in France, Mexico, and Latvia with no ill effects. German doctors, however, were against these inoculations because they considered them risky. Despite their concerns, Deycke inoculated 256 children in Lubeck. Tragically, 77 died from TB and 131 became ill. When it was determined that the vaccine developed in the general hospital was contaminated with pathogens, Deycke was convicted and sent to prison for one year. Neisser's and Deycke's experiments fueled the campaign against unethical experimentation by medical researchers, and the Reich's government responded by promulgating the Guidelines for New Therapy and Human Experimentation in 1931. The guidelines stated that nontherapeutic research was not permitted without the subject's consent. Experimentation on dying patients was not permitted, and the guidelines provided special protection for children. This legislation was way ahead of its time and was never annulled. The Nazis ignored these guidelines and dispensed with all restrictions on human experimentation in the concentration camps (Ley and Ruisinger 2001; Weyers 1998).

VACCINE DEVELOPMENT

Vaccine research opened the door for the criminal unethical research conducted in the concentration camps. Centuries ago Asian physicians crudely vaccinated children with dried crusts from the lesions of people suffering from smallpox to protect them against the disease. Although some developed immunity, others developed the disease. Smallpox was a terrible disease, and in 1796 the British physician Edward Jenner provided protection against it by inoculating people with the cowpox virus (vaccinia), a related virus (Figure 4.2). This protection was considered miraculous. Jenner's principle of vaccination was to use a substance similar to, but safer than, smallpox to confer immunity. Jenner's discovery spurred the development of other vaccines. In 1881 French microbiologist Louis Pasteur developed an anthrax vaccine by injecting sheep with a preparation containing an attenuated, weakened form of the anthrax bacillus.

The challenge of vaccine development is to devise one strong enough to prevent an infection without making the individual seriously ill. Many variations have been developed, but in general vaccines are made of weakened or killed microorganisms or toxins that have lost the ability to cause serious illness but have the ability to stimulate immunity.[2] Vaccines against rabies, polio (the Salk vaccine), some forms of influenza, and cholera are of this type. Since Pasteur's time, medical researchers have conducted a widespread and intensive search for new vaccines. Smallpox has been virtually eradicated worldwide, and polio has been substantially reduced through vaccination.

Figure 4.2: Jenner was instrumental in starting the vaccine hunt. His vaccine against the devastating smallpox disease is best illustrated by this 1800 etching that depicts the history of vaccination from an economic view: a pharmacy for sale, an outmoded inoculist selling his premises, and Jenner, to the left, pursuing a skeleton with a lancet. *Welcome Library, London.*

FRANTIC COMPETITION: VACCINE RESEARCH AND PRODUCTION

In 1941 typhus was highly prevalent among the German troops, in the general government, and in the camps and prisons in Germany owing to bad hygiene, overcrowding, and an influx of Russian POWs. Hundreds of lice-infested German soldiers were dying from typhus every day on the Eastern front. There was a desperate uncoordinated effort to produce typhus vaccines for the German soldiers and civilians. The Robert Koch Institute in Berlin was contracted to provide vaccine for the Luftwaffe.

Institutes in the occupied territories were taken over and plundered for vaccines—for example, in Kiev (Ukraine), Riga (Latvia), Dorplat (Estonia), Dolschi (Belarus), and Kauen, the German name for Kaunas (Lithuania). Behring, an I.G. Farben subsidiary and Germany's leading commercial producer of sera and vaccines, sought control of vaccine production and confiscated 20 million ccs of vaccines from the captured Soviet vaccine institutes (Weindling 1995). Hygiene centers were commandeered and new ones established with typhus research as part of their mission.[3] German pharmaceutical companies, public health institutes, and the SS established competing vaccine production plants in the occupied East.

Production of the typhus vaccine proved to be challenging because rickettsia, the causative organism of typhus, are difficult to culture. No suitable artificial media existed at that time. In 1925 Drs. R.R. Spencer and R.R. Parker developed a vaccine for Rocky Mountain spotted fever, a related disease transmitted by ticks. The vaccine was prepared from tick intestines infected with rickettsiae and an antimicrobial chemical (Gross). Based on this work, Polish zoologist Professor Rudolf Stefan Weigl developed the first successful typhus vaccine at his institute in Lwow, Poland (now Ukraine).[4] His louse-based vaccine was produced on a large scale prior to World War II and was used successfully to reduce the mortality from typhus in China and Ethiopia in the 1930s (Szybalski 1996). However, it did not prevent the disease (Figure 4.3).

The Weigl vaccine was dangerous and tedious to produce (Eyer 1967). The procedure involved inoculating lice rectally with virulent rickettsiae. Lice were kept in small boxes resembling matchboxes with a screen on one side. The lice could then feed on human blood by pricking skin through the screen. The lice had to feed for a week after infection on highly immunized persons, and many of the human feeders, including Weigl, contracted typhus. After a week the lice were killed and their infected stomach and intestinal cells were ground up with phenolized saline to prepare the vaccine. An enormous louse farm had to be maintained for a sufficient quantity of vaccine to be prepared; approximately 100 lice were required to yield enough vaccine for just one subject (Gross 1996; Szybalski 1996).

Because the vaccine did not prevent the disease and large-scale production was problematic, a variety of alternative methods to culture the typhus organism were developed. Herrald Cox of the U.S. Public Health Services found that rickettsiae grew without difficulty in chicken embryos, enabling large-scale production (Gross 1996). The Cox vaccine was popular among U.S. and British forces during World War II, and due to this vaccine and the use of DDT there were only 104 cases of typhus in all the Allied armed forces and no deaths (Kiple 1997). Other vaccines were prepared from mouse liver, mouse lung, dog lung, rabbit lung and chicken embryo (see Chart 1). Otto and Bichardt found mouse lung vaccines to be superior in the protection of guinea pigs in 1942. The Pasteur Institute had links to German and Allied research throughout World War II. In April 1944 for example, the Wehrmacht bought large quantities of rabbit lung vaccine from Professor

A.

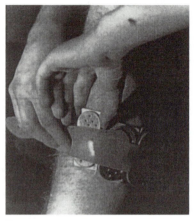

B.

C.

Figure 4.3: A. The Behring Institute, Lemberg, where Weigl's louse vaccine was prepared with much effort and some risk. **B.** Louse feeding box. **C.** Louse feeders wore louse boxes attached to the mid-calf or mid-thigh so they could feed the lice. *Behring Archives, Emil-von-Behring-Bibliothek for Medicine, Philipps University, Marburg, Germany.*

TYPHUS VACCINES TESTED ON BUCHENWALD
CONCENTRATION CAMP PRISONERS

Behring Works
Yolk sac (2 strengths normal/ normal str.) Gildemeister's and Haagen's serum used Cox methodology

Weigl Vaccine
Louse intestine. Institute for Typhus and Virus Research of the Army High Command, Cracow.

Duran-Giroud
Rabbit lung. Pasteur Institute, Paris.

Cantacuzino
Dog lung. Bucharest. Made available by Professor Rose

Ipsen Vaccine
Mouse liver. State Serum Institute, Copenhagen. Made available by Professor G. Rose

Source: E. Kogon, *The Theory and Practice of Hell*. Berkley Books, 1998, p. 156.

Chart 1: Vaccines produced in block 50 Buchenwald concentration camp were for the Wehrmacht. *Photo: Buchenwald Memorial Museum Archives.*

Paul Giroud of the Pasteur Institute in Paris for a substantial sum (28 million francs) (Chevassus-au-Louis, February 13, 2004). Nazi doctor Ernst Ding in 1943 claimed that his studies showed that rabbit lung, dog lung, and Cox vaccines were equally satisfactory and yielded results equal to Weigl's louse vaccine. However, Ding's studies were flawed and unethical, and his findings were invalid.

No sound conclusions on the relative protective value of these different vaccines have been made. None of the vaccines protected individuals against the disease itself, but some shortened the fever, diminished nervous symptoms, and decreased the severity of the disease. Evidence indicates that vaccination does not prevent an attack of the disease if exposure to infection is severe (Wilson et al. 1984).

ESCALATING RESEARCH AND BARBARISM: FROM THE GHETTOS TO THE CAMPS

In 1941 typhus was taking a toll on the front, and there was a shortage of guinea pigs for testing the various typhus vaccines and drugs. The heads of the military and civilian medical services of the Reich, Drs. Handloser and Conti, respectively, held a monumental conference on December 29, 1941. Professor Dr. Joachim Mrugowsky (Waffen SS), Professor Dr. Gildemeister (President of the Robert Koch Institute in Berlin), and Professor Hans Reiter (Office of Reich Health) attended. The Nazi doctors concluded that *as animal tests cannot provide adequate evaluation of typhus vaccines, experiments on human beings must be conducted.* According to one concentration camp doctor, rats were more expensive than concentration camp prisoners. Initially, Professor Dr. Gerhard Rose objected to the idea of using prisoners for experimentation, but Conti argued that German public health was at stake. Rose acquiesced and later initiated a study of the Ipsen mouse liver vaccine from Copenhagen on concentration camp prisoners. The Doctors Trial sentenced Rose to life imprisonment for his involvement in the inhuman typhus experiments (Figure 4.4).

The Nazi doctors and the German pharmaceutical industry began experimenting with vaccines and drugs on Jews in the Cyste Hospital and Warsaw Ghetto as early as 1939 (Wulf 1994). Dr. Ernst Georg Nauck, a pathologist at the Hamburg Hygiene Institute (now Bernard Nocht Institute for Tropical Medicine), headed a typhus research unit in the Warsaw State Institute. He and several other doctors from the Hamburg Institute did their research there and made posters, a film, and other educational materials on typhus. From November to December 1941, Dr. Robert Kudicke tested a new Behring typhus vaccine on 228 Jews under a variety of pretexts; 24 developed severe

Figure 4.4: Professor Gerhard Rose, advisor for Tropical Medicine to the Chief of Medical Services of the Luftwaffe, was initially opposed to using prisoners for human experimentation. In December 1941 he wrote to Professor Gildemeister, director of the Robert Koch Institute, that by doing so they were producing executioners. However in 1943 he provided the Copenhagen and Bucharest vaccines for testing in Buchenwald concentration camp. He is shown here at the Nuremberg Doctors Trial in 1947 making a final plea, "I was far removed from the experiments themselves." *NARA.*

reactions. Nazi doctors forced the staff of the Cyste Hospital in Warsaw to test sulphonamide drugs in typhus cases for I.G. Farben, including the toxic Uliron which caused blueness and death. Jewish doctors wanted to stop the drug trial, but the Germans threatened them with punitive action (Roland 1992; Trunk 1972). Nauck filmed the subjects and autopsied the dead (Figure 4.5).[5]

Figure 4.5: German public health doctors Walter Menk, Peter Mühlens, and Ernst George Nauck, from the Hamburg Tropical Hygiene Institute were involved in medical mass crimes and conducted typhus experiments in the Cyste Hospital using untested sulphonamide drugs, like uliron, on prisoners sick with typhus. They continued their experiments in Langhorn Mental Hospital and Neuegamme concentration camp. None of these perpetrators were tried. Nauck, a rabid anti-Semite who blamed Jews for typhus, became director of the Institute after Mühlens. These doctors were part of the sinister history of what is, since 1945, the Bernard Nocht Institute. *Bernard Nocht Institute, Hamburg.*

Experimentation in the concentration camps was placed under the jurisdiction of the Hygiene Institute of the Waffen SS in Berlin. Dr. Joachim Mrugowsky was the military superior and commander of the hygiene institutes that developed in the course of the war (Figure 4.6). Incredibly, in 1939 Mrugowsky edited a popular book on medical ethics titled *Ethos* (Hufeland, C.W., Das Arzliche, cited in Proctor 1992, p. 298). SS Gruppenführer Dr. Grawitz was his chief from 1943 and reported to SS Reichsfuhrer Heinrich Himmler, who was also head of the Gestapo and the Waffen SS. Himmler would avoid arrest for his crimes against humanity and certain execution. Grawitz later committed suicide (Moorehead 1998, p. 526).

Figure 4.6: Colonel Joachim Mrugowsky was chief SS hygienist and responsible for seeing that Zyclon B reached the gas chambers. He was hanged in Landsberg for his crimes against humanity, including typhus research. From the gallows he shouted, "I die as a German officer sentenced by a brutal enemy." *NARA.*

BUCHENWALD BUTCHERS: CHAIN OF COMMAND

Virus research at Buchenwald was headed by the nefarious SS Captain Ernst Ding. Ding was a typical Nazi physician, who as a student had joined the Nazi Party, the SA Storm Troopers (*Sturmabteilungen*), also known as "Brown Shirts," and the SS (*Schuetzstaffel*), also known as "Black Shirts." He apparently obtained his medical diploma through party relations in 1937, and in 1938 he became a camp physician in Buchenwald (Fleck, L., cited in Cohen and Schnelle 1986). He received some training in bacteriology at RKI, and in 1942 he went to the Pasteur Institute to learn to produce Giroud's rabbit lung vaccine (Chevassus-au-Louis, personal communication, December 2003). Ding was nasty and cruel at times. Ambitious and deceptive, he was more a creature of the SS than an accomplished research scientist. His demeanor suggested a highly trained professional, though in reality he was an incompetent scientist and a fraud. Ding covered his lack of scientific expertise by relying on prisoner researchers and left the execution of the experiments to a criminal prisoner kapo with no medical training (Poller 1960) (Figure 4.7).

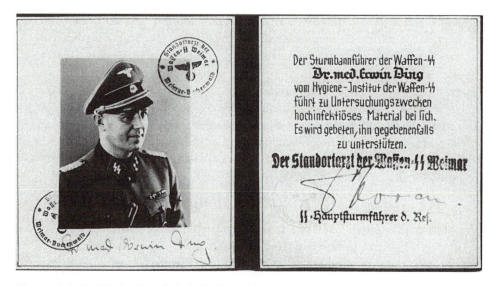

Figure 4.7: Dr. Erwin Ding-Schuler's 1944 identity card allowed him to transport infectious materials. Poller, a Buchenwald conentration camp prisoner, described Ding: "this splendid head intended by nature to carry out valuable work for suffering humanity, had been hollowed out and refilled with the starch of Nazi doctrine." *Buchenwald Memorial Museum Archives.*

The typhus experiments carried out in 1942 and 1943 were under the supervision of Drs. Karl Genzken and Joachim Mrugowsky. Genzken and others arranged for the selection of victims through other branches of the SS and gave directions to their underlings such as Waldemar Hoven and Siegfried Handloser.[6] Requests for human subjects for experimentation were turned over to and filled by the station medical officer of the Waffen SS. The Wehrmacht provided supervision and technical assistance for some experiments, and the eminent Dr. Rose periodically appeared for the Luftwaffe to give expert guidance to Ding.

Ding gave orders but did not spend much time in the typhus blocks because he was hopelessly afraid of typhus. Ironically, he contracted the disease accidentally in the course of conducting experiments (Hackett 1995; Poller 1960). Hoven supervised the experimental station in Ding's absence and remained in charge until he was arrested in September 1943. He was succeeded by the equally vicious SS Captain Dr. Gerhard Schiedlausky (Hackett 1995,

p. 219). In the Nuremberg Doctors Trial Hoven was found guilty of personally conducting brutal experiments; he was hanged in 1948.

BARBARISM: HUMAN GUINEA PIGS AND SECRECY

Beginning in 1941, typhus experiments were conducted at Buchenwald on at least 1000 prisoners (Kogon 1980). Early on, prisoners were enticed to volunteer with promises of food and the deceptive claim that the research was harmless. They were never told that they would be given typhus artificially. They were given extra rations, but after one or two experiments word got out and it became impossible to find more "volunteers." From then on the camp physician or headquarters provided prisoners for the experiments. Initially, those named were supposedly men sentenced to death or serving sentences that had ten or more years to run, but that was evidently not the case.

In January 1943, the typhus clinical station in block 46 was officially named the Division of Typhus and Virus Research of the Institute of Hygiene of the Waffen SS under the control of the Wehrmacht. A special laboratory was set up in block 50 for production of typhus vaccines. The laboratory was well equipped with valuable instruments, microscopes and other apparatus confiscated from Eastern laboratories and purchased or taken as booty from the French (Kogon 1980, p. 161; Hackett 1995, p. 73). Vaccine production began in August 1943, and prisoner scientists and doctors were made to produce 30 to 50 liters of vaccine each month.

In block 46 experiments to test vaccines and drugs were conducted, and the course of the disease was followed. Naturally occurring typhus cases were ostensibly treated as well. No one was allowed to enter without permission, and the block was isolated and enclosed in double barbed wire. The barrack looked like a luxurious hospital with 90 real beds, with clean bedclothes and eiderdowns covered with nice blue and white checkered fabric. The windows were milked out, and there was strict discipline and silence about activities (Waitz and Ciepielowski 1946). The SS avoided the block because they falsely believed one could contract typhus through inhalation.

The experiments conducted on prisoners in Buchenwald concentration camp tested the efficacy of typhus sera of different origins: egg yolk sac cultures using modified Cox methodology by Gildemeister and Haagen; the Weigl louse vaccine, produced from louse gut by the Institute for Typhus and Virus research of the Army High Command at Cracow; and the Durand-Giroud serum prepared from rabbit lungs at the Pasteur Institute, Paris (see Chart 2). Professor Rose, contrary to his earlier reservations about human experimentation, made available a dog lung serum by Cantacuzino, in Bucharest, and a Danish serum from mouse liver, as mentioned earlier, for

TYPHUS SERUM TESTS

Deliberately Infected TP's		No Serum (Controls)	Actually Infected	Fatalities	
Serum Used				With Serum	Controls
Weigl	31				
Cox-Gildemeister-Haagen	35	10	143	1	3
Behring, normal	35				
Behring, normal str.	34				
Durand and Giroud	20	19	59		4
Combiescu & Zotta	20				
Giroud	20	6			
Weigl	25	10	5		
Zurich	20				
Riga	20				
Asid	20			18	
Asid adsorbate	20	10	70	18	8
Weigl	20			9	
Kobenhagen (Ibsen)	17	9	26	3	3
Weimar	5			1	
Giroud	5	5	20		3
Asid	5			1	
Weimar	20	20	60	15	19
Weigl	20				
Total	392	89	383	66	40

A.

TYPHUS THERAPY TESTS

Deliberately Infected TP's		Without Special Therapy (Controls)	Fatalities	
Therapy Test With			Treated TP's	Controls
Acridine	20	7	1 (Infection partly ineffective)	
Methylene Blue	20			
Rutenol	15	9	8	5
Acridine Gran.	15		8	
Typhus Serum Intravenous	10	5	9	4
Intramuscular	10		6	
	90	21	32	9

B.

Chart 2: Experiments were conducted in block 46 Buchenwald concentration camp on prisoners without their consent and regardless of the horrific outcome. **A.** Typhus vaccine experiments. **B.** Typhus drug experiments. (Note: TP = typhus patient; serum = vaccine.) *Source: A. Mitscherlich and F. Mielke,* Doctors of Infamy. *New York: H. Schuman, 1949, pp. 45, 46.*

further experiments in prisoners. In addition to the vaccine experiments, a number of toxic and untested pharmaceuticals, as well as unnamed but numbered preparations, were tested on prisoners without their knowledge or consent. For this experimentation, a third group of prisoners was used as carriers, "human reservoirs," to maintain live typhus strains. The Austrian sociologist Dr. Eugen Kogon, a political prisoner who was ward secretary to Ding from April 1943, was in a unique position to observe the experiments at Buchenwald. His stirring words summarize the horrors he witnessed:

> Every man in Buchenwald knew that barrack 46 was a dreadful place. . . . A dreadful horror seized anyone who was brought into any kind of connection with this block. If people were selected and taken to block 46 through the sick bay, then they knew it was the end of them. The untold horror which was attached to this block made things even worse. . . .
>
> Everyone, therefore, who went to block 46 as an experimental person did not only have to expect death and under certain circumstances a very long drawn out and frightful death, but torture and the complete removal of the last remnants of freedom. In this mental condition these experimental persons waited in the sick bays for an unknown period of time. They waited for the day or night when something was to be done to them; they did not know what it would be, but they guessed it would be a frightful form of death. If they were vaccinated then some of the most horrible scenes took place because the patients were afraid the injections were lethal . . . there were cases of raving madness, delirium, people would refuse to eat, and a large percentage of them would die. Those who experienced the disease in the milder form, perhaps because their constitutions were stronger or because the vaccine was effective were forced continuously to observe the death struggles of others. Experiments produced agonizing deaths (Kogon 1980, p. 94).

By the end of 1944 there had been twenty-four series of documented experiments (Kogon 1980). Although the mortality of typhus was normally 30 to 40 percent in unprotected cases, some experiments carried a 100 percent mortality rate. The experiments were numerous and technically complicated; only a few are mentioned in this chapter to illustrate the unscrupulous unethical behavior of the doctors involved.

HUMAN INCUBATORS FOR TYPHUS ORGANISMS: VACCINES, DRUGS, AND "PASSAGE PERSONS"

A general procedural pattern for experiments was established in Buchenwald and was subsequently followed in other camps. Typhus vaccine experiments

began with the selec-
tion of a group of the
healthiest inmates with
some resistance to the
disease. They were in-
oculated and then in-
fected with typhus to
test the efficacy of the
vaccine. At the same
time, a control group
of prisoners (compari-
son group) were not
vaccinated but in-
fected with typhus.
The experimental vac-
cines rarely worked
(Kogon 1980, p. 158)
(Figure 4.8).

Experiments were
also conducted to de-
termine how the dose
and point of entry of
injections affected the
incubation period, the
Weil-Felix reaction,
and the severity of ty-
phus. Certain drugs—

Figure 4.8: Dr. Eugen Kogon, an Austrian philosopher, sociologist, and prisoner in Buchenwald, testified at the Nuremberg Doctors Trial and provided Ding's incriminating signed diary with experimental details and results. *NARA.*

particularly sedatives used against typhus encephalitis—were also tested, and the effects on the victims were particularly unpleasant. Experiments with the toxic drug acridin caused subjects to develop severe vomiting of blood and other serious side effects. Ding wanted to stop the experiment because of the ill effects, but the pharmaceutical company sponsoring the study insisted the experiment continue.

Artificial infection of the human subjects was accomplished in various ways. The skin was lacerated and infected with a typhus culture, and some-times infected lice were used. In one instance of incompetence at Buchen-wald, Hoven attempted to artificially infect fifteen experimental patients with typhus-infected lice. Nine of the prisoners died, and the lice leaked from the cages and exposed the camp to an epidemic (Kogon 1980).

Initially, a strain of typhus (*Matelska*) from RKI in Berlin was used to pro-duce the disease, but in April 1943 it was found that it had lost its virulence.

In order to maintain live virus, a group of prisoners was deliberately infected with the sole purpose of keeping typhus alive and available in the blood-stream of the inmates. Each month three to five of these prisoners were used as human incubators, or "passage persons." They were repeatedly injected with lethal doses of typhus-infected blood, sometimes twenty-five or thirty times (Waitz 1945).[7] The prisoners used in the study were deceptively called "volunteers" in so-called good physical condition (Ding 1943). The ruthless Arthur Dietzsch, a kapo with no medical background or experience, ran the block and performed the inoculations from man to man. The virulence of this mode of transmission was high and caused such severe infections that within hours virtually all of these victims died (Kogon 1980).

Most of the subjects of the typhus experiments in the camps died, and if they did not die, they were killed after results were recorded (see Chapter 2). Evidence from the Nuremberg Doctors Trials suggests that it was common-place to deliberately infect subjects to induce death. On one occasion, Mru-gowsky ordered an experiment to establish the most effective method of injecting blood from passage persons into otherwise uninfected prisoners (IV or IM). Of the twenty-five victims nineteen died (Kogon 1980).

The value of these atrocious experiments is questionable at best (Berger 1990). The clinical vaccine and drug trials in the ghettos and camps were sci-entifically unsound and statistically flawed. The experimental subjects were emaciated, fatigued, terrorized concentration camp victims and not represen-tative of healthy German troops. Vaccine production was not standardized, and batches were often ineffective. Many prisoners who were inoculated died because the experimental vaccines were too diluted.

The method of infecting prisoners with typhus bordered on lunacy and re-flects the incompetence of the scientists. The experiments tested an artificial infection passed from man to man and not from louse to man, the natural mode of infection. Although the amount of infected blood administered was eventually decreased to one tenth of a cc, the effect was still deadly because the virulence of the strain had increased by transmission through human car-riers. In addition, typhus-infected blood was given by intravenous injection, whereas lice pass the infection through their feces when it is scratched into a louse bite (Kogon 1980, p. 158).

DOCUMENTATION AT BUCHENWALD: DING'S DIARY

> Nowhere will the evidence in this case reveal more wicked and murder-ous course of conduct by men who claim to practice the healing art than in the entries of Dr. Dings diary relating to the typhus experiments.
>
> Medical Trials

Figure 4.9: Captain Waldemar Hoven, former chief doctor at Buchenwald concentration camp, was a "spritz" (syringe) doctor. He was tried and charged with conspiracy to commit crimes against humanity, for participating in the typhus experiments, the euthanasia program, and membership in the SS. *NARA.*

The SS destroyed documentation from the Buchenwald studies before the Americans entered the camp. Fortunately, Dr. Kogon kept a typed diary written retrospectively. What was crucial was that Ding had signed every page, and so this diary served as critical evidence presented at the Nuremberg Medical Trials. The diary provided precise details of the studies undertaken, the number of inmates involved, and the outcome. According to the data in Ding's diary, at least 729 inmates were experimented on with typhus, and at least 154 died as a result of these experiments. The 90 to 120 so-called passage persons who died must be added to the figure. According to the former prisoner Dr. Alfred Balachowsky, the number was much higher than 600. Artificial inoculation of typhus by intravenous injection is invariably fatal (Balachowsky testimony in Padfield 1991 p. 307, note 7 A).

Kogon revealed that Dr. Hoven, the chief camp doctor of Buchenwald, had the reputation of murdering inmates with a syringe. He murdered between ninety and one hundred prisoners per week for almost one and a half years with intracardiac injections of phenol or evipan (Kogon 1980, p. 149). It was known at Buchenwald that when Hoven had finished injecting a whole row of prisoners with sodium evipan, he strolled out of the operating room with a cigarette in his hand whistling "the end of a perfect day." Prisoners suffering from typhus feared that if they came to the hospital (*Krankenhaus*) they would die from an injection from Hoven's syringe (Figure 4.9).

In 1944, when it appeared that Germany was losing the war, Ding changed his name to Schuler, the name of his birth father, in an attempt to conceal his record of human experimentation.[8] He concealed the fact that he worked in a research institute in the heart of the Buchenwald camp and often gave the impression he was stationed in Berlin. He had had great hopes that the Buchenwald experiments would enhance his career. His expectations weren't met, and fearing the worst, after the war he committed suicide.

PHARMACEUTICALS AT ANY EXPENSE: EXPERIMENTS AT AUSCHWITZ

Typhus experiments at Auschwitz were carried out in the hospital blocks of the main camp, mostly in block 20, the contagious disease ward, in the women's camp hospital in Birkenau, and in the Monowitz camp hospital. In September 1942, Dr. Eduard Wirths was transferred to Auschwitz as chief doctor to deal with a raging typhus epidemic that was affecting the SS. Wirths sponsored and facilitated most of the experiments in Auschwitz, particularly those that were of interest to Berlin at a high level. He personally conducted typhus trials in which four Jewish prisoners were artificially infected with typhus. They were all killed even though none developed the disease. He ordered that all subsequent experiments be conducted by someone else, presumably to keep his own hands clean (Lifton 1986).

The infamous Dr. Mengele was another unscrupulous experimenter in the concentration camps. With permission from Himmler and funding from the German Society for Research, Mengele conducted his barbaric twin studies at Auschwitz. In one study he infected twins with typhus. He later had the twins killed and sent their preserved organs to Otmar von Verschuer, his supervisor and mentor in Berlin who headed the Kaiser Wilhelm Institute of Anthropology and Human Heredity and Eugenics (Children as Guinea Pigs 2003) and was never prosecuted.

From 1941 until 1944 a number of physicians are known to have tested new drugs on prisoners in Auschwitz, including Drs. Friedrich Entress, Helmuth Vetter and Eduard Wirths, and to a lesser extent Fritz Klein, Werner Rhode, Hans Konig, Victor Capesius (director of the camp pharmacy), and Bruno Weber, director of the SS Hygiene Institute in Raisko near Auschwitz. Raisko was a subordinate part of the Hygiene Institute of the Waffen SS in Berlin and autonomous from camp administration (Weindling 2000). The pharmaceuticals tested included substances that had not yet been put into general use, many of which were toxic (see Chart 3). They were given in various forms (pills, granulated liquid, intravenous and intramuscular injections, and suppositories) to healthy prisoners and to those suffering from contagious diseases. In many cases, unbeknownst to the prisoners, they were deliberately infected with typhus in order to test the efficacy of these substances. The lethal effects of untested pharmaceuticals like B1034 were carefully recorded and sent to Berlin (Figure 4.10).

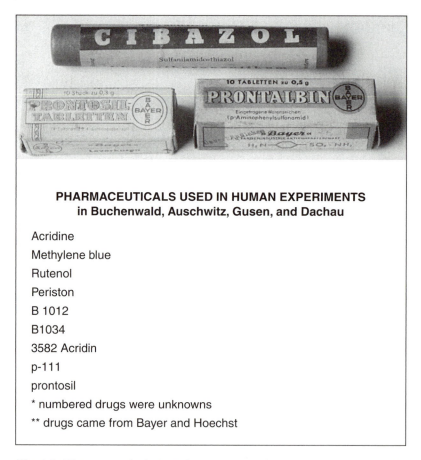

PHARMACEUTICALS USED IN HUMAN EXPERIMENTS
in Buchenwald, Auschwitz, Gusen, and Dachau

Acridine

Methylene blue

Rutenol

Periston

B 1012

B1034

3582 Acridin

p-111

prontosil

* numbered drugs were unknowns

** drugs came from Bayer and Hoechst

Chart 3: Pharmaceuticals tested on concentration camp victims were obtained from Hoechst and Bayer. Many were untested sulphonamides including prontosil and the unknown preparation B-1034. *Photo: Deutches Apothekan-Museum, Heidelberg.*

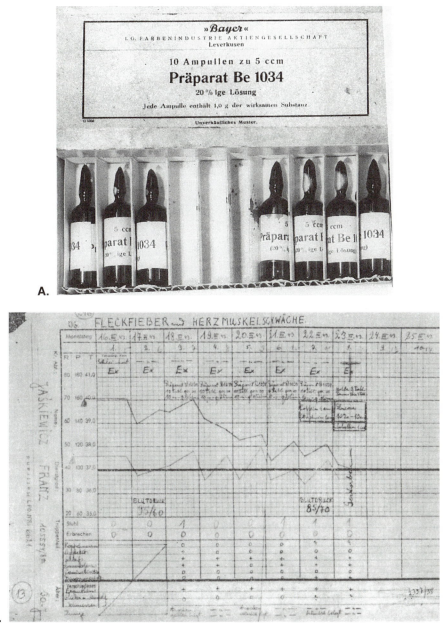

Figure 4.10: A. Bayer preparation B-1034 found on the shelves at Auschwitz. **B.** Detailed records were kept of experiments conducted on prisoners. This chart from Auschwitz concentration camp shows the medical history of a prisoner who was given experimental preparation B-1034 five times and, as a result of the experiment, died on the eighth day. *Auschwitz Concentration Camp Archives.*

DOLLARS AND DRUGS: THE DRIVING FORCE
OF I.G. FARBEN

I.G. Farben, a German economic corporate emporium in the first half of the twentieth century, had a business interest in disease. The acronym I.G. Farben was short for Interessen-Gemeinschaft (interest partnerships), nothing other than a powerful cartel of BASF, Bayer, Hoechst and three other German chemical and pharmaceutical companies.[9] It became extremely powerful after contributing 400,000 marks to Hitler's Nazi Party one year before he seized power (Hunger 1995). Hoven's testimony at the Nuremberg Trials confirms that I.G. Farben was the driving force behind drug experiments:

> It should be generally known and especially in German scientific circles, that the SS did not have notable scientists at its disposal. It is clear that the experiments in the concentration camps with IG preparations only took place in the interest of the IG, which strived by all means to determine the effectiveness of these preparations. They let the SS deal with the—shall I say—dirty work in the concentration camps. It was not the IG's intention to bring any of this out in the open, but rather to put up a smoke screen around the experiences so that [. . .] they could keep any profits to themselves. Not the SS but the IG took the initiative for the concentration camp experiments.
>
> SS Dr. Hoven, Testimony at the Nuremberg Trial

I.G. Farben employed doctors to conduct research on their drugs at Auschwitz, for anti-typhus drugs had tremendous potential commercial value. Drs. Entress and Vetter conducted research on behalf of the Bayer Company, which was part of the conglomerate (Figure 4.11).

Dr. Friedrich Entress came from Poland but considered himself German. He joined the SS early in his career and would not speak or deal with Poles, whom he considered to be beneath him. His specialty in the concentration camps was intracardiac phenol injections, and he ordered them more than anyone else.

Entress was consistently perceived as brutal and was known for his radical therapy of murdering typhus patients. He injected prisoners with typhus to observe the communicability of the disease in at least one series of experiments (Lifton 1986). Entress enjoyed the company of his colleagues at Auschwitz, and in comparison to prior professional positions he wrote to a friend "[from the German] I feel like I am in paradise" (Klee 1997, p. 285).

Bayer paid SS Captain Helmuth Vetter a retainer for conducting drug

I·G·FARBENINDUSTRIE
AKTIENGESELLSCHAFT

Figure 4.11: I.G. Farben initiated pharmaceutical and vaccine experiments and exploited concentration camp prisoners for their own profit. In May 1947 the United States filed an indictment against I.G. Farben's board. They were accused of slavery and mass murder but got off very lightly. It was the Third Reich that was blamed for the crimes against humanity, not I.G. Farben. *Source: I.G. Farben advertisement, Illustrierte Zeitung no. 4956 (1940). Sterling Memorial Library, Yale University.*

experiments on prisoners at Auschwitz and Gusen. Vetter commuted between the camps to supervise the study of the effects of certain drugs
(rutenol and preparation 3582) on medical conditions including typhus. He
had been known among medical colleagues before the war as a traveling
salesman for Bayer products, and after his arrival at Auschwitz, previously
unknown preparations came into use (Tondos, cited in Mikulski 1976). In
order to test these drugs, "healthy" prisoners were intravenously injected
with blood from typhus sufferers and then treated with new Bayer products,
the exact content of which was unknown.[10] According to eyewitness prisoner physicians employed in the camp hospital (Drs. Fejkiel, Klodzinski,
and Tondos), these pharmacological tests had no therapeutic effects and the
drugs were very toxic. Prisoners who were forced to take them developed
gastric distress, persistent bloody vomiting, painful bloody diarrhea containing fragments of mucous membranes, and circulatory impairment. Many
died (Mikulski 1976).

Vetter, however, did not accept the negative findings and always insisted
that he had better results in other camps (Auschwitz data). I.G. Farben eventually put a stop to his meaningless experiments. Vetter was apparently a Nazi
functionary who enjoyed the killing. Like Entress, he found in Auschwitz a
haven for unrestrained experimental research with no peer review, rigorous
judgment, or limits regarding harming or killing research subjects (Lifton
1986, p. 291).

NAZI SCIENTISTS AT NATZWEILER: THE ROLE OF ACADEMIA

The experiments at Natzweiler concentration camp were conducted by
Professor Dr. Eugen Haagen, an officer of the Air Force Medical Service and
professor at the Reich University of Strassburg, a major biological warfare re-
search base (Figure 4.12). In the 1930s, Haagen was a researcher at the
Rockefeller Institute in New York and participated in pro-Nazi bund activities in his spare time. His main work was on hepatitis and typhus vaccines.
Haagen's experimental typhus vaccine was not derived from killed pathogens
but was a dry live, unsterilized product that induced long fever reactions
(Haagen's statement before Trials of War Criminals before the Nuremberg
Military Tribunal, Vol. 1, pp. 496–497). His study was barbaric and brutal:
the prisoners died gruesome deaths after they were injected with the live typhus vaccine.

Haagen obtained concentration camp prisoners for his experiments through
an SS connection at the University of Strassburg, a model Nazi institution.

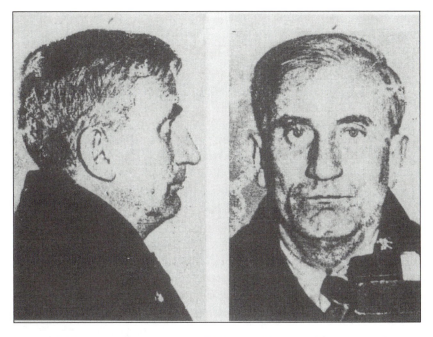

Figure 4.12: The callous, arrogant Professor Haagen of Strasbourg University, carried out bestial experiments on Auschwitz prisoners specially sent to Natzweiler concentration camp for his vaccine experiments. He was finally sentenced by the French court to twenty years imprisonment in 1954 but was released shortly thereafter. *F. Bayle (1950).*

Many of the faculty were SS members whose chemical and biological warfare research consisted of horrific experiments on humans. Chief among these faculty members was the notorious Professor August Hirt of the Anatomical Institute of the Reich University in Strassburg, the official representative of the SS at the university and Haagen's contact. Professor Hirt had a collection of skulls and skeletons of concentration camp victims. At the end of the war he ordered them destroyed. However, after the war, many bodies were found still in the vats. Hirt, through his SS connections also provided other professors with prisoners for lethal experiments. Haagen conducted his experiments on Auschwitz prisoners specially sent to the Natzweiler concentration camp upon his request. In November 1943 he wrote to Dr. Rose about his exciting research. He complained that several of the prisoners who had been sent for experimentation had died on their way from Auschwitz and most were emaciated. He declared them unsuitable for his experiments, and had the survivors killed (Aroneau 1996).

Haagen also injected fresh typhus blood to measure the effectiveness of his dry live vaccine and killed the victims if they had not already died. He changed the vaccine in the hope that it would reduce the side effects, and to test it he inoculated 200 more prisoners in the summer of 1944 (Aroneau 1996). The prisoners suffered awful deaths, but he was impervious to their suffering. He was ambitious and arrogant and considered his work superior to the trials conducted in Buchenwald (Bilik, personal communication 2003). Haagen continued his experiments until 1944 when the inmates were freed. He showed no remorse and believed he deserved the Nobel Prize for his research (Bilik personal communication, citing NMT). Documents detailing Haagen's experiments on Auschwitz prisoners were found in Natzweiler concentration camp. His experimental facilities were hidden in nearby military installations and disguised as an "Electro-technical Institute" (Weindling 2004).

Haagen was arrested in 1945 by the United States, released in 1946, and then rearrested by the British in November 1946 and served as witness for the prosecution at the Nuremberg War Crimes Trial (Hunt 1991). He admitted several of his victims had died after he deliberately infected them with typhus but declared that what he did was to save humanity. Despite his admission of guilt, Haagen was allowed to go free. The incriminating evidence about his studies had not been found at this stage and he was offered a job by the Russians as head of the medical department at the Institute of Medicine and Biology in Berlin in 1946. In 1947 he was tried by a French military court in Metz and in 1952 condemned to life imprisonment. A Parisian court overturned the judgment but in May 1954 the process was reopened in Lyon and he was sentenced to twenty years hard labor (French trial 1954). In the fall of 1955 he was released yet again and went to work in Tübingen at the Federal Institute of Research for Viral Pathology in animals. He received financial support from the Deutsche Forschungsgemeinschaft and was supported in Berlin from 1956–1966 for a book on *viruskrankheiten* of *menschen* (virus diseases of man) (Horrenberger 2004). He had a heart of stone, and he was reckless and arrogant (Weindling 2004; Klee, Bayle 1950). Releasing him was a criminal act.

DECEPTION AND ACCOLADES: PROPAGANDA

The conduct of the Nazi doctors was blatantly unscrupulous and their methods unscientific, yet they were skilled at awarding themselves recognition. Nazi doctors and the pharmaceutical industry widely publicized German "advances" in vaccine research in the media and journals. The Nazi doctors Robert Kudicke and Rudolf Wohlrab were among those decorated for their achievements for vaccine production in Warsaw.

During the war Drs. Ding and Haagen as well as other Nazi doctors gave talks at scientific meetings and published articles on their typhus vaccine experiments in German medical journals. Experimental results were generally falsified. Ding fabricated statistics in at least one typhus study that he supposedly conducted on droplet infection (Kogon 1980). He reported that he had examined 10,000 sputum smears from typhus cases and did not find any organisms. This was a complete fraud, for not a single slide had been prepared, let alone tested (Kogon 1980). Ding, in an article on the comparison of the effectiveness of typhus vaccines, claimed his subjects were healthy volunteers. He did not mention that the study took place in the concentration camps; instead he stated that it was conducted in a Wehrmacht clinic (Ding 1943).

The Lancet was not fooled by the studies. In December 1943 an editorial subtly condemned Ding's paper and deduced that human experiments were carried out on a large group of victims whose ages suggested they were Russian prisoners of war. "Thus, it seems that particularly heavy infections occurred in some hundreds of persons on known days during the investigations of a storm-troop leader. We leave our readers to make their own decisions" (*The Lancet*). Ding's publications on vaccine research eventually became a target of international criticism.

At first, others failed to question Ding's suspicious experiments. Six U.S. army medical corps officers who were deeply involved in typhus research were willing to accept the published results. They referred at length to Ding's report in their 1945 article on typhus, which was written before the camps were liberated and the true nature of the experiments was revealed. According to one of the authors, Dr. Jack Snyder, a retired dean of public health at Harvard University, they did not suspect that torture was involved. Dr. Fox, another U.S. typhus investigator who worked at the University of Washington, assumed the subjects were volunteers: "I was quite willing to accept the published results as fact. . . . It didn't occur to us not to." Fox knew the Nazi publication of the experiment was in the open literature, but although the article did not mention that the study was conducted on concentration camp prisoners, Dr. Fox admitted, "I suspected it was" (Moe 1984).

Nazi doctors in the concentration camps did not have adequate technical expertise, and so they relied on prisoner medical researchers and doctors to do the laboratory work. Kogon stated that during the last two years he spent in block 50 at Buchenwald, he and Dr. Marian Ciepielowsky wrote half a dozen medical papers on typhus, which Dr. Ding published under his name in the *Journal for Infectious Diseases*, the *Journal of Hygiene* and other scientific publications. Ding's contribution was chiefly the insertion of statistical material generally invented (Kogon 1984). Prisoner doctors Wegere and Sitte wrote a doctoral thesis for Hoven on the treatment of silicosis (Kogon 1980, p. 147). Three days before the exam he memorized the thesis and was awarded the degree with distinction from Freiberg University.

PRISONER DOCTORS:
COLLABORATION AND RESISTANCE

SS doctors assigned to the concentration camps tended to be medically undistinguished, strong in their Nazi ties, and personally self-aggrandizing. Most of these SS doctors were more adept at feathering their nests than healing the sick (Kogon 1980, p. 147). At the same time, prisoner doctors participated in the experiments, both willingly and unwillingly. Many survived to report what occurred in their presence and detail courageous acts of resistance. In Buchenwald camp alone, sixty-five of the best available prisoner physicians, bacteriologists, serologists and chemists were selected to operate the vaccine production. Many of the prisoner doctors were experts in their field and came from well-known institutes, among them were Professor Waitz from France, Dr. Ciepielowski from Poland, Dr. Ludwik Fleck, previously of the Lemberg Institute, and Dr. Alfred Balachowsky of the Pasteur Institute in Paris (Hackett 1995).[11] Dr. Balachowsky, a Russian-born French entomologist and leader of a French Resistance group, was involved in supplying weapons and radio receivers and assisting Allied agents and aviators. He was arrested by the Gestapo, and July 1943 he was sent to block 50 Buchenwald concentration camp where he worked on lice research. After the war he was decorated by the French government for his service (Figure 4.13).

Dr. Fleck, an accomplished scientist and philosopher, developed a typhus vaccine and diagnostic test based on human urine in Lvov (Lemberg) Ghetto in 1942; 70 percent of the inmates had typhus, and there were no resources available to them. By contrast to the other typhus experimenters in the ghetto and later in the camps, Fleck demonstrated a superior ethic by first vaccinating himself and his family with the trial vaccine and then a group of 500 volunteers. Fleck and other prisoners who worked in block 50 at Buchenwald had a privileged life and used their privilege to help others and support the camp resistance. Dr. Ciepielowski was in charge of block 50 vaccine production and together with Professors Fleck and Waitz falsified results, sabotaged vaccine production, and organized an undercover resistance in the laboratory (Fleck, cited in Cohen and Schnelle, 1986, p. 23 [see Chapter 3]).

When Fleck was transferred from Auschwitz to help with vaccine production in block 50, he discovered that the typhus vaccine being produced was ineffective. Unable to tell the authorities, the prisoner doctors decided to

Figure 4.13: Dr. Alfred Balachowsky, a French entomologist turned British spy, was transferred, after he was arrested by the Gestapo, to Buchenwald block 50 because of his expertise on lice. This saved his life. In Buchenwald concentration camp he developed a lice laboratory and wrote a paper on lice and fleas. He had utter contempt for Nazi doctors' pseudo-science. *Archives of the Academy of Science, Paris.*

continue production of the ineffective, harmless vaccine for the Wehrmacht as an act of sabotage. Approximately 600 liters of the ineffective vaccine were produced; 30,000 men at the front were injected and for themselves they made 60 liters of an effective serum (Cohen and Schnelle 1986, p. 26; Weindling 1986, p. 369), which they secretly made for their own use and for prisoners in the resistance (Hackett 1995; Kogon 1980).

The Germans did not entirely trust the prisoner doctors and required them to send control samples of the serum to other institutions to be cross-checked. But through Kogon, who took care of all of Ding Schuler's paperwork, Fleck, Ciepielowski, and Waitz sent their high-quality vaccine samples instead of the ineffective vaccine they were producing for the Wermacht

(Fleck, cited in Cohen and Schnelle 1986, p. 26). SS doctors were almost completely inefficient and it was easy to sabotage the vaccine for the German army

(Balachowsky 1991). The Germans were so afraid of typhus that they did not check the research laboratories. After the war the work fell into the hands of a large pharmaceutical firm, which was not able to produce effective serum using the method described. They wrote to Ciepielowski asking for an explanation (Fleck, cited in Cohen and Schnelle 1986).

THE DOCTORS TRIAL AND ITS AFTERMATH

Nazi atrocities were perpetrated in the name of medical science. Members of the German medical profession committed various crimes by tolerating, promoting, and performing horrifically unethical medical experiments. Telford Taylor, prosecutor of the Doctors Trial, described Nazi science as "thanatology," the science of producing death (Taylor in Annas and Grodin 1992) (Figure 4.14). The Nuremberg evidence revealed the murderous intention of the experiments, even when the type of experiment seemed applicable to survival research (Cornwell 2003, p. 359). Many of the perpetrators are known, but few were called to account and sufficiently sentenced at the Nuremberg Doctors Trial of 1946–1947 or other court procedures.[12] Sixteen of the accused were found guilty, seven were sentenced to death by hanging and the other nine were sentenced to imprisonment for at least ten years, but in the 1950s the sentences were reduced (Case no. 1, *United States of America vs. Karl Brandt et al.*) (Figure 4.15).

An indictment on behalf of the United States was filed against twenty-four members of the board of I.G. Farben in May 1947. The crucial crimes were slavery and mass murder, but the Third Reich regime was blamed rather than I.G. Farben. The sentences handed down were laughable and most got off scot-free. A few served light sentences and later assumed high positions in Bayer, BASF, and Hoechst. According to the chief prosecutor Josiah du Bois, the sentences were light enough to satisfy a chicken thief (Hunger 1995).

It is estimated that there were 8000 to 10,000 victims of medical experiments in the concentration camps (Schmalke 2001). Balachowsky calculated that 600 prisoners were sacrificed at Buchenwald to maintain twelve strains of infection (NMT roll 16, frame 916; NAW RG 153 War Crimes Case Number 12-390 The Buchenwald Case, microfilm 5, Kogon cross examination, p. 276). Most victims are no longer alive or traceable. Their names remain unknown, and no research will enable us to comprehend the horrible suffering they experienced. In the year 2000 an agreement between the United States and Germany created a $5 billion fund to compensate survivors of forced labor and experiments at the hands of the Nazis. Many survivors are dissatisfied with the pitiful amount of financial "compensation" (if

Figure 4.14: "Nowhere will the evidence in this case reveal a more wicked murderous course of conduct by men who claim to practice the healing arts than in the entries of Ding's diary relating to typhus experiments." Dr. Telford Taylor, Chief Prosecutor, United States, Doctors Trial, 1946, Nuremberg. *NARA.*

any) received, and lawsuits continue to surface against German pharmaceutical giants Bayer and Schering (Greenhouse 2003).

Modern medicine must acknowledge these crimes to perpetuate the memory of the victims, to apologize to them and their relatives, and most of all to uphold ethical principles that preserve the health and well-being of the individual and human rights (Schmalke 2001). The Nuremberg prosecution, advised by Dr. Leo Alexander and with the assistance of Dr. Ivy, drafted the Nuremberg code of permissible medical experiments that distinguishes criminal medical experiments from lawful experiments (Figure 4.16). German physicians also gave opinions. Many of these principles, such as voluntary and informed consent, stand today, though others have not stood up to scrutiny. The Revised Declaration of Helsinki of the World Medical Association has since superseded the 10 points of Nuremberg to reflect today's more modern complicated research protocols (Deutsch 2003). The importance of such codes lies in where the lines are drawn and whether prevailing laws regulating such experimentation are in force (Cornwell 2003, p. 356).

Figure 4.15: Nuremberg Doctors Trial sentences and commutations. 1st row from left to right: Hermann Becker-Freysing, chief of Aviation Medicine and Air Force Medical Services; Wilhelm Bieglböck, consultant physician to the Air Force; Viktor Brack, chief administrative officer of the NSDAP; Karl Brandt, Reich Commissioner of Health and Sanitation.

2nd row from left to right: Rudolf Brandt, personal administrative officer to Reichsfurer SS Himmler; Fritz Fischer, assistant physician to Gebhardt; Karl Gebhardt, chief surgeon of the Reich Physician SS and president of the Red Cross; Karl Genzken, chief of the medical department of the Waffen SS.

3rd row from left to right: Siegfried Handloser, chief of the Armed Forces Medical Services; Waldemar Hoven, chief doctor at Buchenwald concentration camp; Joachim Mrugowsky, chief of the Hygiene Institute of the Waffen SS; Herta Oberheuser, physician for Ravensbruck concentration camp.

4th row from left to right: Helmut Poppendick, chief of the personal staff of the Reich Physician SS and police; Gerhard Rose, vice president, chief of department for tropical medicine, professor at RKI, and hygienic advisor for tropical medicine to the chief of medical services of the air force; Oskar Schröder, chief of medical services of the air force; Wolfram Sievers, official of the SS Ancestral Heritage Society and director of the Institute for Military Scientific Research. *USHMM.*

Defendant	Sentence	Commutation	
Becker-Freysing, Hermann	20 yrs	10yrs	
Bieglböck, Wilhelm	15yrs	10yrs	
Blome, Kurt	acquitted		
Brack, Viktor	death		
Brandt, Karl	death		
Brandt, Rudolf	death		
Fischer, Fritz	life	15yrs	
Gebhardt, Karl	death		
Genzken, Karl	life	20yrs	
Handloser, Siegfried	life	20yrs	
Hoven, Waldemar	death		
Mrugowsky, Joachim	death		
Oberheuser, Herta	20yrs	10yrs	
Pokorny, Adolf	acquitted		
Poppendick, Helmut	10yrs	served time	
Romberg, Hans Wolfgang	acquitted		
Rose, Gerhard	life	15yrs	
Rostock, Paul	acquitted		
Ruff, Siegfried	acquitted		
Schäfer, Konrad	acquitted		
Schröder, Oscar	life	15yrs	
Sievers, Wolfram	death		
Weitz, Georg August	acquitted		(not pictured)

Source: RG 232, entry 159, box 1, teleconference, War Crimes Operations, 22/8/47:RG238, entry 213, box 1, Nuremberg cases. *NARA*.

Wherever there is an opportunity for research, researchers will seize upon it. For example, two weeks after the liberation of Belsen a small team from the British Medical Research Council arrived to study the relative efficacy of different agents to treat starvation.[13] The side effects of the treatments were so destructive (nausea, vomiting, diarrhea, rigors and blood clots) that inmates began to view them as a "new form of torture." Their trust of medical professionals shattered, prisoners cowered and begged "*nicht crematorium*" at the mere sight of a stomach tube. Hematologist Dr. Janet Vaughan concluded that milk flavored with tea or coffee would have been more appropriate. The project was quickly abandoned and the products were destroyed, producing a paradoxical waste in a time of great need. Vaughan noted that

THE NUREMBERG CODE: PERMISSIBLE MEDICAL EXPERIMENTS

1. The voluntary consent of the human subject is absolutely essential.
2. The experiment should be such as to yield fruitful results for the good of society, unprocurable by other methods or means of study, and not random and unnecessary in nature.
3. The experiment should be so designed and based on the results of animal experimentation and a knowledge of the natural history of the disease or other problem under study that the anticipated results will justify the performance of the experiment.
4. The experiment should be so conducted as to avoid all unnecessary physical and mental suffering and injury.
5. No experiment should be conducted where there is an a priori reason to believe that death or disabling injury will occur; except, perhaps, in those experiments where the experimental physicians also serve as subjects.
6. The degree of risk to be taken should never exceed that determined by the humanitarian importance of the problem to be solved by the experiment.
7. Proper preparations should be made and adequate facilities provided to protect the experimental subject against even remote possibilities of injury, disability, or death.
8. The experiment should be conducted only by scientifically qualified persons. The highest degree of skill and care should be required through all stages of the experiment of those who conduct or engage in the experiment.
9. During the course of the experiment the human subject should be at liberty to bring the experiment to an end if he has reached the physical or mental state where continuation of the experiment seems to him to be impossible.
10. During the course of the experiment the scientist in charge must be prepared to terminate the experiment at any stage, if he has probable cause to believe, in the exercise of the good faith, superior skill and careful judgment required of him that a continuation of the experiment is likely to result in injury, disability, or death to the experimental subject.

[From *Trials of War Criminals before the Nuremberg Military Tribunals under Control Council Law No. 10.* Nuremberg, October 1946–April 1949. Washington, D.C.: U.S. G.P.O., 1949–1953.]

Figure 4.16: The Nuremberg Code derived in part from the 1931 Reich Guidelines in new therapy and human experimentation. *USHMM.*

what they needed most was care and comfort (Trepman 2001, pp. 147, 281–293; Vaughan and Dent 1945, pp. 38, 395–397).

The doctors who tortured concentration camp prisoners to death in their experimental laboratories produced not a single new cure and not a single important medical discovery. Their heinous actions resulted in the 1975 Declaration of Tokyo which was adopted by the World Medical Association (see Appendix 7) to protect victims from degrading inhuman procedures whatever their beliefs or motives, in all situations, including armed conflict and civil strife and prison (World Medical Association 1975) and the modernization of the 2000-year-old Hippocratic Oath. It is not for vengeance that the Nazis' foul deeds should be remembered, but as an episode of history that must not be repeated.

NOTES

1. Two types of pilot vaccines were prepared in Zurich during 1944–1945, according to Dr. Hans Ulrich Gubler, a Swiss microbiologist who worked as a PhD student under the famous Professor Hermann Mooser. One vaccine was an adaptation of Weigl's vaccine. The second vaccine was made from the lungs of mice and was tested on prisoners at Buchenwald (Mooser 1946). "Zurich Vaccine" was tested in Buchenwald barrack 46 (personal communication from Dr. Walter Bossart, head of Diagnostic Department Institute fur Medizinische Virologie [Medical Virology] der Universität, Zurich).

2. A vaccine confers active immunity against a specific harmful agent by stimulating the immune system to attack the agent. Once stimulated by a vaccine, antibody-producing cells, B lymphocytes, remain sensitized and ready to respond to the agent should it ever gain entry to the body. A vaccine may also confer passive immunity by providing antibodies or lymphocytes already made by an animal or human donor. Another type is a subunit vaccine, which is made from proteins found on the surface of infectious agents. Vaccines for influenza and hepatitis B are of this type. When toxins, the metabolic byproducts of infectious organisms, are inactivated to form toxoids, they are used to stimulate immunity as in tetanus, diphtheria, and whooping cough.

3. In 1939 the Warsaw Institute came under German administration, and bacteriologists from the Hamburg Tropical Institute commandeered the State Institute for Hygiene in Warsaw. In 1940 a typhus and viral research center was established at Cracow University, and new Reich institutes were established in Posen and Strassburg, which included typhus research as part of their mission. The Reich University of Strassburg, for example, was funded in 1941 for special tasks, including testing vaccines on prisoners sent from Auschwitz. The Hygiene Institute of the Waffen SS was established in Auschwitz in autumn 1942, expanded in spring 1943, and relocated in Raisko. It was the counterpart of typhus research at Buchenwald concentration camp.

4. The Weigl Institute in Lvov (Lemberg) was a hot bed of anti-Nazi resistance. Because Weigl saved some Jews by smuggling vaccine into the ghetto and giving shelter to a few by making them louse feeders, Yad Vashem honored him as one of the "righteous among nations" (Szybalski 1996). According to Weindling, Weigl collaborated closely with the Germans.

5. Nauck believed that Jews were the carriers of typhus, and when expelled from Spain in the fifteenth century, they brought typhus to Europe. His belief was totally unfounded as it was well known by that time that the spread of typhus was caused by the mercenaries Spain hired in the battle of Granada (Walbaum).

6. Hoven became a captain in January 1941 and in the spring of 1942 chief camp doctor. He was arrested in 1943 for assassinating an SS noncommissioned officer to protect the camp commander.

7. Prisoners were injected first with 10 cc, then 5 cc, and later 2 cc.

8. His natural father was a physician and an explorer, but Erwin was given the name of Ding on adoption.

9. Hoechst tested a new typhus drug "3582," acridin and methylene blue.

10. Among the preparations he used were 3582, a nitroacridine preparation; 1012 and rutenol in combination with preparation 3582 and arsenic acid.

11. Balachowsky was also a British agent.

12. The medical trial started on November 21, 1946 and ended on August 20, 1947.

13. Agents tested included skimmed milk, protein hydrolysate, and amigen, an American enzyme product.

REFERENCES

Annas, G. J. and M. A. Grodin. 1992. *The Nazi Doctors and the Nuremberg Code: Human Rights in Human Experimentation.* New York: Oxford University Press, pp. 81–83.

Aroneau, E. 1996. *Inside the Concentration Camps; Eyewitness Accounts of Life in Hitler's Death Camps.* Trans. by Thomas Whissen. Westport, CT: Praeger Press.

Balachowsky, A. 1991. Testimony cited in P. Padfield, *Himmler: Reichs Fuhrer-SS.* New York: Henry Holt, p. 307.

Baumslag, N. 2000. German Public Health: Typhus for Racial Genocide and Jewish Health Professionals Resistance. Presented at the Remembering the Future conference, Oxford.

Bayle, F. 1950. *Human Experiments in Germany During the Second World War.* The Swastika Counters Caduceus (French) Neustadt: impr. Gault.

Berger, R. L. 1990. "Nazi Science—The Dachau Hypothermia Experiments." *New Engl. Journ. Med.* no. 29, 322:1435.

Bilik, M. 2003. Personal communication (October).

Borkin, J. 1978. *Crime and Punishment of I. G. Farben.* New York: The Free Press.

Buchenwald Memorial, Berichtsammlung, Sign. 31/31.

Caplan, A. L. 1992. *When Medicine Went Mad*. Princeton, NJ: Humana Press, p. 75.

Chevassus-au-Louis, Nicolas. 2003. Personal communication (December 5).

Children as Guinea Pigs. 2003. House of the Wannsee Conference Memorial Education Institute. http://www.ghwk.de/engl/catalog/cateng11a.htm (accessed November 30).

Cohen, E. A. 1988. *Human Behaviour in the Concentration Camp*. Trans. from the Dutch by M. H. Braaksma. London: Free Association Books, pp. 81, 352.

Cohen, R. S., and T. Schnelle. 1986. *Cognition and Fact: Materials on Ludwik Fleck*. Dordrecht: Reidl D. Publishing Co., pp. 19–29.

Cornwell, J. 2003. *Hitler's Scientists: Science and War and the Devils Pact*. New York: Viking.

Cox, H. R. 1938. Public Health Rep. 53, 2241–2247.

Dadrian, V. N. 1986. "The Role of Turkish Physicians in WWI Genocide of Ottoman Armenians." *Holocaust and Genocidal Studies* no. 2, 1:169–169.

Deutsch, E. 2003. The Protection of the Person in Medical Research—German National Report for the XV. International Congress of Comparative Law. http://www.jura.uni-freiburg.de/einrichtungen/gfr/Bristol/Deutsch/Deutsch.pdf (accessed September 12).

Ding, E. 1943. "On the Protective Effect of Different Vaccines in Humans and the Course of Typhus after Immunization." *Zeitschrift fur Hygiene* Infek-Kr, 124, 670.

Eyer, H. 1947. *Munch. Med. Wochen Schr* 42:2185–2191.

Fertig, Howard, ed. 1986. *Nazi Medicine, Doctors Victims and Medicine in Auschwitz, Experimental Typhus in Buchenwald*. New York: International Auschwitz Committee. p. 120.

Fleck, A. 1971. Testimony of Arieh Fleck from Lvov Ghetto, Auschwitz, Gross-Rosen, Buchenwald. Tel Aviv: Yad Vashem Archive.

Fleck, L. 1947. "Specific Antigenic Substances in the Urine of Typhus Patients." *Texas Reports on Biology and Medicine* 6:168–172.

French Trial: 2 German Doctors Sentenced. 1954. *New York Times* (May 15).

Gerber, K., Director of RKI Library. 1996 Personal communication (August 26).

Greenhouse, S. 2003. "Survivor of Nazi Experiments Says $8,000 Is Not Enough." *New York Times* (November 19).

Gross, L. 1996. Perspective: How Charles Nicolle of the Pasteur Institute discovered that epidemic typhus was transmitted by lice; Reminiscences from my years at the Pasteur Institute in Paris. *Proceedings Natl. Acad. Sci.* 93:10539–105470.

Haagen's testimony in *US v Brandt et al.*, M 887, RG 238, NARS.

Hackett, D. 1995. *The Buchenwald Report*. Trans. from Bericht uber das Konzentrationlager Buchenwald bei Weimar. Boulder, CO: Westview Press, p. 73.

Hilberg, R., S. A. Staron, and J. Kermisz. 1968. *The Warsaw Diary of Adam Czerniakoz*. New York: Stein and Day Publishers.

Horrenberger A. 2004. Strasbourg University personal communication (August 30).

Hunger, J. and P. Sander. 1995. *I. G. Farben—From Anilin to Forced Labour.* Stuttgart: Schmetterling Publishers.

Hunt, L. 1991. *Secret Agenda: The United States Government, Nazi Scientists, Project Paperclip 1845–1990.* New York: St. Martin's Press, pp. 11–12.

Kater, M. H. 1989. *Doctors under Hitler.* Chapel Hill: University of North Carolina Press, p. 145.

Kiple, K. F. 1997. *Pox, Plague and Pestilence.* London: Weidenfeld and Nicolson, p. 353.

Klee, E. 1997. *Auschwitz, die NS-Medizin und Ihre Opfer.* Frankfurt-am-Main: S. Fischer Verlag, pp. 287–300.

Kogon, E. 1980. *The Theory and Practice of Hell.* Trans. from the German by Heinz Norden. New York: Berkley Books, p. 154.

Ley, A. and M. M. Ruisinger. 2001. *Gewissenlos Gewissenshaft: Menschenversuche im Konzentrationslager.* Erlangen Institut fur Geschichte der Medizin, Erlangen: Specht Verlag.

Lifton, R. J. 1986. *The Nazi Doctors Medical Killing and the Psychology of Genocide.* New York: Basic Books.

Marsalek, H. 1995. *The History of Mauthausen Concentration Camp.* Vienna: Linz, p. 162.

Mikulski, J. 1976. *Pharmacological experiments in Concentration Camp Auschwitz—Birkenau.* Trans. from the Polish by Krystyna Michalik. Panstwowe Museum W Oswiecimiu, pp. 197–229.

Mitscherlich, A. and F. Mielke. 1949. *The Doctors of Infamy: The Story of Nazi Medical Crimes. Experiments with Typhus and Infectious Jaundice.* New York: Henry Schuman, p. 42–51.

Moe, K. 1984. "Typhus Researchers Didn't Know Torture Had Been Used." *Journal-American* (April 16).

Moorehead, C. 1998. *Dunant's Dream: War, Switzerland and the History of the Red Cross.* London: HarperCollins.

Mooser, H. 1943. "Les Methodes actuelles de l'immunization contre le typhus exan-thematique." *Pathologie and Bacteriologie* no. 112, VI:48–65.

———. 1946. "Twenty years of research in typhus fever." *Schweizerische Medizinische Ochenschrift* no. 37/38, Zurich, p. 877.

NAW RG 153 War Crimes Case No. 12–390: The Buchenwald Case. NMT roll 16, frame 916, microfilm 5, Kogon cross examination, pp. 276.

Poller, W. 1960. *Medical Block Buchenwald.* London: Souvenir Press.

Proctor, R. N. 1992. Nazi Doctors, Racial Medicine, and Human Experimentation. In *The Nazi Doctors and the Nuremberg Code*, G. J. Annas, and M. A. Grodin, eds. New York: Oxford University Press, pp. 17–31.

Roland, C. G. 1992. *Courage under Siege.* New York: Oxford University Press.

Schmalke, T. 2001. Specht Verlag Erlangen. Institute fur Geschichte der Medizin.

Setkiewicz, P. 2003. Personal communication. Archives State Museum of Auschwitz-Birkenau (July 4).

Szybalski, W. 1996. "Professor Dr. Rudolf Weigl (1883–1957) and the Activity of His Typhus Institute in Lvov between 1939 and 1944." *Arch. Hist Filoz Med.* no. 1, 59:77–84.

Taylor, T. 1992. Doctors Trial and the Nuremberg Code, opening statement of the prosecution, December 9, 1946: Typhus (Fleckfieber) and related experiments. In G. J., Annas, and M. A. Grodin, eds. *The Nazi Doctors and the Nuremberg Code.* New York: Oxford University Press, pp. 93–97.

Trepman, E. 2001. "Rescue of the Remnants: The British Emergency Medical Relief Operation in Belsen Camp, 1945." *JR Army Med. Corps* pp. 147, 281–293.

Trials of War Criminals before the Nuremberg Military Tribunals under Control Council Law No. 10. Nuremberg, October 1946–April 1949, Washington, D.C., Superintendent of Documents, U.S. Government Printing Office, 1949–1953, Case no.1, *United States of America vs. Karl Brandt et al.* 1946–1949, pp. 27–74.

Trunk, I. 1972. *Judenrat: The Jewish Councils in Eastern Europe under Nazi Occupation.* Lincoln: University of Nebraska.

"Typhus Vaccines: A Crucial Experiment." 1943. *The Lancet* p. 770 (December 18).

Vaccine. 2003. Encyclopædia Britannica Premium Service (August 2).

Vaughan, J. 1945. "Experience at Belsen." *The Lancet* pp. i, 724.

Vaughan, J., C. Dent, and R. P. Rivers. 1945. "The Value of Hydrolysites in the Treatment of Severe Starvation." *Proc. R. Soc Med* 38:395–397.

Wagner, D. 2003. Personal communication. The Federal Ministry of the Interior from Mauthausen Memorial Archives (June 10).

Waitz, R. 1945. Paper presented and reported in La Presse Medicale (May 26).

Waitz, R. and M. Ciepielowski. 1946. "Experimental Typhus in the Buchenwald Concentration Camp." Trans. from the French by Romney, in *La Presse Medicale* no. 23, pp. 322–324 (May 18).

Walbaum, J. 1946. *Kamf den Seuchen! Deutsche Arte Einsatz in Osten. Die Aufbauarbelt im gesundheitswesen des Generalgouvernement.* Cracca: Buchverlag Deutscher Osten.

Wallace, D. J., and M. H. Weisman. 2003. The Physician Hans Reiter as Prisoner of War in Nuremburg: A Contextual Review of His Interrogations (1945–1947). Seminars in Arthritis & Rheumatism, no.4, 32:208–230 (February).

Weale, A. 2001. *Science and the Swastika.* London: Macmillan, p. 34.

Weindling, P. 1995. "Between Bacteriology and Virology: The Development of Typhus Vaccines between the First and Second World Wars." *Hist. Phil. Life Sci.* 17:88.

———. 2000. *Epidemics and Genocide in Eastern Europe 1890–1945.* Oxford: Oxford University Press.

———. 2005. *The Nazi Medicine and the Nuremberg Trials: From Medical War Crimes to Informed Consent.* New York: Palgrave Macmillan Publishing Company.

Weinrich, M. 1945. Hitler's Professors: The Part of Scholarship in Germany's Crimes against the Jewish People. YIVO, pp. 6–7.

Weissman, G. 1980. In *Quest of Fleck: Science from the Holocaust Hospital Practice*, pp. 48–55 (October).

Wess L. 1993. Experiments on Humans and Policies on Epidemic Diseases: Two Unknown Chapters in the History of German Tropical Medicine. Trans. from the German, Zeitschrift fur Socialgeschichte des 20 und 21, Jahrhundrets [germant] no. 2, 8:10–50.

Weyers, W. 1998. *Death of Medicine in Nazi Germany: Dermatology and Dermopathology under the Swastika*. Philadelphia: Lippincott-Raven, pp. 292–297.

Wilson, G., A. Miles, M. T. Parker, and W.W.C. Topley. 1984. *Topley and Wilson's Principles of Bacteriology, Virology and Immunity*, 7th ed. Baltimore: Williams & Wilkins.

World Medical Association. Declaration of Tokyo. 1975. Adopted by the World Medical Association, Tokyo, Japan (October).

Wroblewski, J., Director, Archives State Museum Auschwitz-Birkenau. 1998. Personal communication (March 12).

Wulf, S. 1994. *Das Hamburger Tropeninstitut, 1919–1945 Auswaertig Kulturpolitik und Kolonialrevisionismum nach Versailles*. Berlin, Hamburg: Dietrich Rema Verlag.

CHAPTER 5

The Red Cross Fails Its Humanitarian Mission

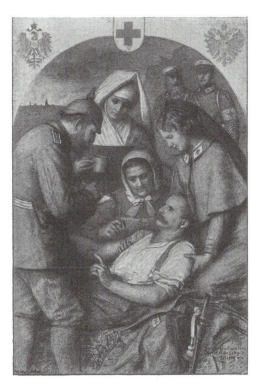

Painting on Red Cross cards sold to raise funds (WWI). *German Red Cross Archives.*

Inter arma caritas

Per humanitatem ad Pacem
    Acknowledged mottos of the ICRC, Statutes of the ICRC, 1998

The WWII era has been engraved in the hearts and minds of inhabitants of the ghetto and concentration camp who survived, as the "period of bitter disappointment with the Red Cross."
                                                        Meier Dworzecki, 1974

The International Red Cross is the world's prevailing provider of medical relief and supplies to victims of war. A driving force behind the evolution of international humanitarian law, it has long been considered the "sacred cow," above reproach (Hutchinson 1996). But the record of the International Committee of the Red Cross (ICRC) during World War II is atrocious and indicative of the inherent weaknesses in the organization. This chapter describes how and why the most recognized humanitarian organization in the world virtually ignored the medical crisis facing Jews and other groups during World War II.[1]

The Red Cross had the experience, resources and authority to combat typhus epidemics, having been at the forefront of epidemic control during World War I. Nevertheless it did not provide medical relief or typhus vaccine to combat the raging epidemics in the ghettos and concentration camps. The Red Cross did provide invaluable food resources, parcels, and medicines to those protected by the Geneva Convention, the international treaty governing the treatment of prisoners of war. It did not provide the same assistance to Jewish and Russian POWs or to civilians in concentration camps, hiding behind technicalities of the convention and a plagued concept of Swiss "neutrality."

The IRC faced unprecedented responsibility in its efforts to alleviate the plight and suffering of the people in Nazi-occupied territory. The Nazi regime opposed all relief and rescue programs designed to help the Jews and generally denied the ICRC access to the labor and extermination camps. They claimed that the Geneva Convention did not obligate them to protect the civilian population in times of war. The Germans did not want their campaign of murder exposed to the world, and the ICRC was not about to confront them. Despite documented knowledge of the ongoing atrocities, the organization chose not to expose the Nazis' genocidal program because the majority of the leadership feared it might jeopardize other relief work (*The Holocaust Chronicle*, p. 539).

HUMANITARIAN VISIONARY: JEAN-HENRI DUNANT

The Red Cross was the inspiration of Jean-Henri Dunant, a young humanitarian from Geneva (Figure 5.1). While on a business trip, Dunant by chance

Figure 5.1: Jean-Henri Dunant, humanitarian, envisioned the formation of the Red Cross. *The German Red Cross, Berlin.*

witnessed the devastation caused by the battle of Solferino in 1859. The French and the Sardinians were at war with Emperor Francis Joseph's army for the liberation of Lombardy from Austrian rule. There were few doctors, nurses, medicines, dressings, and military field hospitals to care for the thousands of wounded soldiers who were abandoned by the armies and left to die. Ironically, the French forces had four veterinarians for every 100 horses, but only one doctor for every 1000 soldiers and no instruments for amputations (Moorehead 1998, p. 3). Dunant noted that soldiers taken prisoner were maltreated. He delayed his trip so that he could help in whatever way he could, procuring first aid supplies, water, and other necessities. He also persuaded local women from a temporary field hospital, established in a church in Castiglione, to take food and water to the wounded soldiers, wash their wounds, and comfort them and the enemy wounded as well. These women forgot their nationality and worked together with the men as brothers and sisters.

In 1861, deeply distressed by the suffering he had witnessed and in particular the treatment of the soldiers who fell into enemy hands, Dunant wrote and published at his own expense a small but very important book titled *A Memory of Solferino* in which he recorded the dreadful sight:

> Bodies of men and horses covered the battlefield; corpses were strewn over roads, ditches fields. . . . The poor wounded men were ghostly pale and exhausted. Some who had gaping wounds already beginning to show infection, were almost crazed by suffering. They begged to be put out of their misery, and writhed with faces distorted in the grip of the death struggle . . . Many were disfigured . . . their limbs stiffened, their bodies blotched with ghastly spots, their hands clawing at the ground, their eyes staring wildly, their moustaches bristling (Dunant cited in Moorehead 1998, p. 3).

A Memory of Solferino contained two key proposals: first, to create a society in each country to provide relief to the wounded during times of conflict, and second, to adopt an international convention that would provide a legal basis for the protection of military hospitals and medical personnel (ICRC, General Introduction 1998). He called for voluntary bodies that would not replace the army medical authorities but would act as a link between them. He sent copies of his book to influential people all over Europe, urging them to recognize the need for voluntary aid societies that would improve army medical services, handle the care of war victims, provide supplies, and train nurses (Figure 5.2).

Genevan philanthropist Gustave Moynier, who was often asked for money, received a copy of the book in 1862 (Figure 5.3). Intrigued by Dunant's project, he arranged to meet him. Their subsequent meeting led to

Figure 5.2: The battle at Solferino. *The German Red Cross, Berlin.*

the origin of the ICRC. The five members of the founding committee were Jean-Henri Dunant, Gustave Moynier, Theodore Maunoir, General Dufour, and Lois Appia. Dunant provided the vision, and Moynier the organization. While some call Moynier the real architect of the Red Cross it was Dunant who recognized that the organization should be nongovernmental with governmental support, have its own national organization, and be voluntary and neutral. Dunant continued to press his ideas despite financial hardship and falling out of favor with the ICRC. In 1901, Dunant was justly awarded the Nobel Peace Prize together with Frederic Passy, the oldest and most highly regarded pacifist. Dunant was honored for his efforts to mitigate the horror of war (Moorehead 1998, p. 168). His vision and humanitarianism continue to be recognized.

Figure 5.3: Gustave Moynier was a lawyer in search of a cause when he received Dunant's book. In a rare and touching passage of self-revelation, written many years later, he said his legal studies had left him with a lawyer's mind devoid of originality and prone to doubt everything except the infallibility of the law. *The German Red Cross, Berlin.*

FROM IDEAS TO ORGANIZATION

By 1863 Dunant obtained support from the Geneva Society for Public Welfare to found the International Committee for the Relief of Military Wounded. In 1864 the Geneva Convention for the amelioration of conditions of the wounded in armies in the field was drafted and approved. In 1867 the International Committee for the Relief of Military Wounded was renamed the International Red Cross Committee (see Appendix 7).

The Swiss took the lead and organized a conference in Geneva to improve conditions for the war wounded and prison conditions for political prisoners, offer assistance to refugees, and help track people parted by war. The conference resulted in the founding of the International Red Cross (ICRC), which started as a Swiss organization and remains one today. Headquartered in Geneva, the emblem of the IRC is a reversed Swiss flag, a red cross on a white field; the Swiss flag is a white cross on a red field. In Muslim countries the Red Crescent was adopted instead of the Red Cross, but it is still basically part of the same organization.[2] The Geneva Convention, the first treaty of contemporary international humanitarian law, also established international legal protection to personnel and ambulances bearing the Red Cross emblem (ICRC, The Geneva Conventions 1998).[3]

Currently, the International Red Cross, also known as the International Red Cross and Red Crescent Movement, has 178 national societies and 97 million workers. It is a large network of nongovernmental organizations, including the International Federation of Red Cross and Red Crescent Societies and all national Red Cross and Red Crescent Societies. Each society is independent but shares the same mission: to provide services to victims and prisoners of war. The ICRC, the governing body of the Red Cross, has not changed its structure since its inception. It is a private, independent, discreet organization accountable to no outside body (Moorehead 1998). All the members are Swiss citizens, in part due to the origins of the Red Cross in Geneva and in part to establishing "neutrality" so that any country in need can receive aid. The committee assembles ten times a year to ensure that the ICRC fulfills its mission as promoter of international humanitarian law and guardian of the fundamental principles of the Red Cross: "humanity, impartiality, neutrality, independence, voluntary service, unity and universality" (ICRC, The Fundamental Principles 1995).

FULFILLING THE MANDATE: THE GREAT WAR AND THE INTERWAR YEARS

Early failures of the International Red Cross to fulfill its mandate foreshadowed its spectacular failure during World War II. The ICRC did nothing, for example, in 1900 when the British invented concentration camps to confine Boer women and children in disease producing, starving conditions (Moorehead 1998, p. 344). But during World War I the ICRC had taken on a larger role than it ever had before. At the outbreak of war the ICRC recognized twenty-nine (national) Red Cross and Red Crescent societies. The Red Cross traced missing soldiers, sent 2 million parcels and letters to POWs, inspected interned civilian and POW camps, and even evacuated civilians from occupied districts (Penkower 1988, p. 230). During the war and the interwar years, the organization was very much in the forefront of typhus epidemics as well as relief work extending from Rumania to Russia.

The American Red Cross sent a "mercy ship" to war-torn Europe in 1914 with teams of doctors and nurses and a cargo of supplies on board. Their mission was to provide relief to the wounded regardless of nationality and to stem typhus epidemics.[4] A "great white train" made epoch journeys to typhus-ridden villages (Figure 5.4). They also adapted tobacco sheds as hospitals and set up clinics and disinfecting stations. They ran hospitals, dispensaries, mothering classes, and elementary home nursing and hygiene programs. As typhus overran Serbia, the American Red Cross responded by sending a sanitary commission, partly financed by the Rockefeller Foundation, to combat the epidemic. The commission of American, English, and French sanitarians helped rid Serbia of typhus by the end of the summer. The Americans had not yet learned how to protect themselves from the infected lice with special suits fitted tightly at the ankles, wrists, and neck; as a result, many relief doctors contracted typhus.

After World War I the American Red Cross worked to control the raging typhus epidemic in Poland and other Baltic countries (Dock et al. 1922,

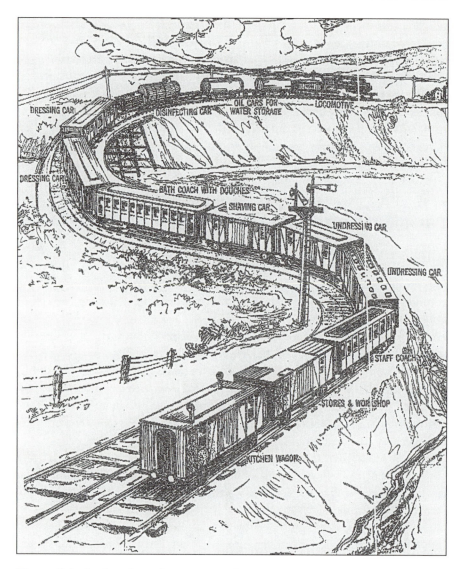

Figure 5.4: An American doctor, to combat a typhus epidemic in Romania, devised a bath train to provide delousing and hygiene. He converted oil tanks into laundries. American Red Cross Magazine *(December 1917)*.

p. 139). The American Red Cross commission went into Poland in February 1919 with the purpose of combating typhus and famine. They organized delousing, bathing, and hair clipping stations and distributed clean clothes, soap, disinfectants, food, and other supplies. The League of the Red Cross Societies (the precursor to the International Federation of the Red Cross) and the American Red Cross in March 1919 jointly established the Typhus Research Hospital in Warsaw, where a large number of nurses observed typical and critical cases (Kernodle 1940). Although the team of mercy nurses and doctors was relatively small, they believed that they saved thousands of lives.

The sanitary commissions established in the Allied countries were gradually withdrawn in the early 1920s, with the exception of Poland where continued relief was badly needed. The Rockefeller Foundation believed that the Red Cross accomplished little and that a massive government effort was needed to combat the typhus epidemic (see Appendix 8). The IRC continued to provide humanitarian service during the interwar years, sending two medical missions to the Ukraine from 1921 to 1923 and assisting political prisoners throughout Europe (Penkower 1988, p. 230).

ESSENCE OF THE GENEVA CONVENTION

Lessons learned from World War I led the Red Cross to consider how it could better protect victims of war through international law (Sommaruga, 1996).[5] In 1929 the ICRC held an important conference resulting in the revision of the Geneva Convention, which remains the internationally recognized Magna Carta of the rights of prisoners of war. The treaty was signed by forty-seven nations; Japan and the USSR did not sign. In addition to guaranteeing the fair treatment of POWs and neutral inspection of POW camps, the convention specifically declared that hygiene must be maintained in the camps so as to prevent epidemics and medical care should be provided to all inmates.

The Red Cross also prepared resolutions to specifically protect civilian internees, reflected in the Tokyo Project of 1934. Although most of the governments followed the resolutions, the document did not receive international ratification prior to World War II: It was considered "particularly inappropriate for the IRC to recommend including civilians in the 1929 Geneva convention," because the state of "general optimism which reigned at the time" led various representatives to conclude that such a resolution "would be regarded in international circles as almost equivalent to betraying the cause of peace" (Grossman 1988). (See Appendix 9.) The German Foreign Office was among the first to assure the ICRC that Germany would protect civilians in times of war. Under the Geneva Convention of 1929 over 150,000 civilians had the same legal status as POWs (Favez 1988). They were protected under law because, unlike Jews, they were not stripped of their citizenship.

The ICRC stated that during hostilities its tasks were, first, the application of the Geneva Convention and the exchange of news and information, and second, the provision of material assistance to war victims (Favez 1988,

p. 47). In the years leading up to World War II, the International Red Cross would progressively loosen its interpretation of the Geneva Convention so as to avoid antagonizing the Nazi regime. The American Red Cross would also relinquish its nursing role and legacy of epidemic control in Eastern Europe.

NAZIFICATION OF THE GERMAN RED CROSS

In November 1933 a German statute destroyed the independence of the German Red Cross (*Deustches Rote Kreutz*) and made the organization an instrument of the government. Over the next few years the German Red Cross, which had a million and a half ardent members, all in close contact with the medical profession, was effectively nazified. Red Cross nurses were militarized and assigned to the new medical military corps of the army, navy, and air force.[6] Gauleiters, local political officials under the Nazi regime, were appointed heads of local nursing associations, and nurses were indoctrinated with Nazi dogma. Flags bearing the swastika and the Red Cross symbol hung side by side (Figure 5.5). The distinctive German Red Cross official

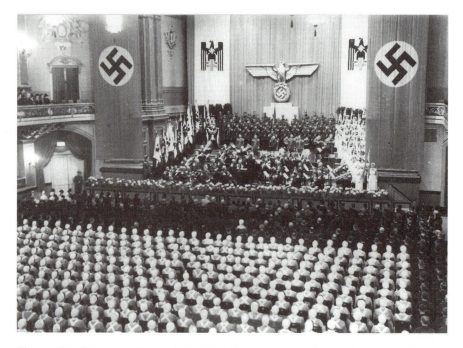

Figure 5.5: The swastika and the Red Cross became intertwined.   **A.** German Red Cross Helferinnen (helpers) during a swearing-in ceremony in the philharmonic, Berlin. *The German Red Cross, Berlin.*

B. One of the many gatherings of Red Cross and auxiliary nurses in which swastikas and the Red Cross hung side by side. *The German Red Cross, Berlin.*

decoration—a white cross with a black eagle—was replaced by a red cross in a white circle. The center depicted an eagle bearing a golden wreath with a swastika in its talons (Moorehead 1998, p. 357) (Figure 5.6).

Himmler appointed Dr. Ernst Grawitz, then head of the Health Service of the SS and the Police, as acting president of the German Red Cross, effective January 1937.[7] One of his first tasks was to transform the organization according to nationalist socialist principles and oversee its smooth absorption into the Nazi Party (Figure 5.7). When president of the IRC, Max Huber, was notified that Grawitz was in charge of the German Red Cross, despite the fact that he knew that the organization was being nazified, he sent a telegram wishing the society a smooth translation of its "high aims and ideals" into practice (Moorehead 1998) (Figure 5.8).

Figure 5.6: The German Red Cross (Das Deustche Rote Kreuz) became an instrument of the Third Reich, with a new emblem and policy. *The German Red Cross, Berlin.*

Figure 5.7: Dr. Ernst Grawitz, a staunch Nazi, became acting president of the German Red Cross in 1937. He advised Himmler to use gas for mass murder. *The German Red Cross Berlin.*

Grawitz was an amoral and ambitious person who epitomized the moral treachery of the Nazi doctors (Moorehead 1998, p. 356). He groveled to superior officers, particularly Himmler, whose orders he carried out devoutly. A large staff of SS officers and SS doctors were at his disposal. He selected doctors for senior positions who were supportive of the Nazi regime and the euthanasia program. Grawitz was also in charge of the health services in concentration camps, which he entrusted to the murderous Dr. Enno Lolling.

After World War II, Grawitz was found responsible for all the medical atrocities and criminal experiments performed by SS doctors in the camps. When the Allied forces approached Berlin, he committed suicide to escape the death sentence. Grawitz's successor as chairman of the German Red Cross was Professor Karl Gebhardt, Heinrich Himmler's personal physician. Gebhardt, too, was found guilty of war crimes at Nuremberg and sentenced to death.

Figure 5.8: Professor Max Huber was a widely respected scholar and judge who taught International Public Law at Zurich University. Legal adviser to the Swiss government's political department, he was pro-German and profited greatly during the war from arms factory and slave labor. *ICRC.*

THE GERMAN RED CROSS: DECEPTION

The whole medical apparatus was décor to disguise massacre.

Eli Cohen

In the rest of the world the Red Cross was a symbol of hope, but for Nazi Germany it served to camouflage and facilitate mass murder (Nahon 1989, p. 98). Vans disguised as Red Cross vehicles were in reality mobile gassing units used to murder Jews. The vans were used at Zemun concentration camp near Belgrade and later transferred to Riga. Reports of the gas vans reached Warsaw Ghetto in May 1942 and confirmed their fears that they were to be exterminated (Weindling 2000, p. 296). For the purposes of "pest control" (*für schädlingsbekämpfung*), ambulances bearing the insignia of IRC transported concentration camp doctors and Zyclon B to the gas chambers (Yahil 1987, p. 366). A German Red Cross car escorted each transport en route for the Birkenau crematorium (Nahon 1989, p. 98) (Figure 5.9).

In the ghettos throughout Poland, Latvia, Lithuania, White Russia (Belarus), and Ukraine, typhus was rife, and Jews were quarantined and denied typhus vaccines and basic health care. For most people, however, there was no help. At the beginning of 1942 a Jewish refugee from Germany visited the Joint Commission of the Red Cross and reported that some of the Jews deported were in the Riga Ghetto. He stated that cases of typhus had been noted in the ghetto, and he asked the Red Cross to send drugs and vaccines (German Jews at Riga 1948). The Joint Commission undertook an inquiry. By June the chief medical officer at the central hospital of the ghetto reported to the Joint Commission

Figure 5.9: Red Cross vehicles were used to transport Zyclon B to the gas chambers. In this photo taken in 1940, Heinrich Himmler was inspecting the sanitary service (from left to right): Heinrich Himmler, Karl Genzken, Karl Wolff, Erwin Ding, and Werner Kirchert. Note the Red Cross vehicle in the background. *Buchenwald Memorial Museum Archives. Photo: J. M. Suard, Paris.*

(through the German Red Cross) that sanitary conditions were good in the ghettos and the surrounding area. There were sufficient nurses and doctors and no lack of medical stores, but typhus vaccine was urgently needed. In late October 1942, the Red Cross sent vaccine to the ghetto through the German Red Cross, and as late as April 1944 the chief medical officer of the hospital acknowledged receipt of the vaccine through the office of the German Red Cross. It is unclear where the vaccine went because the Riga Ghetto hospital no longer existed at that time (Ezergailis 1996).

The German Red Cross went to extremes to deceive the world. Grawitz was primarily concerned with serving the Nazi regime and used the supposedly humanitarian organization to spread propaganda. The ICRC either swallowed the propaganda or pretended not to see or acknowledge reports of the Nazi crimes and atrocities. ICRC member Jacques Cheneviere of the ICRC in autumn 1939 stated that it was difficult to refuse the German Red Cross something because it seemed much more advanced than other Red

Cross societies when it came to organizing its services. His comments were related to the DRK order requesting those keeping horses, cows, or pigs to acquire a Red Cross veterinary box (Moorehead 1998, p. 467).

THE ICRC FAILS TO CONFRONT THE NAZIS

> With its internationally recognized standing and contact with virtually
> all governments, the IRC stood in a unique position to relieve the tragic
> plight of European Jewry.
>
> Monty Noam Penkower

The ICRC knew early on that the German Red Cross was part and parcel of the Nazi oppression, but ICRC president Huber decided it was best to support them and not to make things worse by taking any action. As early as December 1933, Camile Drevet, secretary of the International League of Peace and Freedom, wrote to Huber urging him to send a delegate to investigate conditions in German police stations, prisons, and concentration camps.

The ICRC asked repeatedly for permission to visit the concentration camps. In September 1935 an unsigned eyewitness report from Dachau published in the *Manchester Guardian Weekly* described the atrocities and terrible conditions in the concentration camp (*Manchester Guardian Weekly,* September 27, 1935). Three weeks later Himmler and Reinhard Heydrich, the head of the security service (*Sicherheitsdienst* [SD]) Gestapo and German intelligence, respectively, finally granted ICRC representative Professor Carl Jacob Burkhardt permission to visit the camps at Esterwegen, Lichterberg, and Dachau (Figure 5.10). Burkhardt reported to the ICRC that conditions were military, harsh, and even brutal and that many political prisoners were in poor condition, held without trial, and "treated like dogs." His report was never published, but he discussed his findings with Heydrich and other prominent members of the Nazi regime and requested that the prison commander at Esterwegen be removed. The commander was instead promoted to commandant of Dachau concentration camp (Moorehead 1998).

In the spring of 1936 Burkhardt was allowed to visit Germany again. Though he did not visit any camps and had only spoken to a number of released prisoners, he reported that conditions had improved and that Jewish detainees were treated exactly the same as families of Aryan prisoners (Moorehead 1998, p. 353). Meanwhile, Huber wrote some "warm and ingratiating letters" to the duke of Saxe Coburg, nominal figurehead of the

Figure 5.10: Professor Carl Jacob Burkhardt was ICRC president in all but name during WWII. Arrogant and conservative, he overestimated the chances of a German victory. *ICRC.*

German Red Cross. It was evident that Huber and Burkhardt were not willing to challenge the Nazis.

The Red Cross also turned a blind eye when Jewish prisoners of war were separated and treated differently from other POWs. Poland and Germany had both signed the Geneva Convention, which specifically forbade ethnic or religious segregation of prisoners of war. By September 1939 there were 420,000 Polish POWs, and 15 percent were Jewish. The Germans separated the Jewish POWs from the others, assembled them in different camps, reduced their rations, and forced them to wear clothing with a special triangle on their back. In 1940, they were released and then deported and persecuted as civilian Jews. In other places they were murdered, as in Lublin concentration camp, where 700 Jewish POWs were sent on a death march. Russian POWs didn't fare any better because the Russians never signed the Geneva Convention. As such, the Germans considered millions of those they detained to be unprotected by international law (Yahil 1987, p. 237).

The Germans were anxious for the Red Cross to protect German POWs and German civilians held in countries fighting against Nazi Germany. In return, the IRC was allowed to protect POWs in Germany and to distribute food, medicine and clothing in specified quantities to the population of occupied countries. The IRC did not threaten to deny treatment to German POWs or civilian internees because that would betray its mission to protect individuals regardless of nationality. The IRC, however, accepted Germany's classification of Jews as "detained civilians" rather than "civilian internees" and failed to protect millions (Penkower 1988, p. 231).

In September 1939, the Geneva office of the World Jewish Congress (WJC) offered its services to the ICRC, as it well knew the unique danger facing Jews in Germany and the occupied territory. The name on the WJC's letterhead was changed to RELICO (Committee for Relief of the War Stricken Population) so as to avoid provoking Germany (Penkower 1988, p. 230). After long negotiations with the ICRC and the American Red Cross in late 1939, RELICO sent food, clothing and medicine to the Jewish community in Warsaw through the ICRC and the German and Polish Red Cross (Penkower 1988, pp. 230–231). Later on money and supplies sent by Jewish relatives, organizations and relief agencies were never distributed to the Jews in the ghettos or concentration camps. Packages of food and medical supplies continued to arrive even when 90 to 95 percent of Jews had been exterminated (Dworzecki 1974, pp. 71–106).

In December 1939 Huber inquired about the fate of Jews deported to Poland from Vienna. The German Red Cross refused Huber's request to inspect the camp conditions and indicated that the fate of interned Jews was not up for debate. From then on, the ICRC admits it had a policy of only indirectly inquiring about their status (ICRC, The ICRC and the Holocaust 1998). In April 1942 the German Red Cross officially informed the ICRC that it would not relay any information about "non-Aryan" detainees. But the ongoing genocide could not be kept secret, and the international community became increasingly suspicious. Drawing on local German sources, Burkhardt in November 1942 confirmed reports of the Nazis' annihilation plan for the United States minister in Berne (Penkower 1988, p. 233).

The ICRC had over 3000 employees in Switzerland assigned to the central agency for POW relief. There were 180 delegations posted in sixteen different countries. More than any other institution, it was in a position to see and know what was going on (Perl 1989, p. 224). ICRC delegates paid more than 11,000 visits to POW camps and arranged for the distribution of 470,000 tons of relief supplies to POWs and civilian internees mostly in Germany. According to the American Red Cross, 99 percent of American POWs returned home alive due to food packages and typhus vaccine delivered from America till the end of the war. The joint relief commission delivered 165,000 tons of food, medicines, and other relief supplies to people in need throughout Europe but practically nothing to the suffering Jews.

The Red Cross delegates and staff approached the suffering in a manner that was professionally neutral and diplomatically evasive. The terms used to describe the unimaginable were at best diplomatic and at worst terribly inadequate (Favez 1988, p. 10). The insight was also woefully lacking. When one of the committee members, Marie Frick, learned of the medical experiments conducted on concentration camp prisoners, she wrote: "if nothing can be done, the wretched victims should be sent the means of committing suicide, this perhaps would be more humane than giving food" (Favez 1988, p. 43).

SWISS "NEUTRALITY" AND ANTI-SEMITISM

> The mission of the Red Cross is to serve, and only that. Neither attacks, nor thanks, nor prestige will alter anything.
>   Max Huber, ICRC president during World War II

During World War II the International Red Cross steered a very careful path, taking care not to endanger Switzerland. Antagonizing the Nazis might result in the German occupation of Switzerland, thereby affecting the nation's economic prosperity. High-ranking Swiss diplomat Edouard de Haller was given the sole task of supervising ICRC's relations with the Nazi authorities so as to prevent "mistakes" from being made (Alpern 1988). As such, the organization was not independent or neutral in any real sense. Protecting Switzerland and its "neutral" status was considered more important than upholding the IRC charter. By 1942, reputable sources had notified members of the IRC and their delegates in Berlin of the Nazi atrocities, but they did not publicly condemn the Nazis for their inhuman treatment and murder of Jews, Roma (gypsies), and Slavs (Favez 1988).

In autumn of 1942 two Auschwitz escapees gave graphic details to the world press, and a copy of their report was given to the ICRC. Huber cautioned the ICRC not to react, but two members recommended a public protest (Penkower 1988, pp. 233–234). The ICRC met in October 1942 and prepared a public call to appeal against the worsening conditions for civilians caught in the war, though it did not specifically mention the Jews. A majority of members (twenty-one out of twenty-three) voted to go public (Favez 1988). Swiss authorities felt it would antagonize the Nazis and put Switzerland's neutrality at risk. A meeting was held to discuss the ICRC's action plan. Max Huber was unable to attend and had Philippe Etter, then president of the Swiss Confederation and member of the ICRC, attend the meeting on his behalf. It was the only ICRC meeting that Etter ever attended, and it is apparent that he came specifically to influence the ICRC to remain silent. Unfortunately, he was successful (Favez 1988, p. 6). Through his political maneuvering the committee was persuaded to keep silent and continue working with the German Red Cross in a guarded manner.

Anti-Semitism also influenced Swiss decisions. When the Third Reich declared Jews noncitizens and stripped away their rights, the Swiss government feared a mass influx of German Jewish refugees. In 1938 the Swiss arranged

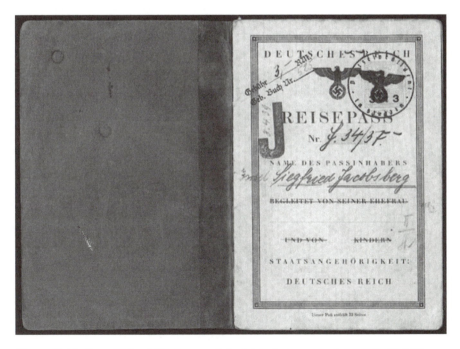

Figure 5.11: Passports of German and Austrian Jews were stamped with "J" to restrict their immigration to Switzerland. *USHMM.*

with the Germans to stamp a "J" on the passports of German and Austrian Jews so that they could identify them and refuse them entry into Switzerland (Figure 5.11). In August 1942 the Swiss passed a law that hermetically sealed Swiss borders to fleeing Jews. Etter signed the order. The driving force behind the legislation was Heinrich Rothmund, head of the Swiss police division in the federal department of police and justice (LeBor 1997, p. 145). Anti-Semitism was apparent in national Red Cross societies as well (Favez 1988, p. 6). In France the Red Cross did not allow Jews to attend nursing school, or volunteer to assist the war wounded—another blot against the "neutral" Red Cross (Cohn 2002).

DECEPTION AND PROPAGANDA AT THERESIENSTADT

The Nazis staged elaborate deceptive presentations of concentration camp facilities and used the ICRC to present their fraud to the world. The SS did not allow outside access to the concentration camps, and all visits were meticulously controlled. Concentration camps like Amersfoort in the Netherlands were decorated for Red Cross visits, and inmates were given new clothing to perpetuate the fraud. Musical events were even staged to show that living conditions were agreeable (The Holocaust Chronicle 2003, p. 325). In preparation for a Red Cross visit to Westerbork, a transit camp for Dutch Jews in the Netherlands, a barrack was specially prepared with plump pillows and crisp sheets covering each bunk. The Red Cross was tricked into believing that prisoners were well treated and had decent living quarters. Ironically, the fraud was financed by money confiscated from the Jews (*The Holocaust Chronicle* 2003, p. 347).

The biggest hoax was carried out at Theresienstadt in Czechoslovakia, where the so-called ghetto was in fact a concentration camp. The Nazis had established Theresienstadt (also known as Theresienstadt Ghetto/ Familienlager) as a model ghetto for propaganda purposes. The prisoners, mostly wealthy and privileged Jews, had more food, medicines, vaccines, and doctors and less crowding than the other ghettos and concentration camps. Still, conditions were terrible. To enhance the illusion that people were treated decently, in December 1942 the Nazis opened second-hand clothing shops, a bank, and a café in the main square for Jews to socialize and listen to music. The name Ghetto Theresienstadt was changed to "Jewish Settlement Theresienstadt." In reality, the camp operated as a waystation to the death camps.

After 400 Jewish Danes were deported to Theresienstadt, King Christian requested the Danish Red Cross to demand permission to visit the camp (Moorehead 1988, p. 465). The request was finally granted in June 1944. The reason for the delay, unbeknownst to the ICRC, was that the Nazis were implementing a grotesque intensive beautification program to transform the ghetto into a Potemkin-like village. The Nazis perpetrated this massive fraud by painting buildings and adding gardens, showers, an orchestra, art, and a fake restaurant with pastries and other delicacies not readily available to most people. Tombstones were even placed over graves in the cemetery. In preparation for the visit, the Nazis had also cleaned the area and added washbasins to the shower room. Just before the scheduled Red Cross visit more than 17,000 Jews (mainly the elderly) were sent to Auschwitz Birkenau concentration camp to decrease the crowding. The Theresienstadt prisoners were warned that if they complained or revealed the deception they and their families would be murdered.

The visiting delegation included Frants Hvass, head of the Political Department of the Danish Foreign office, Dr. Juel Henningsen, representative of the Danish Red Cross, Dr. Maurice Rossel, representative of the Berlin delegation of the ICRC, Dr. Heidenkampf of the German Red Cross, two representatives of the SS, representatives of the German Foreign Office, and several high-ranking German officers and members of the German Red Cross. Two delegates from the Swedish Red Cross were granted permission to participate, but for some reason they did not attend. The visit lasted six hours and included a special dinner. The delegates failed to inspect the fortress at Theresienstadt, known for incredible brutality, which was reserved for political prisoners and selected Jews.

Dr. Maurice Rossel, a Swiss doctor and the ICRC delegate in Berlin, had been told by the Nazis to evaluate the place positively, and he did just that (Moorehead 1988, p. 465). Rossel presented a report that praised Theresienstadt, its independent Jewish administration, ample supply of food, and good living conditions. Rossel's report, which also included photographs, stated falsely that the camp was not a transit camp but an *endlager*, from which there were no deportations (Rossel 1944) (Figures 5.12 and 5.13). The Danish representatives were concerned because a quarter of the Jewish Danes they were looking for had disappeared. If Rossel had noted the age composition of the population, it would have been obvious to him that Theresienstadt was a transit camp. Rossel's report caused a wave of protests from Jewish organizations. The Nazis were overjoyed, while the Jews, acutely aware of the deception, were outraged but unable to expose it (Dworzecki 1974, p. 98). Three months after the visit to Theresienstadt, the ICRC visited Auschwitz. Once again the delegates failed to report and expose the true conditions of the camp. They failed to notice that the "shower rooms" were really gas chambers with fake shower heads and absent drains (Report of the Joint Relief Commission, 1948).

Figure 5.12: The photos of the staged beautified Theresienstadt concentration camp taken by ICRC Berlin delegate Dr. Rossel, during his official visit in June 1944 show: **A.** A normal community with children playing. *ICRC (HIST-01160-29)* .

B. A choir and orchestra performance. The ICRC did not suspect they had been duped but were concerned that Theresienstadt was not representative of other camps. *ICRC (HIST-01161-24).*

Figure 5.13: Theresienstadt fortress was not inspected during the ICRC visit. *N. Baumslag.*

Documentary filmmaker Claude Lanzmann interviewed Dr. Rossel after the war and Rossel revealed that he was more interested in preserving his own status than in seeing that Theresienstadt was thoroughly investigated. At the outbreak of World War II, he was stationed in a Swiss army border patrol camp and was able to obtain a position in the ICRC delegation in Berlin through a friend. He insisted that he did not join the Red Cross for any missionary or humanitarian reason. He was simply bored on the border. Life in Berlin was quite comfortable for him, and his post gave him access to the concentration camps, including the Auschwitz extermination camp, which he visited to satisfy his curiosity. Rossel's positive report to the IRC on the Theresienstadt Ghetto pleased the Germans and protected his status and lifestyle in Berlin.

In April 1945 there was complete chaos in Theresienstadt with the constant arrival of inmates from other concentration camps. Typhus became rampant, and by early May the Nazis turned Theresienstadt over to Swedish Red Cross workers, who were left to deal with the typhus epidemic. Shortly after the war on May 5 Red Cross representative Paul Dunant saw and heard from survivors how Theresienstadt had been staged (Moorehead 1988, p. 466). He also learned that three weeks after the "official visit" ghetto inhabitants were sent for extermination (Dworrzecki 1974, p. 99; Favez 1988; Moorehead 1998).

ACTION AT THE LAST HOUR: CHANGING SIDES

ICRC delegates Friedrich Born and Robert Schirmer distinguished themselves from the otherwise helplessly silent members of the ICRC. In 1944 the two delegates managed to bluff the Arrow Cross, the fascist and anti-Semitic Hungarian ruling party, that the Jews in Budapest were in fact protected under the convention. Thousands of lives were saved as a result (Penkower 1988, p. 234). Such courage and success strongly suggests that the ICRC was capable of doing more to protect Jews and other groups during the war.

The ICRC finally made a move as the Allies gained on the Nazi war machine and it became clear that the Germans were losing. They sent a letter to the German Foreign Ministry in October 1944 asking Germany to respect the Tokyo Project of 1934 and guarantee the safety of all foreign workers, political detainees, and foreign Jews in Germany and German-occupied territories. While the ICRC waited for a response, a conference was held in November to discuss joint action to pressure Germany to safeguard the rights of *all* civilian internees. Red Cross delegates from Rumania, Yugoslavia, Poland, and the Netherlands and representatives from the governments of France, Greece, Italy, Norway, and Belgium and the World Jewish Congress attended and agreed there was a need for a united front to confront Germany's treatment of Jews (Penkower 1988, pp. 234–237).

Professor Burkhardt succeeded Huber officially as ICRC president in January 1945 and maintained that ICRC's interference with Germany's treatment of Jews would jeopardize other Red Cross activities. A second meeting was called in February to generate an action plan. Burkhardt agreed to meet with Himmler to negotiate the liberation of surviving camp prisoners before the final surrender of Germany. The Swiss government guaranteed that it would allow them entry. Himmler gave Gestapo Head, Ernst Kaltenbrunner, power to negotiate with the ICRC on his behalf. Kaltenbrunner agreed to speed the delivery of food to POWs and allow Red Cross observers to permanently live in the POW camps and concentration camps. Himmler later agreed to surrender the camps and the inmates to advancing Allied troops (Penkower 1988, pp. 240–243).

But the Nazis had one card left to play. Reports surfaced that in preparation for the evacuation of the camps, Polish Jews were segregated from other groups, a clear violation of the Geneva Convention of 1929. Burkhardt stubbornly refused to acknowledge the violation and continued to support the Nazi argument that Jews were not covered by the convention.

DARK SECRETS REVEALED

The ICRC released copies of its files from World War II in 1996. The files included first-hand accounts and reports about the persecution of the Jews from 1939 to 1945, verifying that the organization was aware of what was happening in concentration camps. The files also reveal that the Red Cross rescued thousands of Jews in Hungary and Romania and provided assistance to Jews at Ravensbruck camp in Germany, but the assistance came mainly at the end of the war and was relatively little (Molotsky 1996). After the war, a number of dark secrets were and continue to be exposed about the relationship between the Nazi regime and the International Red Cross.

After the war it was revealed that ICRC president Max Huber was a war profiteer and owned plants in Germany, one of which used slave labor to supply the Nazi war effort and earned Huber millions (Zuckerman 1998). American intelligence documents, declassified in 1996, showed that the Red Cross was used as a cover for Nazi agents. The Allies suspected twenty-eight Red Cross officials were German agents (Bower 1997). Some Red Cross employees exploited their positions to smuggle money and jewelry to Switzerland. The ICRC investigated and announced that it had found three cases of serious misconduct by former employees.[8] Police found Giuseppe Beretta, a Red Cross official in Turkey in 1945, in possession of gold coins he had received from a Nazi agent. The ICRC further claimed that only eighteen of the forty-nine people identified in the documents had worked for the Red Cross during the war (Reuters 1997).

As late as 1984, the ICRC would not allow the Simon Wiesenthal Center to access the emigration files in their archives to identify hundreds of Nazi perpetrators (Simon Wiesenthal Center, 1988 Appendix 10). According to a government-sponsored commission on Nazi activities in Argentina, Nazis who faced charges for war crimes used Red Cross passports issued in their real names (Zadunaisky 1998). The ICRC unwittingly provided travel papers to at least ten Nazis including the notorious Dr. Josef Mengele, Adolf Eichmann, and Klaus Barbie (Jackish 1999). Applicants for passports had only to supply an identity document, proof of permission to leave the country, and permission to enter the country. Mengele presented an Italian residency document with the false name Gregor Helmut as well as proof of permission to enter Argentina in 1949. It is not known who helped him (Figure 5.14). He managed to escape despite mammoth efforts to hunt him down (Figure 5.15). The Red Cross admitted pain and regret.

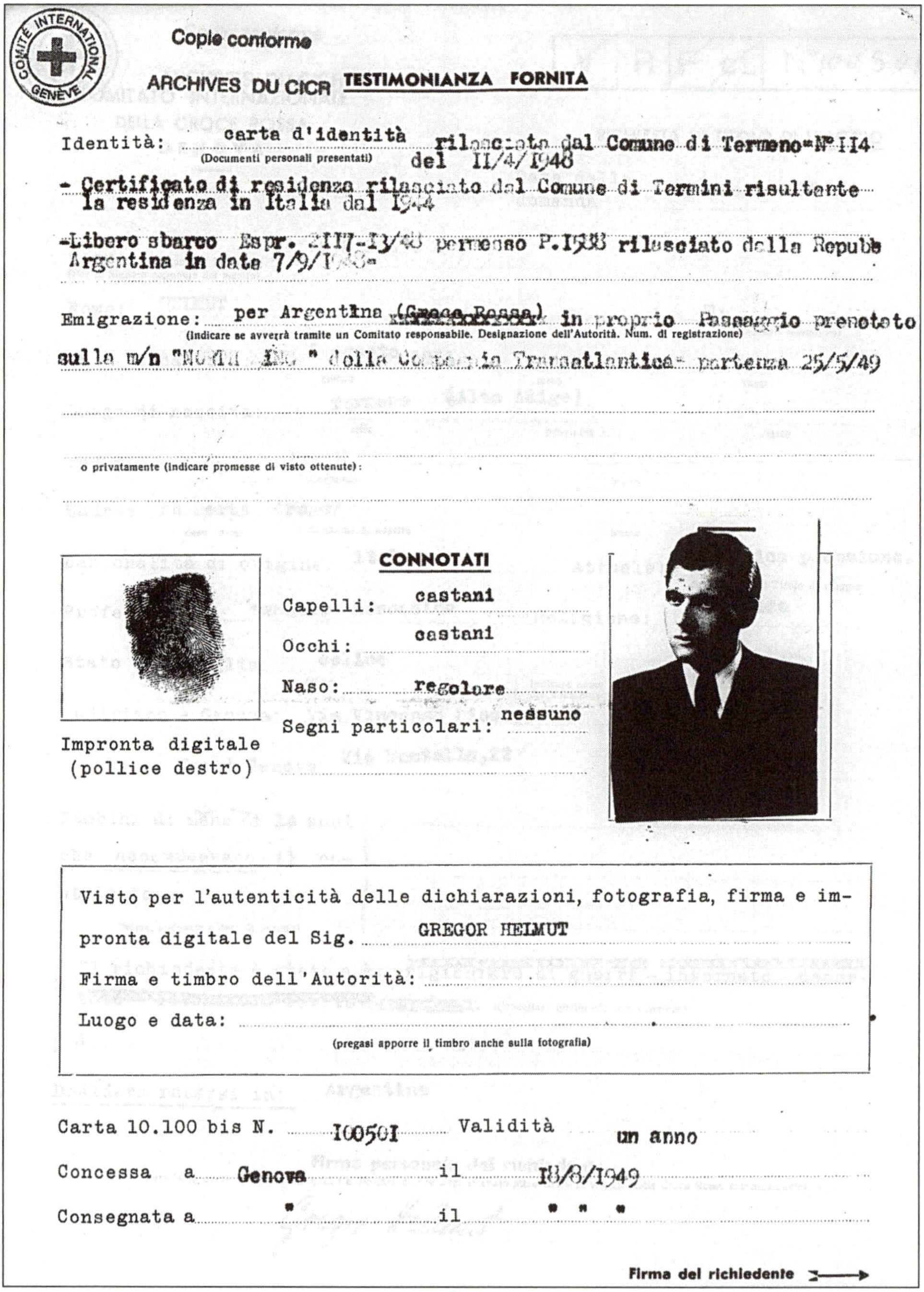

COMITÉ INTERNATIONAL GENÈVE

Copie conforme

ARCHIVES DU CICR **TESTIMONIANZA FORNITA**

Identità: carta d'identità rilasciato dal Comune di Termeno-Nº II4 del II/4/I948
(Documenti personali presentati)

- Certificato di residenza rilasciato dal Comune di Termini risultante la residenza in Italia dal I944

-Libero sbarco Espr. 2II7-I3/48 permesso P.I588 rilasciato della Repubb Argentina in date 7/9/I948-

Emigrazione: per Argentina (Croce Rossa) in proprio Passaggio prenotato sulla m/n "NORTH KING" della Compagnia Transatlantica- partenza 25/5/49
(indicare se avverrà tramite un Comitato responsabile. Designazione dell'Autorità. Num. di registrazione)

o privatamente (indicare promesse di visto ottenute):

Impronta digitale (pollice destro)

CONNOTATI

Capelli: castani

Occhi: castani

Naso: regolare

Segni particolari: nessuno

Visto per l'autenticità delle dichiarazioni, fotografia, firma e impronta digitale del Sig. GREGOR HELMUT

Firma e timbro dell'Autorità:

Luogo e data:

(pregasi apporre il timbro anche sulla fotografia)

Carta 10.100 bis N. I00501 Validità un anno

Concessa a Genova il I8/8/1949

Consegnata a " il " " "

Firma del richiedente

Figure 5.14: ICRC passport issued to Josef Mengele that allowed him and other Nazis to escape justice for their heinous crimes by fleeing to Argentina. *ICRC Archives, Geneva.*

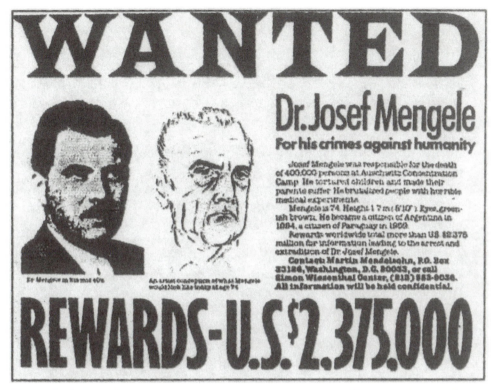

Figure 5.15: This Wanted poster was widely circulated by the Simon Weisenthal Centre. Mengele was never captured or tried for his crimes against humanity. *SWC*.

THE RED CROSS AND INTERNATIONAL HUMANITARIAN LAW

> The committee's failure to speak out to take the high moral ground in a way that is seldom offered to any one individual or any one organization, has haunted it ever since.
>
> Caroline Moorehead

The history of the Red Cross reveals past and potential weaknesses in the enforcement of universal standards for the treatment of prisoners of war, civilian detainees, and other victims of armed conflict. The Red Cross was one body that could have made a significant difference and saved millions of lives during World War II (see Appendix 10). They had some leverage but failed to use it. They could have offered to help control epidemic disease, particularly typhus, which was rampant in the camps. Revealing Nazi atrocities to the world could have saved lives. Instead the German Red Cross was part and parcel of Nazi medicine, and the International Red Cross was weak and did not take a stand. The ICRC has admitted that it failed in its mission by not speaking out against the Nazi genocide. It has issued a rather weak report in response to inquiries on the subject, which may be interpreted as a watering down of a staggering failure. There can be no doubt that much of the catastrophe of the Holocaust could have been prevented had the ICRC lived up to its own standards (Perl 1989, p. 326).

The ICRC has increased its role as guardian of international humanitarian law. The United Nations granted the ICRC observer status in 1990, allowing the organization to participate in its proceedings (International Review of the Red Cross, 1990). Fundamental principles underlying international humanitarian law have also dramatically increased in scope since World War II. With millions of civilian casualties, the Geneva Convention was expanded in 1949 to specifically protect civilian persons in occupied territories and civilian detainees in times of international and noninternational armed conflict. Two additional protocols were adopted in 1977 that extended that protection (Sommaruga 1996).

The independence and neutrality of the Red Cross remain in question. To this day the IRC does not recognize the Israeli equivalent of the Red Cross (Magen David Adom) but has recognized the Red Crescent. Jean-Henri Dunant would be turning in his grave had he known this. Herzl called him a Christian Zionist for favoring in 1876 Jewish settlement in Palestine (Simon Wiesenthal Center 1988).

Today violent terrorists target Red Cross workers, perhaps viewing the organization as an instrument of an occupying force. The publication of a confidential ICRC report on prison conditions at U.S.-run prisons in Iraq indicated that the organization was aware of abuses for over a year and chose to complain to the United States in private. The prison abuse scandal at Abu Ghraib prompted significant media attention and raised questions about what would have happened had the Red Cross gone public with its findings. The ICRC maintains that its policy of confidentiality is what enables them to visit and protect victims of war (Higgins 2004).

The Red Cross aims to be the primary humanitarian organization operating in each nation, with independent humanitarian operations clearly distinguished from governmental and intergovernmental efforts (Sommaruga 1996). The startling difference in the actions of the Red Cross during World War I and World War II suggests that the organization is not neutral, not international, and certainly vulnerable to political conditions. If the organization is to live up to its mission, some fundamental changes must be made.

The ICRC organization must prioritize humanitarian relief over Swiss or other national interests. Creative solutions must be found so that such a colossal humanitarian failure never happens again.

NOTES

1. Information from the Red Cross and Red Crescent in Latvia, Lithuania, and Poland remain, but the other archives were destroyed during and after World War II. The German Red Cross has been most helpful.

2. The Israeli Red Cross uses a red Star of David as a symbol, which remains unrecognized under international humanitarian law.

3. The Geneva Convention for the amelioration of the condition of the wounded in armies in the field was signed by twelve states in 1864.

4. When the United States entered the war, its role shifted to primarily serving American soldiers.

5. The 1907 Hague Regulations previously governed the treatment of prisoners of war.

6. Many Norwegian Red Cross nurses traveled to Germany to join the German Red Cross to help wounded German soldiers. After the war they were convicted of supporting the enemy of Norway, sentenced to imprisonment and lost their nursing rights. Denmark is also reported to have had some Red Cross nurses on the eastern front, though there appear to have been no consequences for these nurses.

7. Though his role was that of a figurehead, Carl Eduard Herzog von Sachsen-Coburg und Gotha was president of the German Red Cross from 1933 till 1945.

8. Giuseppe Beretta, Jean-Roger Pagan, and Jean Sublet were three Red Cross employees involved in misconduct (Reuters).

REFERENCES

Alpern, J. 1988. "Red Cross: We failed the Jews." *Jewish Chronicle* (September 2).
American Red Cross. 1915. *Battling with Typhus.* By the editor, p. 180 (May).
————. 1915. *The Scourge of War and some American Heroism.* By the editor, no. 4, 10:137–143 (April).
Anti Typhus Train Checked Epidemics in Camps and Cities in Siberia. 1919. *Atlantic Division Times* Letter (August 4).
Bower, T. 1997. *Blood Money: The Swiss, the Nazis and the Looted Billions.* London: Macmillan, p. 40.
Cohen, E. 1988. *Human Behaviour in the Concentration Camp.* London: Free Association Books.
Cohn, M. 2002. *Behind Enemy Lines: The True Story of a French Jewish Spy in Nazi Germany.* New York: Harmony Books, pp. 89, 98.

De Forest, C. B. 1917. "Fighting the Plague in Rumania." *American Red Cross Magazine* (December).

Dock, L., et al. 1922. *A History of American Red Cross Nursing.* New York: The Macmillan Company, p. 139.

Dworzecki, M. 1974. The International Red Cross and Its Policy Vis-a-vis the Jews in the Ghettos and Concentration Camps in Nazi-occupied Europe: Rescue attempts during the Holocaust. In Proceedings of the Second Yad Vashem International Conference, Jerusalem, pp. 71–106.

Ezergailis, A. 1996. The Holocaust in Latvia 1941–1944. The Historical Institute of Latvia and the United States Holocaust Memorial Museum.

Favez, J. 1988. *The Red Cross and the Holocaust.* Ed. and trans. by John and Beryl Fletcher. Cambridge: Cambridge University Press.

German Jews at Riga—Delivery to the Riga Ghetto Hospital. 1948. In Report of the Joint Relief Commission of the International Red Cross, 1941–1948, p. 209.

Higgins, Alexander. 2004. "Red Cross Faces Pressure in Abuse Scandal." Associated Press (May 11).

Hogan, D. 2003. "The Red Cross." In *The Holocaust Chronicle: A History in Words and Pictures.* Lincolnwood, IL: Publications International.

The Holocaust Chronicle: A History in Words and Pictures. 2003. Lincolnwood, IL: Publications International.

Hutchinson, J. F. 1996. *Champions of Charity: War and the Rise of the Red Cross.* Boulder: Westview Press.

ICRC Activities during the Second World War. 1996. International Review of the Red Cross, no. 314, pp. 562–567 (September 1).

"The ICRC Is Granted Observer Status at the United Nations." 1990. International Review of the Red Cross, no. 279 (December 31). http://www.icrc.org/web/eng/siteeng0.nsf/iwpList109/9C01CEE818E27505C1256B66005B1CF3 (accessed January 8, 2004).

International Committee of the Red Cross. 1957. The Fundamental Principles: Extract from XXVIth International Conference of the Red Cross and Red Crescent (January 1). http://www.icrc.org/Web/Eng/siteeng0.nsf/iwpList74/86084FD590E1112DC1256B6600593B20 (accessed June 10, 2004).

———. 1998. General Introduction, Founding and Early Years of the ICRC (1863–1914) (June 4). http://www.icrc.org/web/eng/siteeng0.nsf/iwpList288/FAFDE5C21CBC5ACDC1256B66005B0E39, (accessed May 30, 2004).

———. 1998. The Geneva Conventions. Founding and Early Years of the ICRC (1863–1914) (January 15). http://www.icrc.org/web/eng/siteeng0.nsf/iwpList74/932347283AACD598C1256B66005B107B (accessed May 30, 2004).

———. 1998. The ICRC and the Holocaust, (July 14). http://www.icrc.org/web/eng/siteeng0.nsf/iwpList418/359CC4EF8A1E5C72C1256B66005B2171 (accessed January 23 2004).

Jackish, C. 1999. BBC News (February 17).

Kernodle, P. B. 1949. *The Red Cross Nurse in Action 1882–1948*. New York: Harper Brothers Publishers, p. 192.

Lanzmann, C. 1997. *A Visitor from the Living*. Films Adelph, Cineteve, New Yorker Films, New York.

LeBor, A. 1997. *Hitler's Secret Bankers: The Myth of Swiss Neutrality During the Holocaust*. Secaucus, NJ: Carol Publishing Group, p. 145.

Manchester Guardian Weekly, September 27, 1935.

Molotsky, I. 1996. "Red Cross Admits Knowing of the Holocaust During the War." *The New York Times* (December 19).

Moorehead, C. 1998. *Dunant's Dream: War, Switzerland and the History of the Red Cross*. London: HarperCollins.

Nahon, M. 1989. *Birkenau: The Camp of Death*. Tuscaloosa: University of Alabama Press, p. 98.

Nebehay, S. 1995. "ICRC President Admits 'Moral Failure' in Holocaust." Reuters (May 30).

Nyiszli, M. 1993. *Auschwitz: A Doctor's Eyewitness Account*. Trans. by T. Kremer and R. Seaver. New York: Arcade Publishing.

Penkower, M. 1988. *The Jews Were Expendable: Free World Diplomacy and the Holocaust*. Detroit: Wayne State University Press.

Perl, W. R. 1989. *The Holocaust Conspiracy: An International Policy of Genocide*. New York: Shapolsky Publishers, pp. 322–326.

Post, W. M. 1915. "Our Ottoman Branch: Typhus and Wounds Give American Red Cross Chapter Much to Do in the Sublime Porte. It Is Operating Fifteen Hospitals." *Red Cross Magazine*, pp. 215–220 (June).

RAC Rockefeller Foundation 1.1/785/2/15. 1921. George Vincent to John D. Rockefeller, Jr. (August 9).

Red Cross during the Holocaust. 2002. Jewish Social Studies, EBSCO Publishing.

Report of the Joint Relief Commission of the International Red Cross 1941–1946. 1948. Geneva: International Committee of the Red Cross League of Red Cross Societies.

Reuters. 1997. "Red Cross Finds 3 Aides at Fault in Nazi Era." *The New York Times* (March 4).

Rossel. 1944. Aktennotiz. Beruch von Theresienstadt (June 27).

Simon Wiesenthal Center. 1988. Press Release (August 29).

Sommaruga, C. 1996. The International Committee of the Red Cross and International Humanitarian Law. Intervention by Dr. Cornelio Sommaruga, President, International Committee of the Red Cross, Comenius University, Bratislava (May 20). http://www.icrc.org/web/eng/siteeng0.nsf/iwp List109/96EA842943A5CF97C1256B66005A02C6 (accessed January 8, 2004).

Strong, R. P. 1915. "Conquering the Typhus Plague." *American Red Cross Magazine* no. 8, p. 267 (August).

————. 1915. "Delivering a People from Pestilence." *American Red Cross Magazine* no. 11, 10:339.

Weindling, P. 2000. *Epidemics and Genocide in Eastern Europe, 1890–1945*. Oxford: Oxford University Press, pp. 296, 313.

Wiesenthal, S. 1989. Rote Kreuz, Documentationszentrum Des Bundes Judischer Verfogter Des Naziregimes, Vienna (July 27).

Yahil L. 1987. *The Holocaust: The Fate of European Jewry 1932–1945*. Trans. from the Hebrew by Ina Freedman and Haya Galai, New York: Oxford University Press.

Zadunaisky, D. 1998. Associated Press (March 9).

Zuckerman, M. B. 1998. "Switzerland's Secret Shame." *U.S. News and World Report* vol. 124, no. 24 (June 22).

CHAPTER 6
Germ Warfare:
From Bodies to Bombs

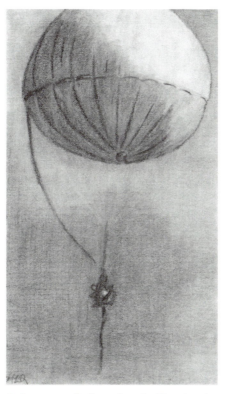

A Japanese balloon bomb. *Drawing by
M. Zelaya Quesasa.*

> If the world was so shocked at what it discovered to be extremes to which experimental medicine would go, it has as yet to condemn the method and find means to control it.
>
> Raoul Hilberg

During World War II the Nazis intended the total annihilation of Jews and other groups, and epidemic typhus undeniably furthered that goal. Disease has been used as a weapon of war through the ages. The military has merely progressed over time from the crude catapulting of diseased corpses over castle walls to large-scale production of lethal organisms dispensed by intercontinental ballistic missiles.

Biological warfare—the use of bacteria, viruses, or toxins during war to cause disease or death—long predates any scientific understanding of germs or the spread of disease. In the earliest stage of biological warfare, diseased bodies were hurled at the enemy even when it was not known how disease spread. Later, as scientific knowledge increased, biological warfare became more sophisticated. Disease was intentionally spread to enemies through fomites (objects capable of carrying germs from an infected person to another person, like clothes or bedding). With the era of bacteriology in the nineteenth century came the knowledge that specific organisms caused certain diseases and that each disease was spread in its own way. This knowledge made it easy to cultivate organisms for epidemics.

It can sometimes be difficult to determine whether an increased incidence of infectious disease is due to biological warfare or is merely a natural consequence of social disruption caused by war. In 1812 Napoleon's army was devastated by typhus during their attempt to invade Russia; 300,000 French soldiers died of the disease. According to Nettleman, it could have been intentional and thus a form of biological warfare, but there is no evidence that this was so. The devastation caused by natural epidemics during wartime is unpredictable and indiscriminate, and serves as a warning of how devastating biological weapons can be.

The Nazis' method of containing typhus can be considered the second stage in the development of biological warfare. The Nazis went to great lengths to protect themselves from epidemics, while at the same time forcing Jews and others to struggle to survive in conditions where typhus was sure to flourish. The negligence was intentional; the strategy discounted the prevailing knowledge of typhus and proven methods of epidemic prevention and control. Their draconian methods instilled fear and caused cases to be concealed, further spreading the disease. The countless murders that were committed in the name of typhus control and the deliberate infection of prisoners in the name of drug and vaccine research constitute a direct manipulation of typhus as a weapon. When the Nazi doctors in Buchenwald concentration camp injected typhus-infected blood from patient to patient (instead of the natural way by patients getting typhus from infected lice), they also increased the virulence and severity of the disease (Kogon 1980).

The current stage of biological warfare developed from harnessing natural epidemics to harvesting and cultivating germs—the most dangerous stage. Growing organisms has become easy, and engineering and altering biological germs can increase their virulence markedly. Biological engineering has made it possible to dry germs, extend their shelf life, and encapsulate them in special coatings, making them hardy enough for aerosol sprayers. Toxins, deadly chemicals derived from biological agents, are also used in biological weapons. Botulism toxin is a potent example.

Generally, modern biological warfare includes a carrying device like a missile or bomb that is used to deliver and disseminate biological agents. New types of munitions have been developed to spread these organisms, such as spray tanks, bomblets, flechettes, generators, supersonic rockets, and special weapon rounds. The airborne delivery of biological weapons through aerosols is the traditional and most effective way of mobilizing microbes for war causing inhalation of biological agents leading to disease or death. Aerosols are difficult to detect because they are generally invisible, odorless, and tasteless, and the symptoms they produce are often delayed for several days (Marty 2001, p. 429). These weapons are attractive to the military because they are excellent for clandestine operations.

Biological weapons are also easier and far less expensive than chemical and nuclear weapons. The devastation of one square kilometer of enemy territory could cost $2000 with conventional weapons, $800 with nuclear weapons, and $600 with chemical weapons, but only $1 with biological weapons (Livingston and Douglas 1984). To kill the same number of persons, it would cost $2 million for nuclear, $2000 for chemical, and only $2 for biological weapons (Marty 2001, p. 429)—hence the attraction of biological weapons. A financial motive also seemingly underlies the Nazis' use of disinfection chemicals in the gas chambers. It took comparatively little Zyclon B to gas a large group of people, but large amounts to effectively delouse an entire camp.

But biological weapons have some serious defects. They constitute a particularly dangerous threat because they are alive and uncontrollable once released. Furthermore, since they can reproduce, they have the unique potential to make an environment more dangerous over time. Biological weapons are weapons of mass destruction, whose effects are irregular and indiscriminate, not confined to their specific target population. They can multiply exponentially and spread like wildfire, and the danger could boomerang and affect the attacker. Biological warfare development centers also constitute a danger to citizens living in the surrounding area and the environs, just as nuclear development sites have proven to have catastrophic effects. This also applies to chemical warfare, which depends on wind and vapor and is not easily monitored and controlled. The effects, however, are short term, whereas biological warfare can wreak havoc for years. For most organisms prevention is not possible. Thus, the dangers presented by the proliferation of germ warfare are enormous and unpredictable.

EARLY DAYS OF BIOLOGICAL WARFARE

Germs and warfare are old allies. More than two millennia ago Scythian archers dipped their arrows in blood, manure and rotting corpses to increase their deadliness. Hannibal, the Carthaginian general, threw poisonous snakes onto enemy ships. Even though bacteria and viruses were unknown, the practice of poisoning enemy wells with bodies of dead soldiers to spread diseases is as old as war itself (Metcalfe 2002, p. 272). In 1340 at a castle in northern France, the besiegers catapulted dead animals over the castle walls, with the stench eventually forcing the other side into a truce. At the siege of Kaffa, a Crimean port, the invading Tartars suffered an outbreak of plague. The troops threw infected human corpses over the city walls, causing the residents to flee. The residents then carried "Black Death" outbreaks back to Europe.

There are countless examples of the deliberate spread of pathogens. Spaniards in 1495 put the blood of leprosy patients into the wine of the French; the Polish general Siemenowics put the saliva of rabid dogs into hollow spheres to hurl against his enemies; Russians hurled plague-infested bodies at the Swedes; the Iroquois threw contaminated animal skins into water to kill English soldiers. Fortunately some biological warfare strategies were not enthusiastically accepted. When an Italian chemist offered a biological weapon to Louis XIV, the king put him on a full pension on the understanding he never divulge his invention (Metcalfe 2002, p. 272).

Smallpox was commonly employed as a biological weapon in North America in the eighteenth century. The British army employed the disease as a weapon against the Continental army and Native Americans. During the war in North America the British saw to it that their troops were vaccinated against smallpox, while at the same time they forced the disease on the civilian population in the hope that as the population fled from the cities, they would carry smallpox back to the rebel forces (Marty 2002, p. 423). This strategy proved successful in Quebec, as smallpox spread throughout the Continental army and forced them to retreat. Smallpox-contaminated fomites were also delivered to the Chippewa, Blackfeet and Pawnee Indians and rebel families (Marty 2002).

During the French and Indian War (1754–1767) Sir Jeffrey Amherst, commander of British forces in North America, after whom Amherst College was named, suggested the deliberate use of smallpox to "reduce" Native American tribes hostile to the British. In 1763 when an outbreak of smallpox occurred in Fort Pitt on the Pennsylvania border, Amherst approved a plan to give smallpox-infected blankets and a handkerchief from the fort's infirmary to the Delaware Indians in a peace ceremony. He recorded the following in his journal: "I hope it will have the desired effect" (Sipe 1929). Primitive biological warfare was again waged during the American Civil War. Confederate troops contaminated wells and ponds with animal carcasses during their retreat from Vicksburg in July 1863. Clothing infected with smallpox and yellow fever was sold to Union troops.[1] The U.S. Army responded by issuing General Order No. 100 in 1863, stating that "the use of poison in any manner, be it to poison wells, or food, or arms, is wholly excluded from modern warfare" (Discovery Channel 2004).

THE TWENTIETH CENTURY: MILITARIZATION OF SCIENTISTS

Large-scale use of biological weapons occurred first during World War I. Great strides in medical knowledge enabled individual bacteria to be identified and isolated. Much more was known about how disease spread, and German scientists and military officials used this knowledge in World War I to target livestock with animal diseases like glanders, a highly infectious disease in horses. The hope was that by infecting a few animals the illness would spread and kill larger populations or incapacitate their cavalry. This method, however, proved to be less effective than the chemicals used in the trenches. During the same period, German spies were caught allegedly trying to spread plague bacteria in Russia. The methods they used were relatively simple. Today's methodologies are much more sophisticated.

During World War I eminent scientists like Dr. Fritz Haber joined the military effort and devoted their talents to producing chemicals for killing.

When Germany's supply of explosives was depleted in 1915, a substitute weapon was needed to penetrate enemy trenches. The source of explosives as well as other new weapons became crucial, and many of the leading German chemists mobilized their talents for the war effort. Dr. Fritz Haber, who directed the Kaiser Wilhelm Institute of Physical Chemistry and Electrical Chemistry in Dahlem, was part of an elite group of the Kaiser's chemists. Haber's evil but ingenious idea was to release poisonous chlorine gas from cylinders under proper wind conditions near enemy lines. This required no artillery. The first experiment with the gas took place at Ypres on the Western front and was disguised as "disinfection." This surprise attack had a resounding horrific effect. Haber turned his scientific complex into a tactical military research center and by 1917 had 1500 people on staff. His efforts only served to prolong the war and intensify the horrors. Haber's wife Clara Immerwahr, the first woman to receive a doctorate in chemistry at a German University, was appalled when she saw her husband's transformation from a benefactor of humanity to a military weapons scientist. She committed suicide as a protest and plea for "human science" (Johnson 1996).

In the late 1920s, the Soviet Union started a biological weapons program. One of the key events that prompted the Soviets to explore biological weapons was the Russian typhus epidemic that had raged from 1918 to 1922. During this period, 12 million people contracted typhus, and 2 to 10 million died as a result. The Soviets realized that if they could harness this destructive and disruptive disease, they would create a very powerful weapon (Alibek 1998).

WORLD WAR II: FIELD TRIALS AND HUMAN EXPERIMENTATION

Germ warfare was again used in World War II, but not to the same extent as in World War I. Japan did not sign the Geneva Protocol and used biological weapons extensively in attacks against China. In 1935 the Japanese set up a brutal and vicious germ warfare center at Harbin in Manchuria, which was later moved to Pingfan, a village close to the South Manchuria railway line. This center, Unit 731, operated under the guise of the "anti-epidemic water supply unit" and was under the command of the notorious doctor lieutenant General Shiro Ishii. As early as 1936, Japanese scientists started experimenting with disease organisms such as anthrax, typhus, cholera, and plague on human subjects. The research was criminal and killed as many as 10,000 persons. Strapped naked to posts, the victims, or logs (as they were known), were cut open in the cruelest manner. The gruesome experiments studied disease, pathogeneses and the effect of drugs in live and healthy Chinese, U.S., Korean

American, and other POWs. The center also produced 20 million doses of vaccine annually and eight tons of bacteria per month (Harris 1994). They also manufactured weapons to disperse anthrax, plague, and botulism in particular. Over 2000 *Uji* bombs and a deadly *ha* bomb were designed to shatter into thousands of pieces of shrapnel and spread anthrax spores. A single shrapnel scratch could cause illness and death in 90 percent of victims (Harris 1994).

The Japanese during WWII field-tested the germs they produced by dropping fleas infected with plague and typhus on Chinese cities. It is estimated that approximately 50,000 people were killed as a result of these attacks. Plague-contaminated rice and fleas were used to spread an epidemic in the Chinese town of Chuhsien and other provinces (Noah et al. 2002). The Japanese also intended to spread the plague in California. Codenamed "Cherry Blossoms at Night," the planned kamikaze operation entailed dropping balloon bombs containing plague-infected fleas on San Diego. The plan was later scrapped as the war drew to a close (Cooper 2004).

When the leaders of Unit 731 saw Japan's imminent defeat, they burned their records, destroyed their facilities, and killed the remaining victims. American officials granted Shiro Ishii and several of his associates immunity from prosecution for their war crimes. In exchange they provided voluminous records of the Japanese BW program and help in deciphering them. Dr. William Patrick from the U.S. biological warfare program considered these materials a windfall. The U.S. scientists never questioned the ethics, use, or quality of the results. No senior Japanese official was tried for having waged biological warfare and only nine Japanese doctors and nurses were convicted after the war for having conducted experiments on eight American fliers (Miller 2001). The Japanese are just beginning to learn about this horrendous research.

In their own small way, the Polish and Russian resistance used simple biological weapons. In December 1942, the Gestapo reported to Himmler that they had discovered a house in Warsaw used by the Polish underground with three flasks of typhus bacilli, seventeen sealed rubber tubes presumably containing bacteria, and one fountain pen with instructions for spreading bacteria. According to the Polish resistance, a few hundred Nazis were assassinated by means of typhoid fever microbes and typhoid fever lice. It was probably typhus as typhoid fever is not associated with lice. The raid on the house did not stop the Poles from continuing to use germ warfare (Paxman 1990).

Germany's biological warfare program was years behind that of the Allies. In July 1943 they created an institute for the production of bacterial cultures and vaccines in Buchenwald mainly for typhus (Kogon 1980). The BW program started in 1943 was centered in the military medical academy at Posen under the supervision of Professor Kurt Blome. Experiments were carried out on concentration camp inmates at Natzweiler, Dachau, Buchenwald, and Auschwitz where prisoners were deliberately infected with typhus, other lethal organisms, and poisons. A center at the Reich University of Strassburg was established for special tasks, including biological and chemical warfare. Chemical vaccines and drugs were tested on prisoners in Natzweiler, and victims were ordered from Auschwitz concentration camp. The Nazis' effort was not anywhere as extensive as that of the British and Americans, but the capability was there as well as the intent to use it (Paxman and Harris 1990).

OFFENSIVE WEAPONS:
GREAT BRITAIN AND THE UNITED STATES

The British biological warfare project was born in February 1934. The Committee for Imperial Defense formed a microbiological warfare committee in 1936, and Britain began to stockpile vaccines while searching for offensive biological weapons. A secret new laboratory was established at Porton Down in 1940, presided over by Dr. Paul Fildes. This effort was detached from the British Medical Research Council biological section, which refused to have anything to do with medical research used for destructive purposes and regarded this as a morally indefensible perversion of knowledge.

In October 1941 the British turned to Dr. Fildes at Porton for help when they started planning "Operation Anthropoid" for the assassination of the formidable Reinhard Heydrich, head of the SS and Gestapo, also known as "the man with the iron heart." Fildes had been working at Porton on a botulism toxoid (BTX), the most toxic substance known to man. He turned it into a weapon known as "X". Heydrich was ambushed by the Czech resistance and shot with a specially prepared bullet loaded with BTX. The wound was minor but the effect of the BTX was devastating. He developed dry skin, unresponsive pupils, dizziness, progressive muscular weakness, and respiratory failure. Within days the toxin paralyzed his diaphragm and caused his death. German intelligence never recovered from this loss, and the reprisals against the Czechs were malicious and horrible. The whole town of Lidice was razed and all the men were killed. The Czechs did not rise up against the Nazi regime as it was hoped, and 50,000 Czech workers in Prague demonstrated against what they called a "British-inspired" act (Paxman and Harris 1990, p. 93).

The ties between Porton Down and Camp Detrick, the U.S. Biological Weapons base, were extremely strong. The British liked to think that they were the brains and the United States the money. Washington began mobilizing in 1942 under the direction of a civilian agency, the War Reserve Service. U.S. biological research centers were established at the Camp Detrick Health Farm, a field testing station at Horn Island in Pascogoula, Mississippi, a large-scale production plant at Vigo near Terre Haute, Indiana, and a field testing station near Dugway in Utah.[2] The organisms mainly studied at Camp Detrick included anthrax, brucellosis, plague, typhus, and yellow fever (Christopher 1997).

George Merck was chosen to lead the United States secret anthrax program. Anthrax is caused by a bacterium that is not contagious, but is highly lethal and easily dispersed. Small particles penetrate the lung. One single invader could produce millions of offspring. Patrick and coworkers at Camp Detrick spent decades investigating how to increase the potency of anthrax and make lethal dissemination as efficient as possible. A single gallon held up to 8 billion doses, enough to kill every man, woman, and child on the planet. Botulinum toxin was concentrated so that if properly dispersed a pound could kill a billion people (Miller 2001). From 1942 on the British and the Americans pooled their resources on biological weapons trials, and over the next three years the United States invested $40 million in plants and equipment and employed 4000 people for biological warfare research (Gould 1997).

THE COLD WAR

Both the United States and the Soviet Union stepped up their biological weapons programs in the years following World War II. Various bacteria, viruses, and toxins were researched as well as their means of dispersion. U.S. army tests in the 1950s and 1960s demonstrated that biological agents can be broadly dispersed in a variety of discreet, nonexplosive ways. Bacteria and chemical agents were sprayed at San Francisco from a boat offshore, dispensed from slow-moving cars in Minneapolis and St. Louis, and released from light bulbs dropped in the New York subway. The agents posed some risks to the exposed populations but were not as dangerous as agents used in warfare (Chemical and Biological Warfare 2004). The U.S. military in 1969 had a fleet of ships in the Pacific Ocean loaded with caged animals to test biological agents. At the end of that year, however, President Nixon terminated the biological warfare program and ordered these biological warfare weapons destroyed. Further research was limited to defensive weapons.

But the ban did not last long. The research and stockpiling of organisms continues (Miller 2001). The budget of the U.S. Army Biological Defense Research Program grew by 400 percent to $558 million from 1980 to 1988. Colleges, universities, army bases, agencies, and private businesses nationwide shared in the research. By 1987, the U.S. Defense Department was spending $119 million annually for biotechnology, a sum second to the National Institute for Health budget (Gould 1997, p. 106; Wright 1990). The Department of Defense procurement program for biological and chemical defense cost $659,339 in fiscal year 2003 and $547,401 in 2004 (Department of Defense 2004).

The former Soviet Union also proved adept at turning germs into weapons, producing an arsenal capable of crippling millions. The Russians had 50,000 scientists and technicians and over 40 facilities devoted to research and production of offensive biological weapons. In 1979 an outbreak of respiratory anthrax in Sverdlovsk killed over sixty civilians and an unknown number of military personnel. The Russian government eventually admitted that the outbreak was the result of an accident at an illegal biological weapons facility. After 1989 with the dissolution of the Soviet Union, the laboratories went into disrepair and there was high unemployment. In 1992 Russian president Boris Yeltsin declared that he would terminate Russia's germ warfare program, though no reliable procedure exists to verify the claim (Falkenrath 1993–2004). There is a lot of concern about the danger of organisms getting into dangerous hands, as the Russians have a huge supply of smallpox virus.

THE GENEVA PROTOCOL AND THE BIOLOGICAL WEAPONS COMMISSION

International public fear and outrage over the use of chemical weapons during World War I led to the Geneva Protocol in 1925, which banned the use of chemical weapons and "bacteriological methods of warfare." But the Protocol allowed the development, production, testing, and stockpiling of chemical and biological weapons. Ironically, it was the Geneva Protocol's ban on biological warfare that opened the door for the biological arms race. Alternatives to mustard gas that were allowed within the scope of the Geneva Protocol were sought. The United States was the last major power to ratify the Protocol in 1975, and by 1986 a total of 108 countries had signed off on the agreement (Gould 1997, p. 100). Vaccine production also opened the door for germ warfare research. Mass immunization offered a chance to overcome a major disadvantage of using disease as a weapon for both chemical and biological warfare.

The Biological Weapons Convention (BWC) of 1972 (Appendix 11), the first treaty to outlaw an entire class of weapons, went into effect in 1975. It prohibits signatory states to develop, produce, acquire, or retain microbial or other biological agents and toxins, as well as weapons carrying them and their means of production. It also prohibits stockpiling, transfer, or delivery except for prophylactic, protective, and other peaceful purposes (Wright in Gould 1997). The BWC did not, however, establish a procedure to verify compliance. By August 1994, 134 states had signed.[3] Negotiations to add a verification protocol have been underway since 1994, although there are numerous obstacles to creating an effective system. Biological weapons development is exceedingly difficult to detect and monitor. The biotechnology industry warns of the potential for monitoring to provide a cover for industrial espionage (Falkenrath 1993–2004).

Although germ warfare has been relatively rare in modern times and has been condemned widely as unethical and inhumane, the threat has been far from eradicated (Humphrey 1987). Some experts are currently exploring alternatives to the verification protocol to prevent future biological warfare. Some argue for the further stigmatization of biological weapons. Others press for an international treaty outlawing the possession or use of biological weapons. Just as it is difficult to assess the current threat, it is equally difficult to predict future developments.

FROM SABOTAGE TO TERRORISM

Traditionally, biological weapons have been regarded as weapons of terror because of their morally reprehensible nature as well as their delayed and unpredictable effects. Military strategists generally consider them ill-suited for virtually all tactical military purposes (Falkenrath 1993–2004). But the use of biological weapons by terrorists presents a persistent serious threat. An enemy or terrorist could expose millions of people to disease-causing organisms by a variety of simple techniques. As terrorists traditionally seek to draw the attention of the international community to their cause, the morally reprehensible nature of biological weapons should act as a deterrent, but they also represent an affordable way to compensate for an inferior military force. The Al Qaeda terrorist organization supposedly has an anthrax program, which thus far has failed to obtain a strain that can be easily spread (CBS News 2003).

The Iraqi biological warfare program was, as far as is known, initiated in 1974, but the program did not progress. The scientists were imprisoned for unknown reasons. The program was restarted in 1979 but initially lacked expertise. Iraq unleashed chemical weapons in the 1980s both during the Iraq–Iran War and against the Kurds in northern Iraq when they rebelled. It is suspected that as the Soviet Union's programs began to fall apart in the

1990s and scientists' salaries dropped, some expertise may have been obtained from Russian scientists. By 1990 Iraq had prepared missiles and many air delivery bombs with aflotoxin, anthrax, and botulism organisms for the Gulf War, but they were never used. After years of surveillance and the invasion of Iraq, these weapons of mass destruction have as yet not been found. There are many unanswerable questions (Roffey 2002).

But biological terrorism is by no means restricted to so-called rogue regimes or international terrorist networks. The domestic use of biological weapons by Americans against Americans has surfaced numerous times in the United States since the 1980s. In 1984 members of the Rajneesh cult in Oregon, followers of the Indian guru Bhagwan Shree Rajneesh, living on a compound in rural Oregon, sprinkled Salmonella they had cultured on salad bars throughout the county. The Rajneesh's scheme was to sicken local citizens and prevent them from voting in an upcoming election. The trial they ran was successful and caused more than 750 cases of food poisoning; 45 required hospitalization. The Centers for Diseases Control and Prevention (CDC) declared it a natural outbreak. It took an independent police investigation to discover the true source of this first bioterrorism attack in the United States.

The first and only casualties of biological terrorism in the United States occurred in 2001 when five of the twenty-two Americans infected with anthrax died. Two years after the postal anthrax attacks, a small metal vial of ricin was found at a post office in Greenville, South Carolina, and in February 2004 ricin was found in the mailroom of Senator Bill Frist (R-Tenn). Ricin is a deadly bio-toxin made from the easily procurable castor bean and can be produced easily and safely in a home laboratory. A particle the size of a pinhead could kill an adult man if injected directly into the bloodstream. Lethal in tiny doses, a slightly larger dose (roughly a pinch) is fatal if swallowed or inhaled. It is water soluble and virtually odorless, so it can be used to contaminate water or food on a small scale and not arouse suspicion. When the powder form is enhanced with dimethyl sulfoxide, ricin can be absorbed through the skin, causing respiratory distress, internal bleeding, organ failure, and death within thirty-six to seventy-two hours. Victims may be unaware of it, and there is no known antidote. The U.S. army patented the use of ricin as a biological weapon in 1962 (ABC News 2003). In 2004 the recipe was removed from the archives of the U.S. Patent Office, but it remains in foreign databases and can be found on the Internet.

THE ROLE OF MEDICAL PROFESSIONALS IN BIOLOGICAL WARFARE

Medical professionals must be prepared to speak out against the use of biological weapons, whether they take the form of missiles laden with anthrax or the negligent medical treatment of targeted groups. Lessons learned from the Nazi experience indicate that medical professionals play a unique role in society, not only as guardians of public health but also policy creators and enforcers. It was not cultural propagandists who organized the infamous "special treatment" of the Jews; it was the public health officials, the scientific journals, the physicians, the administrators, and the lawyers who feared that the very presence of the Jews would endanger their families and ultimately their lives. Sadly, threats posed by biological weapons will increase if no serious steps are taken to prevent the proliferation of germ warfare laboratories and lethal weapons.

Theodor Rosebury, a microbiologist at Camp Detrick during World War II, in 1949 pleaded in his book *Peace and Pestilence* that expertise should be used for attacking infectious diseases since the outcome of germ attacks would always be impossible to predict and control (Miller 2001, p. 41). The role of public health professionals and epidemiologists should be to collaborate in preparing for the aftermath of a biological attack. The early detection of chemical or biological agents, physical shelter from the agents, decontamination of exposed materials and clothing, and appropriate medical treatments may help to contain an epidemic and avoid further death and devastation.

The development of counter vaccines has become a big industry. There is no totally effective vaccine against anthrax, the organism that has received the most research and trials for the purposes of biological weapons. Much research focuses on the development of vaccines, pharmaceuticals, and prophylactic agents to mitigate the threat of biological attacks. Such research presents a particular ethical challenge, as current standards are designed for naturally occurring diseases. Biological weapons research inevitably involves exposing human subjects to highly toxic agents, which many view as a clear violation of medical ethics. The risks of deliberately harming patients must be independently weighed against the potential benefits. The Environmental Protection Agency has refused experiments intended to establish "safe levels" of toxicity in human subjects, but national security concerns encourage similar high-risk studies. Such research will likely progress quickly, and guidelines must be established. The need to balance transparency of the research with national security concerns also raises important questions (Caplan and Sankar 2002).

Scientific technology and expertise can help humankind but can also present a terrible threat when misused (Pearson 1998). Advances in genetics, microbiology, bacteriology, and other areas of biomedicine have tremendous implications for biological weapons research. Billions of dollars have been and are being invested in biological warfare, and thousands of scientists and researchers employed in hundreds of institutions, universities, and industries in the United States are involved. Doctors and scientists are actively engaged in making lethal germ weapons that are grown to be resistant and that can be dispersed through sophisticated technology. The involvement of doctors represents a dangerous assault on traditional medical ethics, as put forth in the simplest language of the Hippocratic Oath and human rights declarations.

NOTES

1. The use of fomites against humans continued as evidenced by the smearing of pungi sticks with excrement by the Viet Cong in the early 1960s.

2. Through a cloud chamber project, like the British Cuinard tests, they proved that a bacteriologic bomb or aerosol was a feasible vector.

3. The United States ratified the BWC in 1974.

REFERENCES

ABC News. 2003. Investigators: Anyone Can Get the Recipe for a Bio-Terror Weapon More Deadly Than Cyanide. New York-WABC (February 6).

Alibek K. 1998. "Behind the Mask: Biological Warfare." *Institute of the Study of Conflict, Ideology, and Policy, Perspective* vol. 9, no. 1. http://www.bu.edu/iscip/vol9/Alibek.html (accessed September 9, 2004).

Caplan, A. L., and P. Sankar. 2002. "Human Subjects in Weapons Research." *Science* vol. 1 (November).

CBS News. 2003. Is Al Qaeda Making Anthrax? (October 9). http://www.cbsnews.com/stories/2003/10/09/eveningnews/main577395.shtml (accessed June 3, 2004).

Chemical and Biological Warfare. 2004. Microsoft® Encarta® Online Encyclopedia. http://encarta.msn.com.

Cooper, A. 1999. Japan Must Address the Actions of Its Wartime "Killing Machine." (April 26). http://aohwa.dyndns.org:7999/00/7.html (accessed June 3, 2004).

Cristopher, G. 1997. "Biological Warfare a Historical Perspective." *JAMA* no. 5, 278:412–417 (August 6).

Department of Defense Chemical/Biological Defense Program Overview. www.defenselink.mil/controller/defbudget/fy2005/budget_justification/pdfs/procurement/CBD.pdf (accessed February 2004).

Discovery Channel. Bioterror Through Time. http://dsc.discovery.com/anthology/
    spotlight/bioterror/history/history2.html (accessed June 3, 2004).
Fabre, J. 1997. "Hip Hip Hippocrates Extracts from the Hippocratic Doctor." *British
    Medical Journal* 315:20–27 (December).
Falkenrath, R. A. Unconventional Arms: The Threat of Biological and Chemical
    Weapons. Microsoft® Encarta® Encyclopedia. http://encarta.msn.com.
Gould, R., and N. D. Connell. 1997. "The Public Health Effects of Biological War-
    fare." In *War and Public Health*, B. Levy, and W. Sidel, eds. New York: Ox-
    ford University Press, pp. 98–116.
Grossman K. to Kubowitzki, August 26, 1943, and December 28, 1943, WCJA,
    265. Jean S. Pictet, ed., *The Geneva Conventions of 12 August 1929* (Geneva
    1958), IV, 3–5, cited in Penkower, 1988.
Harris, S. H. 1994. *Factories of Death*. New York: Routledge.
Hilberg, R. 1985. *Destruction of European Jewry*. New York: Holmes and Meier.
History of Biological Warfare. 2003. http://library.thinkquest.org/21659/agents/his-
    tory.html (accessed July 7).
Humphrey, J. H. 1987. "Biological Weapons—Banned But Gone Forever?" *Medicine
    and War* pp. 323–330.
Johnson, J. A. 1996. "Poison Gas." *Humanities* (November/December), p. 26.
Khan, A. S., S. Morse, and S. Lillibridge. 2000. "Review, Public Health Preparedness
    for Biological Terrorism in the USA." *The Lancet* 356:1179–1182 (Septem-
    ber 30).
Kogon, E. 1980. *The Theory and Practice of Hell*. Trans. from the German by Heinz
    Norden. New York: Berkley Books.
Livingston, N. C., and J. D. Douglas. 1984. *CBW: The Poor Man's Atomic Bomb*.
    Cambridge, MA: Institute of Foreign Policy Analysis.
Marty, A. M. 2001. "History of the Development and Use of Biological Weapons."
    Clinics in Laboratory Medicine no. 3, 21:421 (September).
Metcalfe, N. 2002. "A Short History of Biological Warfare." *Medicine, Conflict and
    Survival* 18:271–282.
Miller, J., S. Engelberg, and W. Broad. 2001. *Biological Weapons and America's Secret
    War Germs*. New York: Simon and Schuster, p. 37.
Nettleman, M. D. 1991. "Biological Warfare and Infection Control." *Infection Con-
    trol and Hospital Epidemiology* pp. 368–372 (June).
Noah, D. L., K. H. Huebner, R. G. Darling, and J. F. Waeckerle. 2002. "The History
    and Threat of Biological Warfare and Terrorism." *Emergency Medicine Clin-
    ics of North America* no. 2, 20:1–10.
Paxman, J., and R. Harris. 2002. *A Higher Form of Killing. The Secret Story of Chem-
    ical and Biological Warfare*. New York: Random House Trade Paperbacks.
Pearson, G. S. 1998. "The Threat of Deliberate Disease in the 21st Century." *Henry
    L. Stimson Centre Report* no. 24, Washington, D.C.
Power, S. 2003. *A Problem from Hell: America and the Age of Genocide*. New York:
    Perennial, pp. 57, 171–173.

Regis, E. 2000. *Biology of Doom: The History of America's Secret Germ Warfare Project.* New York: Henry Holt and Co.

Roffey, R., A. Tegnell, and F. Elgh. 2002. *Biological Warfare in a Historical Perspective: The Official Publication of the European Society of Clinical Microbiology and Infectious Diseases.* Oxford: Blackwell Science, pp. 8, 450–454.

Sipe, C. H. 1929. *The Indian Wars of Pennsylvania.* Harrisburg, PA: Telegraph Press.

Wright, S. 1990. *Text of the 1972 Biological Weapons Convention in Preventing a Biological Arms Race.* Cambridge, MA: MIT Press.

———. 1991. "Biowar Treaty in Danger." *Bulletin of Anatomic Scientists* no. 7, 47:36–37.

Appendices

Appendix 1. Hippocratic Oath—modern version.

Appendix 2. Draft Revision of the Hippocratic Oath—British Medical Association.

Appendix 3. Experimental Transmission of Typhus Exanthematicus by the Body Louse. Note by M. M. Charles Nicolle, C. Comte, and E. Conseil.

Appendix 4. Secret communication from Privy Council's Office, Whitehall, re: Professor Buxton's lice proofing belt.

Appendix 5. Pasteur Institute Paris Archives. September 1943 invoice from Pasteur Institute to the Commandant of a military installation for the purchase of 10,000 ccs of vaccine totaling 333,000 francs.

Appendix 6. World Medical Association Declaration of Tokyo (1975).

Appendix 7. Convention for the Amelioration of the Condition of the Wounded in Armies in the Field. Geneva, August 22, 1864.

Appendix 8. Letter from George Vincent to Mr. John D. Rockefeller, Jr. August 9, 1921.

Appendix 9. World Medical Association Declaration of Geneva (1995).

Appendix 10. Simon Wiesenthal Center condemns the IRC defense of the Holocaust silence (1988).

Appendix 11. Convention on the prohibition of the development, production, and stockpiling of bacteriological (biological) and toxin weapons and on their destruction (1972).

Appendix 12. Circular of the Minister of the Interior of the German Reich concerning guidelines for innovative therapy and human experimentation (1931).

APPENDIX 1

Hippocratic Oath—
Modern Version

I swear to fulfill, to the best of my ability and judgment, this covenant:

I will respect the hard-won scientific gains of those physicians in whose steps I walk, and gladly share such knowledge as is mine with those who are to follow.

I will apply, for the benefit of the sick, all measures which are required, avoiding those twin traps of overtreatment and therapeutic nihilism.

I will remember that there is art to medicine as well as science, and that warmth, sympathy, and understanding may outweigh the surgeon's knife or the chemist's drug.

I will not be ashamed to say "I know not," nor will I fail to call in my colleagues when the skills of another are needed for a patient's recovery.

I will respect the privacy of my patients, for their problems are not disclosed to me that the world may know. Most especially must I tread with care in matters of life and death. If it is given me to save a life, all thanks. But it may also be within my power to take a life; this awesome responsibility must be faced with great humbleness and awareness of my own frailty. Above all, I must not play at God.

I will remember that I do not treat a fever chart, a cancerous growth, but a sick human being, whose illness may affect the person's family and economic stability. My responsibility includes these related problems, if I am to care adequately for the sick.

I will prevent disease whenever I can, for prevention is preferable to cure.

I will remember that I remain a member of society, with special obligations to all my fellow human beings, those sound of mind and body as well as the infirm.

If I do not violate this oath, may I enjoy life and art, respected while I live and remembered with affection thereafter. May I always act so as to preserve the finest traditions of my calling and may I long experience the joy of healing those who seek my help.

Written in 1964 by Louis Lasagna, Academic Dean of the School of Medicine at Tufts University, and used in many medical schools today.

APPENDIX 2

Draft Revision of the Hippocratic Oath

The practice of medicine is a privilege which carries important responsibilities. All doctors should observe the core values of the profession which center on the duty to help sick people and to avoid harm.

I Promise my medical knowledge will be used to benefit people's health. They are my first concern. I will listen to them and provide the best care I can. I will be honest, respectful and compassionate towards patients. In emergencies I will do my best to help anyone in medical need.

I will make every effort to ensure that the rights of all patients are respected, including vulnerable groups who lack means of making their needs known, be it through immaturity, mental incapacity, imprisonment or detention or other circumstance.

My professional judgment will be exercised as independently as possible and not be influenced by political pressures nor by factors such as the social standing of the patient. I will not put personal profit or advancement above my duty to patients.

I recognize the special value of human life but also know that the prolongation of human life is not the only aim of health care. Where abortion is permitted, I agree it should take place only within an ethical and legal framework.

I will not provide treatments which are pointless or harmful or which competent patient refuses.

I will ensure patients receive the information and support they want to make decisions about disease prevention and improvement of their health. I will answer as truthfully as I can and respect patients' decisions unless that puts others at risk of harm. If I cannot agree with their requests. I will explain why.

If my patients have limited mental awareness, I will still encourage them to participate in decisions as much as they feel able and willing to do so.

I will do my best to maintain confidentiality about all patients. If there are overriding reasons which prevent my keeping a patients confidentiality I will explain them.

I will recognize the limits of my knowledge, and seek advice from colleagues when necessary. I will acknowledge my mistakes. I will do my best to keep myself and colleagues informed of new developments and ensure that poor standards or bad practices are exposed to those who can improve them.

I will show respect for all those with whom I work and be ready to share my knowledge by teaching others what I know.

I will use my training and professional standing to improve the community in which I work. I will treat patients equitably and support a fair and humane distribution of health resources. I will try to influence positively authorities whose policies harm public health. I will oppose policies which breach inter-national accepted standards of human rights. I will strive to change laws which are contrary to patients' interests or to my professional ethics.

Source: BMA Draft revision of the Hippocratic Oath in Annual Report of council 18996–7. *British Medical Journal* (London) 1997–26.

APPENDIX 3

Experimental Transmission of Typhus Exanthematicus by the Body Louse

Note by M. M. Charles Nicolle, C. Comte, and E. Conseil, transmitted by M. Roux.*

Study of the recent epidemics of typhus which have raged in Regency, particularly at Tunis, Metlaoui and Redeyef (phosphate company of Gafsa) and on the Kerkennah Islands, have led us to consider an insect as the probable agent in the transmission of the disease.

Typhus in upper Africa, is a result of crowding and poverty; it rages among the people who are the poorest and the least careful of hygienic rules; it is not contagious in a clean house, or in the wards of a well-kept hospital. Under these conditions, only the parasitical insects of the house, clothing and body can be suspected, lice, fleas and bedbugs. The usual time of appearance of typhus (spring) makes the role of mosquitoes, ticks and stomox very improbable.

Many observations have led us to limit our hypothesis to the louse. At the hospital of Tunis, the patients on admission are washed and re-dressed with clean clothing; no case of inside contagion has been observed, notably during the epidemics of 1902 and 1906, in spite of the absence of any isolation and the presence of numerous bedbugs in the wards. The only cases of contagion observed have been among the personnel in charge of receiving and disinfecting the personal effects of those admitted. On the Kerkennah Islands, an epidemic foyer of typhus, bedbugs are rare. In Djerid, where the disease appears as elsewhere, there are no *fleas*. These insects multiply on the contrary in the tunnels of the phosphate mines; they attack there both Europeans and natives, and moreover, the latter alone are affected with typhus. Finally two observations are known to us, where, after the duration of ordinary incubation, typhus followed obviously the bite of a *louse*.

These observations were known to us when one of us succeeded in inoculating a chimpanzee with typhus and after passing it through the chimpanzee to a bonnet-macaque (*macacus sinicus*). Also since the beginning of our investigations, we have attempted the transmission of the disease from monkey to monkey by means of the *body louse*.

Our experiments have been carried out thus: We placed upon bonnet-macaque I, infected with the blood of the chimpanzee at the 16th day of inoculation and during the hours which followed the appearance of the eruption, 29 lice obtained the day before from a man and kept fasting for 8 hours.

In the morning and on the following days, we placed them upon two bonnet-macaques A and B. Monkey A was bitten for 6 consecutive days by 15, then 12, 13, 8, 6 and 3 lice; and monkey B 12 days by 14, then 15, 13, 9, 5, 5, 6, 5, 5, 4, 2 and 1 louse. Every day after biting, the lice were mixed and kept at a temperature of 16° to 20°.

The two monkeys, A and B, had been previously employed for some experiments upon kala-azar: both of them had recovered at the time of their inoculation and another important fact was that their temperature had been taken twice daily for 5 months (monkey A) and 1 year (monkey B) and had never shown any elevation of temperature.

Monkey A—Nothing noticeable until the 22nd day of the inoculation. On this date, there was an elevation of temperature to 39.2° and 32.9° then a fall the 23rd and 24th day. Then temperature climbed again on the 25th day and reached or passed 40° the 26th, 27th and 28th day. Slow defervescence from the 30th to 34th day. The 39th day, the temperature rose, relapse for five days with a classical fever curve (maximum 40.5° the 41st day). Death the morning of the 44th day.

The general condition was good until the 30th day; on this date depression, the animal ate less, was easier to seize. No eruption. Extreme agitation during the second febrile period. Violet coloration of the lips the last two days. At autopsy, no lesion except an irregular ulceration of the caecum covered with a diphtheroid exudate.

Monkey B.—Nothing until the 40th day of inoculation. The 41st day, an elevation of temperature corresponding to the second attack of fever in Monkey A. The 44th day, temperature of 40° defervescence from the 46th day and the same day, an eruption. The only symptoms observed were some weakness and less appetite; almost immediate return to health.

These experiments show that it is possible to transmit the typhus of the infected bonnet-macaque to a new monkey, by means of the body louse. The application of this finding to the etiology and the prophylaxis of the disease in man, is important. Measures to combat typhus should have as their aim, a destruction of the parasites; they live principally on the body, linen, clothes and bedclothes of the patients.

* *Compt. rend. Acad. d. sc.*, Paris, 1909, CXLIX, 486.

Source: R. H. Major, *Classic Descriptions of Disease* (Oxford: Blackwell Scientific Publications, 1955) 178.

Secret Communication from Privy Council's Office, Whitehall, Re: Professor Buxton's Lice Proofing Belt

MINISTRY OF INFORMATION,

Malet Street, W.C.1.

F.P.150/18/1.

January 26th, 1942.

Dear Lord Hankey,

Professor Buxton of the London School of Hygiene and Tropical Medicine recently showed me the belt he has devised for proofing men against lice, the carriers of typhus and certain other diseases. I have independent evidence from our Entomologists at Rothamsted of the efficacy of the method which seems to be beyond doubt, and it can almost certainly be applied to large bodies of men as the materials are available and relatively inexpensive.

In view of the presence of typhus in Eastern Europe, and the almost certain prevalence of lice in the regions into which the Russians are now advancing, it would seem opportune to consider the advisability of sending Professor Buxton out to Russia with a stock of his material in order that he could demonstrate his procedure to the Russian medical authorities.

At the same time, as the louse may yet prove a potent ally, it is undesirable that the method should get into German hands.

Should this suggestion commend itself to you Professor Buxton would be prepared to attend and give full information.

Yours sincerely,

(Sgd.) E.J. RUSSELL.

Sir John Russell,
Adviser to the Soviet
Relations Branch.

The Rt. Hon. Lord Hankey,
   Privy Council Office,
      Whitehall, S.W.1.

PAYMASTER GENERAL'S OFFICE,

PRIVY COUNCIL
OFFICE,

WHITEHALL 1234.

WHITEHALL, S.W.1.

SECRET.

6th February, 1942.

Dear Warner,   M.I. 4/5

In continuation of my letter
of yesterday about Professor Buxton and
his belt, I enclose a copy of a letter
I have just received from Sir Edward
Mellanby, from which it appears that
Professor Buxton is about to start for
Cairo on his way to Iran, where he will
be able to test his belt: and that it
is unlikely that Buxton would allow his
belt to be sent to Russia to be tested
as he has not yet tested it on troops in
the field.

In the circumstances I think
we can drop the proposal to take further
soundings with the Soviet Government.

Yours sincerely,

Hankey

C.F.A. Warner, Esq.,
     FOREIGN OFFICE.

229

September 1943 Invoice from Pasteur Institute to a Military Commandant for Vaccine

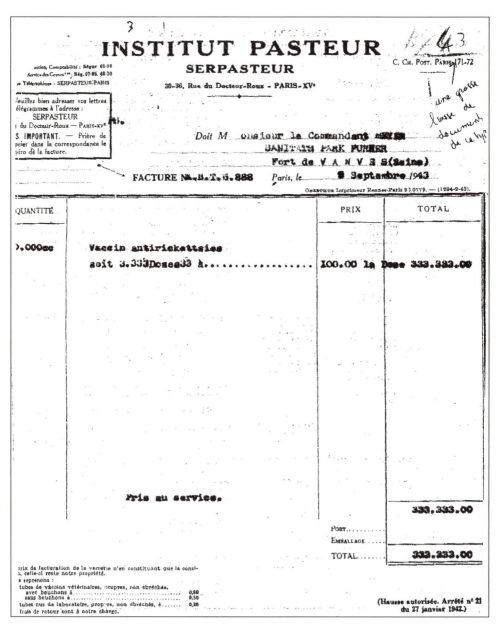

Source: Pasteur Institute Paris Archive.

World Medical Association Declaration of Tokyo (1975)

Guidelines for medical doctors concerning torture and other cruel, inhuman or degrading treatment or punishment in relation to detention and imprisonment adopted by the World Medical Assembly, Tokyo, Japan, October 1975.

PREAMBLE

It is the privilege of the medical doctor, to preserve and restore bodily and mental health without distinction as to persons, to comfort and to ease the suffering of his or her patients. The utmost respect for human life is to be maintained even under threat, and no use made of any medical knowledge contrary to the laws of humanity.

For the purpose of this Declaration, torture is defined as deliberate, systematic or wanton infliction of physical or mental suffering by one or more persons acting alone or on the orders of any authority, to force another person to yield information, to make a confession, or for any other reason.

DECLARATION

The doctor shall not countenance, condone or participate in the practice of torture or other forms of cruel, inhuman or degrading procedures, whatever the offence of which the victim of such procedure is suspected, accused or guilty, and whatever the victims' belief or motives, and in all situations, including armed conflict and civil strife.

The doctor shall not provide any premises, instruments, substances or knowledge to facilitate the practice of torture or any other forms of cruel, inhuman or degrading treatment or to diminish the ability of the victim to resist such treatment. The doctor shall not be present during any procedure during which torture or other forms of cruel, inhuman or degrading treatment are used or threatened.

A doctor must have complete clinical independence in deciding upon the care of a person for whom he or she is medically responsible. The doctor's fundamental role is to alleviate the distress of his or her fellow men, and no motive whether personal, collective or political shall prevail against this higher purpose.

Where a prisoner refuses nourishment and is considered by the doctor as capable of forming an unimpaired and rational judgement concerning the consequences of such voluntary refusal of nourishment, he or she shall not be fed artificially. The decision as to the capacity of the prisoner to form such a judgement should be confirmed by at least one other independent doctor. The consequences of the refusal of nourishment shall be explained by the doctor to the prisoner.

The World Medical Association will support, and should encourage the international community, the national medical associations and fellow doctors to support the doctor and his or her family in the face of threats or reprisals resulting from a refusal to condone the use of torture or other forms of cruel, inhuman or degrading treatment.

Convention for the Amelioration of the Condition of the Wounded in Armies in the Field. Geneva, August 22, 1864

Art. 1. Ambulances and military hospitals shall be recognized as neutral, and as such, protected and respected by the belligerents as long as they accommodate wounded and sick. Neutrality shall end if the said ambulances or hospitals should be held by a military force.

Art. 2. Hospital and ambulance personnel, including the quarter-master's staff, the medical, administrative and transport services, and the chaplains, shall have the benefit of the same neutrality when on duty, and while there remain any wounded to be brought in or assisted.

Art. 3. The persons designated in the preceding Article may, even after enemy occupation, continue to discharge their functions in the hospital or ambulance with which they serve, or may withdraw to rejoin the units to which they belong. When in these circumstances they cease from their functions, such persons shall be delivered to the enemy outposts by the occupying forces.

Art. 4. The material of military hospitals being subject to the laws of war, the persons attached to such hospitals may take with them, on withdrawing, only the articles which are their own personal property. Ambulances, on the contrary, under similar circumstances, shall retain their equipment.

Art. 5. Inhabitants of the country who bring help to the wounded shall be respected and shall remain free. Generals of the belligerent Powers shall make it their duty to notify the inhabitants of the appeal made to their humanity, and of the neutrality which humane conduct will confer. The presence of any wounded combatant receiving shelter and care in a house shall ensure its protection. An inhabitant who has given shelter to the wounded shall be exempted from billeting and from a portion of such war contributions as may be levied.

Art. 6. Wounded or sick combatants, to whatever nation they may belong, shall be collected and cared for. Commanders-in-Chief may hand over immediately to the enemy outposts enemy combatants wounded during an engagement, when circumstances allow and subject to the agreement of both parties. Those who, after their recovery, are recognized as being unfit for further service, shall be repatriated. The others may likewise be sent back, on condition that they shall not again, for the duration of hostilities, take up arms. Evacuation parties, and the personnel conducting them, shall be considered as being absolutely neutral.

Art. 7. A distinctive and uniform flag shall be adopted for hospitals, ambulances and evacuation parties. It should in all circumstances be accompanied by the national flag. An armlet may also be worn by personnel enjoying neutrality but its issue shall be left to the military authorities. Both flag and armlet shall bear a red cross on a white ground.

Art. 8. The implementing of the present Convention shall be arranged by the Commanders-in-Chief of the belligerent armies following the instructions of their respective Governments and in accordance with the general principles set forth in this Convention.

Art. 9. The High Contracting Parties have agreed to communicate the present Convention with an invitation to accede thereto to Governments unable to appoint Plenipotentiaries to the International Conference at Geneva. The Protocol has accordingly been left open.

Art. 10. The present Convention shall be ratified and the ratifications exchanged at Berne, within the next four months, or sooner if possible.

If faith whereof, the respective Plenipotentiaries have signed the Convention and thereto affixed their seals.

Done at Geneva, this twenty-second day of August, in the year one thousand eight hundred and sixty-four.

APPENDIX 8

Letter from George Vincent to Mr. John D. Rockefeller, Jr. August 9, 1921

August 9, 1921

My dear Mr. Rockefeller:

I am returning Mr. Spargo's letter, which I read with deep interest. The subject of aid to Russia was informally discussed at the meeting of the Executive Committee yesterday. Those present were: Dr. Buttrick, Mr. Rose, Mr. Fosdick and Mr. Straus.

Even on the assumption that Mr. Hoover's organization could be set up in Russia under satisfactory conditions, the prevailing sentiment of the group seemed to be distinctly against any participation by the Foundation in an emergency relief undertaking. The chief points which were urged in defense of this position were:

1. The relief of Russia as a part of a deferred war program cannot be convincingly presented. The project would be a new one, closely analogous to relief for the Chinese famine, in which the Foundation, you will remember, did not participate.

2. The only sound policy for the Foundation is to adhere to a policy of constructive cooperation in foreign countries in the fields of medical education, public health training and demonstrations in the field. This will call for all the available funds of the institution for a long time. To engage in emergency relief work, would create difficult precedents and compel the Foundation either to make invidious distinctions or to divert its funds from its main purposes.

3. The Russian crisis is so vast, that only government aid and that in generous amounts can possibly cope with the situation. Private subscriptions, especially under existing conditions in the United States, would make almost no impression and might even do harm by relieving the government of a sense of responsibility.

4. The Russian problem involves political complications. The
    Soviet government will undoubtedly attempt to take credit
    for whatever amelioration is secured. The United States
    and the allied powers, which for political reasons will
    insist on sharing in the relief project, will on the other
    hand do their best to undermine the Soviet influence.
    (Mr. Spargo's letter throws interesting light on this point).

5. Even medical relief measures cannot be adequately dealt with
    by agencies like the Red Cross. Again government coopera-
    tion on a large scale will be necessary if a fight is to be
    made against such diseases as typhus, cholera, etc. The
    Red Cross campaign against typhus in Poland accomplished
    practically nothing, although Colonel Gilchrist and four-
    hundred men with government cooperation did what they could.

6. When the time comes, the Foundation will be able to render
    fundamental service to Russia by aiding in the rehabilitation
    of medical schools, training of public health officials,
    nurses, and others, in cooperating in establishing training
    centers, etc., etc. It might be well for the Foundation to
    take steps and announce its determination to render this sort
    of aid to Russia at the earliest opportunity.

I must confess that my first feeling that the Foundation

ought to have some part in a relief program was radically modified by the

discussion yesterday. My desire to express good-will and to lay the

foundations for future work in Russia, I fear misled my judgment.

Mr. Spargo's letters to Mr. Hughes and Mr. Hoover are strong

and appealing documents. His arguments, however, seem to tend con-

vincingly toward government appropriations, rather than to the appeal to

private support, which I am convinced would be utterly unequal to the

almost overwhelming need.

In all the circumstances, I should think it would be wise for

you in acknowledging Mr. Spargo's letter, to emphasize the fact that the

Foundation has withdrawn from the field of emergency relief, that it

believes only government aid can cope with the present Russian problem

and that at the earliest possible opportunity, the Foundation expects

to do all in its power to develop a constructive medical education and

public health program in Russia.

Yours sincerely,

GEORGE E. VINCENT

Source: Rockefeller Archive.

APPENDIX 9
Declaration of Geneva (1995)

At the time of being admitted as a Mentor of my profession:

I solemnly pledge myself to consecrate my life to the service of humanity:

I will give to my teachers the respect and gratitude which is their due;

I will practice my profession with conscience and dignity;

The health of those in my care will be my first consideration;

I will respect the secrets that are confided in me, even after the patient has died;

I will maintain by all means in my power, the honor and noble traditions of my profession;

My colleagues will be my sisters and brothers;

I will not permit considerations of age, disease or disability, creed, ethnic origin, gender, nationality, political affiliation, race, sexual orientation, or social standing to intervene between my duty and my patient;

I will maintain the utmost respect for human life from its beginning, even under threat, and I will not use my specialist knowledge contrary to the laws of humanity;

I make these promises solemnly, freely and upon my honor.

Source: World Medical Association Declaration of Geneva London WMA, 1995.

Simon Wiesenthal Center Condemns IRC Defense of Holocaust Silence (1988)

FOR IMMEDIATE RELEASE   August 29, 1988

PRESS INFORMATION

WIESENTHAL CENTER CONDEMNS IRC DEFENSE OF HOLOCAUST SILENCE –
SWISS PRESIDENT SAID TO INTERVENE TO BLOCK 1942 PROTEST
OF NAZI ATROCITIES

LOS ANGELES--The Simon Wiesenthal Center has blasted
the head of the International Red Cross (IRC) for defending the
relief agency's official WWII policy of silence about the
ongoing systematic murder of six million Jews during the
Nazi Holocaust.

Jacques Moreillon, the IRC's executive director, defended
his agency's policy of official silence about Nazi atrocities
claiming that "public protest" would have "jeopardized its
humanitarian work in Nazi Germany" during WWII. His comments
were made to the BBC in reaction to the charges made by Swiss
historian Jean-Claude Favez that the IRC should have spoken
out as early as 1942 about Nazi atrocities. Ironically,
Mr. Moreillon, who originally arranged to open IRC WWII archives
to Mr. Favez, rejected Favez's conclusions as mere "hindsight."
In fact, Favez's research uncovered records which showed
that a draft of a proposed public protest was approved in
October 1942 by 21 of the 23 Red Cross' international representatives.
The majority vote, however, was overruled by the organization's
vice president Carl-Jacob Burckhardt and by Philippe Etter,
president of Switzerland and a Red Cross committee member.

"It is shocking that the very mentality of silence and
apathy which helped seal the fate of millions of innocent
men, women and children during the Holocaust, still lives today
at the very address entrusted by the international community to stand
with and for the innocent victims of oppression," said Rabbi
Abraham Cooper, associate dean of the Simon Wiesenthal Center.
"However, the Wiesenthal Center is not totally shocked by
this outrageous attempt to defend the indefensible, considering

that for most of the years since the Holocaust, the IRC
has done virtually nothing to help bring Nazi war criminals
to justice," he added.

As recently as 1984, efforts by the Wiesenthal Center
to gain access to critical emigration files held by the Red
Cross, which could have helped Nazi hunters trace the whereabouts
of Nazi war criminals, were turned down. Since that time, however,
the Wiesenthal Center has succeeded in obtaining duplicates of
that data, which have helped lead to the opening of hundreds
of new cases of accused Nazi war criminals in the U.S., Canada,
Australia and Great Britain.

# # #

APPENDIX 11

Convention on the Prohibition of the Development, Production, and Stockpiling of Bacteriological (Biological) and Toxin Weapons and on Their Destruction (1972)

ARTICLE I

Each State Party to this Convention undertakes never in any circumstances to develop, produce, stockpile or otherwise acquire or retain:

(1) Microbial or other biological agents, or toxins whatever their origin or method of production, of types and in quantities that have no justification for prophylactic, protective or other peaceful purposes;

(2) Weapons, equipment or means of delivery designed to use such agents or toxins for hostile purposes or in armed conflict.

ARTICLE II

Each State Party to this Convention undertakes to destroy, or to divert to peaceful purposes, as soon as possible but not later than nine months after the entry into force of the Convention, all agents, toxins, weapons, equipment and means of delivery specified in article I of the Convention, which are in its possession or under its jurisdiction or control. In implementing the provisions of this article all necessary safety precautions shall be observed to protect populations and the environment.

ARTICLE III

Each State Party to this Convention undertakes not to transfer to any recipient whatsoever, directly or indirectly, and not in any way to assist, encourage, or induce any State, group of States or international organizations to manufacture or otherwise acquire any of the agents, toxins, weapons, equipment or means of delivery specified in article I of the Convention.

ARTICLE IV

Each State Party to this Convention shall, in accordance with its constitutional processes, take any necessary measures to prohibit and prevent the development, production, stockpiling, acquisition, or retention of the agents, toxins, weapons, equipment and means of delivery specified in article I of the Convention, within the territory of such State, under its jurisdiction or under its control anywhere.

ARTICLE V

The States Parties to this Convention undertake to consult one another and to cooperate in solving any problems which may arise in relation to the objective of, or in the application of the provisions of, the Convention. Consultation and cooperation pursuant to this article may also be undertaken through appropriate international procedures within the framework of the United Nations and in accordance with its Charter.

ARTICLE VI

(1) Any State Party to this Convention which finds that any other State Party is acting in breach of obligations deriving from the provisions of the Convention may lodge a complaint with the Security Council of the United Nations. Such a complaint should include all possible evidence confirming its validity, as well as a request for its consideration by the Security Council.

(2) Each State Party to this Convention undertakes to cooperate in carrying out any investigation which the Security Council may initiate, in accordance with the provisions of the Charter of the United Nations, on the basis of the complaint received by the Council. The Security Council shall inform the States Parties to the Convention of the results of the investigation.

ARTICLE VII

Each State Party to this Convention undertakes to provide or support assistance, in accordance with the United Nations Charter, to any Party to the Convention which so requests, if the Security Council decides that such Party has been exposed to danger as a result of violation of the Convention.

ARTICLE VIII

Nothing in this Convention shall be interpreted as in any way limiting or detracting from the obligations assumed by any State under the Protocol for the Prohibition of the Use in War of Asphyxiating, Poisonous or Other Gases, and of Bacteriological Methods of Warfare, signed at Geneva on June 17, 1925.

ARTICLE IX

Each State Party to this Convention affirms the recognized objective of effective prohibition of chemical weapons and, to this end, undertakes to continue negotiations in good faith with a view to reaching early agreement on effective measures for the prohibition of their development, production and stockpiling and for their destruction, and on appropriate measures concerning equipment and means of delivery specifically designed for the production or use of chemical agents for weapons purposes.

ARTICLE X

(1) The States Parties to this Convention undertake to facilitate, and have the right to participate in, the fullest possible exchange of equipment, materials and scientific and technological information for the use of bacteriological (biological) agents and toxins for peaceful purposes. Parties to the Convention in a position to do so shall also cooperate in contributing individually or together with other States or international organizations to the further development and application of scientific discoveries in the field of bacteriology (biology) for prevention of disease, or for other peaceful purposes.

(2) This Convention shall be implemented in a manner designed to avoid hampering the economic or technological development of States Parties to

the Convention or international cooperation in the field of peaceful bacterio-logical (biological) activities, including the international exchange of bacteri-ological (biological) agents and toxins and equipment for the processing, use or production of bacteriological (biological) agents and toxins for peaceful purposes in accordance with the provisions of the Convention.

ARTICLE XI

Any State Party may propose amendments to this Convention. Amendments shall enter into force for each State Party accepting the amendments upon their acceptance by a majority of the States Parties to the Convention and thereafter for each remaining State Party on the date of acceptance by it.

ARTICLE XII

Five years after the entry into force of this Convention, or earlier if it is re-quested by a majority of Parties to the Convention by submitting a proposal to this effect to the Depositary Governments, a conference of States Parties to the Convention shall be held at Geneva, Switzerland, to review the opera-tion of the Convention, with a view to assuring that the purposes of the pre-amble and the provisions of the Convention, including the provisions concerning negotiations on chemical weapons, are being realized. Such re-view shall take into account any new scientific and technological develop-ments relevant to the Convention.

ARTICLE XIII

(1) This Convention shall be of unlimited duration.

(2) Each State Party to this Convention shall in exercising its national sover-eignty have the right to withdraw from the Convention if it decides that ex-traordinary events, related to the subject matter of the Convention, have jeopardized the supreme interests of its country. It shall give notice of such withdrawal to all other States Parties to the Convention and to the United Nations Security Council three months in advance. Such notice shall include a statement of the extraordinary events it regards as having jeopardized its supreme interests.

ARTICLE XIV

(1) This Convention shall be open to all States for signature. Any State which does not sign the Convention before its entry into force in accordance with paragraph (3) of this Article may accede to it at any time.

(2) This Convention shall be subject to ratification by signatory States. Instruments of ratification and instruments of accession shall be deposited with the Governments of the United States of America, the United Kingdom of Great Britain and Northern Ireland and the Union of Soviet Socialist Republics, which are hereby designated the Depositary Governments.

(3) This Convention shall enter into force after the deposit of instruments of ratification by twenty-two Governments, including the Governments designated as Depositaries of the Convention.

(4) For States whose instruments of ratification or accession are deposited subsequent to the entry into force of this Convention, it shall enter into force on the date of the deposit of their instruments of ratification or accession.

(5) The Depositary Governments shall promptly inform all signatory and acceding States of the date of each signature, the date of deposit of each instrument of ratification or of accession and the date of the entry into force of this Convention, and of the receipt of other notices.

(6) This Convention shall be registered by the Depositary Governments pursuant to Article 102 of the Charter of the United Nations.

ARTICLE XV

This Convention, the English, Russian, French, Spanish and Chinese texts of which are equally authentic, shall be deposited in the archives of the Depositary Governments. Duly certified copies of the Convention shall be transmitted by the Depositary Governments to the Governments of the signatory and acceding states.

IN WITNESS WHEREOF the undersigned, duly authorized, have signed this Convention.

DONE in triplicate, at the cities of Washington, London and Moscow, this tenth day of April, one thousand nine hundred and seventy-two.

Circular of the Minister of the Interior of the German Reich Concerning Guidelines for Innovative Therapy and Human Experimentation (1931)

The Reich Health Council has placed great value on meeting the concern that all doctors receive knowledge of the following guidelines and be unanimous in the decision from this point of view, whereby all doctors upon entry in institutions of closed and open care of the sick or doctors active in care of the sick should be required in writing to observe these guidelines.

1. Medical science, if it is not to come to a standstill, cannot give up, introducing in appropriate cases New Therapy using agents and methods that have yet to be tested sufficiently. Also, medical science cannot dispense completely with Human experimentation. Otherwise progress in the diagnosis, treatment, and the prevention of disease will be hindered or even made impossible.

The physician under these new Guidelines has a special duty to always acknowledge great respect for the life and health of every individual, undergoing innovative therapy or human experimentation.

2. The term *innovative therapy* used in these Guidelines defines therapeutic experimentation and modes of treatment of humans, which serve the process of healing, also there will be distinguished in specific individual cases the treatment for the recognition, healing or prevention of an illness or suffering, or the removal of a bodily defect, even though the effects and consequences of the therapy cannot yet be adequately determined on the basis of available knowledge.

3. The term *human experimentation*, as defined in the Guidelines, means operations and methods of treatment of humans undertaken for research

purposes without serving a therapeutic purpose in an individual case, and whose effects and consequences cannot be adequately determined on the basis of available knowledge.

4. Each new healing treatment must be in accord with the principles of medical ethics and the rules of the medical art and science, both in design and its realization. A consideration and calculation of possible harms must be undertaken to determine whether they stand in suitable relationship to the expected benefits. Innovative therapy may only be initiated after first being tested in animal experiments, where this is at all possible.

5. Innovative therapy may only be undertaken if after the affected person or his legal representative has declared himself unambiguously in accord after undergoing instruction for that purpose. Innovative therapy may only be introduced without consent if it is urgently required, and cannot be postponed because of a need to save life or prevent severe damage to health, and if prior consent could not be obtained owing to special circumstances.

6. The use of innovative therapy in the treatment of children or minors under 18 years of age requires especially careful consideration.

7. Medical ethics rejects any exploitation of social hardship in order to undertake innovative therapy.

8. Innovative therapy with living microorganisms requires heightened caution, especially in the case of live pathogens. Such therapy may only be considered permissible if the procedure is relatively harmless and if the achievement of equal benefits by other means cannot be expected under any given circumstances.

9. In medical clinics, polyclinics, hospitals, other health care institutions, innovative therapy may only be conducted by the chief physician himself or, at his specific request and with his full responsibility, by another physician.

10. A written report is required on any new type of treatment, and must contain information about the design, justification, and administration of therapy. Such a report shall state specifically that the subject, or his or her legal representative has been informed of the purpose of the therapy and has given consent. If innovative therapy is given without consent, according to article 5.2 the report must specify the preconditions clearly.

11. The publication of the results of innovative therapy must respect the patient's dignity and the commandments of humanity in every manner.

12. Numbers 1 to 11 of these Guidelines apply equally to human experimentation (article no. 3). In addition, the following requirements for such experimentation apply:

a) Without consent. Under no circumstances is nontherapeutic research permissible. Under any circumstances.

b) Any human experiment which can be carried out in animal experiments is not allowed. Only after all basic information has been obtained should human experimentation begin. The information should first be obtained by scientific or laboratory research and from animal experiments for clarification and safety. Under these requirements, given these premises, unfounded or random human experimentation without reason or plan is not permissible.

c) Experiments on children or youth under 18 years are illegal if it endangers the child or youth in the slightest degree.

d) Experiments on dying persons are not in accord with the principles of medical ethics and are not permissible for that reason.

13. Assuming that in accordance with these Guidelines physicians and in particular, responsible directors in charge of medical institutions show a strong feeling of responsibility toward the sick entrusted to their care, it also is hoped that they will maintain receptive to their responsibility to seek relief, improvement, protection, or cure for the patient along new paths, when the accepted and actual state of medical science, according to their medical knowledge, no longer seems adequate.

14. In academic teaching, every opportunity should be taken to stress the special duties of a physician in regard to undertaking innovative therapy or human experimentation; these special responsibilities also apply to the publication of the results of innovative therapy and human experimentation.

Source: Circular of the Reich Minister of the Interior. February 28, 1931. Printed from Reich Health Paper 6,55 (1931). 174 f. Trans. from the German by Nathan Snyder, Judaica Librarian, University of Texas Libraries, The University of Texas at Austin.

Resources

I received incredible support and information from many people and institutions. Their names are merely listed here, but they made this book possible. The following people working in archives, institutions, and organizations have my heartfelt thanks. The Auschwitz Archives, Jerzy Wroblewski; Auschwitz-Birkenau State Museum, Dr. Piotr Setkiewicz, Director; Niedersächsische Landeszentrale für Politische Bildung Gedenkstatte, Bergen Belsen, Dr. Thomas Rahe; Dokumentation Gedenkstatte, Bergen Belsen, Klaus Tatzler; The Buchenwald Archives, Dr. Wolfang Röll; KZ-Gedenkstatte Dachau Archive, Albert Knoll; State Museum in Majdanek Archive, Director, Professor Janina Kielbon; Mauthausen Memorial Museum Archives, Dr. Wagner and Stephan Matyus (photo archives); Historie e Memorie, Natzweiler Memorial Museum, Jean Pierre Husson; Sachsenhausen Memorial and Museum Archives, Dr. Ingrid Ley; Memorial and Museum Sachsenhausen/Brandenburg Memorials Foundation, Dr. Horst Seferens; Archiv Sachsenhausen Gedenkstatte und Museum Bibliotek, Monica Liebacher; Stutthof Memorial Museum, Danuta Drywa; Stautarchiv Nuremberg, Gerard Jochem; Bundesarchiv Koblenz, Berit Pastora; Latvian Historical Archives, Irina Weinberger; Services Archives Academy of Science, Paris, Claudine Poret; Robert Koch Institute, Dr. Thomas Zeise; Musee de la Resistance et la Deportation, Besançon, France, Marie-Claire Ruet; DOEW Documentationsarchiv des Wilderstandes, Austria, Dr. Elizabeth Klamper; German Red Cross, Berlin, Petra Lieber; British Red Cross, Helen Hughes; American Red Cross, Andrew Nichols and Jean Wadman; International Federation of the Red Cross and Red Crescent Societies, Grant Mitchell; Historical Archives ICRC,

Fabrio Bensi; ICRC Library and Research Division, Helene Vincent; ICRC documentalist, New York, Alan Dorsey; ICRC assistant to the head of the delegation, Linda Allain; Lithuanian Red Cross, Kaunas Archives, Vitalye Gircyte and Dr. Juaonas Rimkus; Lithuania State Archives Vilnius, Galina, Baranova; Pasvalys Museum; Vilnius Medical School, Lithuania, Dr. Andrius; Infectious Disease Hospital Kaunas, Dr. Panavas, Director; Vilna Goan Jewish State Museum; Jewish Museum Prague, Macova Pavla and Dr. Alexandr Putnik; Bernard Nocht Institute, Dr. Martina-Christine Koschwitz; Pasteur Institute; Simon Wiesenthal Center Library; YIVO Jewish Institute for Research; Yad Vashem Photo Archives, Masha Odin; National Records and Administration Archives (NARA); Library of Congress Prints and Images, Mary Ison; United States Holocaust Memorial Museum (USHMM) photo archives, Maren Read; Rockefeller Institute and Archives, Tom Rosenbaum; History of Medicine Museum, Charite, Berlin, Professor Dr. Thomas Schnalke and Dr. Marz; Institute fur Medizinsche Virologie der Universitat Zurich, Dr. Walter Bossart; Welcome Library, London, Katrina Robinson; Deutsches Apotheken-Museum im Heidelberger Schloss, Elizabeth Huwer, Director; Emil-von-Behring-Bibliothek for History and Ethics of Medicine, Philipps–University Marburg, Germany, Dr. Kornelia Grundmann, Robert Koch Institute, Dr. K. Gerber, Director of the Library; Senckenbergisches Institut Geschichte der Medizin Frankfurt, Michaela Edelmann; Museum Okregowe w Rzeszowie, Professor Dr. Hab. Sylvester Czopek; Otis Historical Archives National Museum of Health and Medicine Armed Forces Institute of Pathology, Michael Rhode; Special Collections Librarian, Galter Health Science Library, Northwestern University, Chicago, Rom Sims; University of Strasbourg, France, Annelise Horrenberger; Ghetto Fighters House Archive, Western Galilee Israel, Judy Grossman; Archiv der Max-Planck-Gesellschaft, Berlin, Susanne Uebele; Florida Center for Instructional Technology, Dr. Roy Winkelman.

Index

About the Author

DR. NAOMI BAUMSLAG is a Clinical Professor of Pediatrics at Georgetown University Medical School and President of the Women's International Public Health Network. She is an expert in public health and has been an advisor to many international agencies and a member of human rights committees. Born in Johannesburg, South Africa she obtained her M.D. at the Witwatersrand University Medical School, Johannesburg and her M.P.H. at Johns Hopkins School of Hygiene and Public Health, Baltimore. Dr. Baumslag worked in clinics in South African townships and in the United States for underserved populations. She has written nine books and over one hundred journal articles. She has extensively researched the relationship of health professionals and human rights both during the Holocaust and in apartheid South Africa. Dr. Baumslag lectures widely both nationally and internationally.